THROUGH
THE LENS
OF ISRAEL

SUNY series in Israeli Studies
Russell Stone, editor

THROUGH THE LENS OF ISRAEL

Explorations in State and Society

JOEL S. MIGDAL

State University
of New York
Press

Published by
State University of New York Press, Albany

© 2001 State University of New York

For information, address State University of New York Press,
90 State Street, Suite 700, Albany, NY 12207

Production by Susan Geraghty
Marketing by Anne M. Valentine

"Civil Society in Israel" reprinted by permission of University of Washington Press from
Ellis Goldberg, Resat Kasaba, and Joel S. Migdal, *Rules and Rights in the Middle East:
Democracy, Law and Society*, 1993.

"Vision and Practice: The Leader, the State, and the Transformation of Society"
reprinted by permission of Sage Publications Ltd. from Joel S. Migdal, "The Leader, the
State and the Transformation of Society," (*International Political Science Review*: 1988).

"The Odd Man Out, Arabs in Israel" reprinted by permission of The Free Press, A
Division of Simon & Schuster, Inc from Baruch Kimmerling and Joel S. Migdal,
Palestinians: The Making of a People, 1993.

"Laying the Basis for a Strong State: the British and Zionists in Palestine" reprinted by
permission of Princeton University Press from Joel S. Migdal, *Strong Societies and Weak
States*, 1988.

Library of Congress Cataloging-in-Publication Data

Migdal, Joel S.
    Through the lens of Israel : explorations in state and society / Joel S. Migdal.
        p. cm. — (SUNY series in Israeli studies)
    Includes bibliographical references and index.
    ISBN 0-7914-4985-8 (alk. paper) — ISBN 0-7914-4986-6 (pbk. : alk. paper)
        1. Israel—Politics and government. 2. Israel—Social conditions. 3. Civil society—Israel.
I. Title. II. Series.

JQ1830.A91 M54 2001
306'.095694—dc21

                                                                        00-058764

10 9 8 7 6 5 4 3 2 1

To Ariela and Ethan
Tamar
and
Amram

CONTENTS

ACKNOWLEDGMENTS

My fascination with Israel long pre-dated any writing I did on the topic. In fact, it was not until the middle 1980s, about fifteen years after my first academic publication, that I began to put pen to paper on issues of Israeli state and society. Part of the reason for the delay in research and writing, I think, was that I did not initially trust my instincts. As I explain in chapter 1, the decades of the 1960s and 1970s were ones in which I was coming to terms with the myths I held and those I found in the academic literature about Israel, holding them up to my actual observations and experiences in the country. That difficult process was eased by numerous conversations with others writing honest, original material on Israel, including Myron Aronoff, Baruch Kimmerling, and Aharon Klieman among many others. My debt to them for their insights and good company is immeasurable.

The writing of the essays in this book stretched from the mid-1980s through the end of the 1990s. Different colleagues through this period commented on various pieces. Among them were Michael Barnett, Uri Ben-Eliezer, Raymond Duvall, S. N. Eisenstadt, Ellis Goldberg, Steven Heydemann, Reşat Kasaba, Michael Keren, Baruch Kimmerling, and Ian Lustick. My deepest thanks goes to all of them. Special thanks go to several people who commented on all the articles, Eva Bellin (in a superb job for SUNY Press), Ben Smith, and Patricia Woods. In addition, my gratitude goes to Michael Barnett, Mickey Glazer, Penina Glazer, and Niall O Murchu for their reading of the introductory essay, "Myths and Models." Support for work on the book came from the Robert F. Philip Professorship at the University of Washington. I also received invaluable research assistance from Chandni Gupta, Tina Smith, Zoë Stemm, and Cathy Vuong.

As always, my greatest support came from my life partner, Marcy Migdal. Together, we introduced our children to Israel and all its complexities, and their lives became deeply intertwined with Israeli society. It is to them that I lovingly dedicate this book.

PART I

Introduction

CHAPTER 1

Myths and Models:
The State-in-Society Approach
and the Experience of Israel

USING THE STATE-IN-SOCIETY MODEL TO STUDY ISRAEL

The essays in this book develop an unorthodox way of understanding Israeli politics and society and, by extension, domination and change in other societies, as well. Israel serves as a lens, as the title of the book indicates, through which one can view the innards of critical social and political processes determining who obeys and who commands, whose life is marked by exultant privilege and whose by abject subjugation. With the breakup of the Soviet Union and other twentieth-century states, the three central themes of this book—state formation, society formation, and the mutually constitutive roles of state and society—are especially cogent at the dawn of the new century.

I have developed the state-in-society approach in a number of books over the last dozen or so years, in addition to the essays in this book.[1] The questions that I try to get at through the model are fairly conventional. How do particular societies and states end up with their distinctive character? How are the rules that shape everyday behavior determined? Who gains from these rules and who loses? And how and when do these rules and patterns of privilege change?

The search for the answers to these questions through the state-in-society approach begins with the premise that one cannot speak of a singular set of *The Rules*. By "rules," I mean both formal and informal types of sanctioned behavior. No single set of dictates shaping daily life or sorting out conflicting demands on people exists in Israel, or anywhere else, for that matter. Different groups and powerful figures promote a variety of codes that clash with one another. Some of these struggles are contained within a framework, such as state law, that mediates among the different claims through the use of courts or other agencies. But there are differences, too, that go beyond such frameworks of conciliation. It is then the delicate task of individuals and groups to pick

3

their way through the maze of competing, potentially punitive, claims on their behavior and loyalties. The distinctive patterns that characterize any society come from the outcomes of the struggles over the conflicting sets of rules.

To be sure, the preferences of those groups with multiple rewards and sanctions at their disposal, especially violence, are much easier to discern in the way people actually behave than the rules put forth by weak groups. Still, people's behavior is not the simple product of any one group's preferences—even, as in Southeast Asian cases described by James C. Scott, where that group may be vastly more powerful than others.[2] The "hidden transcripts" and weapons of the weak, as Scott and others have shown, have some impact, too.[3] No, day-to-day behavior is not the simple reflection of the codes and preferences of any single group but is the outcome of the ongoing, if often veiled, struggles among multiple groups. Additionally, the very engagement of groups with each other in the battle over rules continually transforms the tactics, goals, and even structure of the groups themselves.

The state-in-society model, then, does not view the structures of domination as the outgrowth of the intentionality or design of a particular figure or group. They are seen, rather, as constructed by the process of hidden and open conflict of varying sets of rules and their promoters, including the negotiations, networks, alliances, and fabrications that are part of that process. Chapters 2 and 6 focus on precisely this point. They analyze Israel's experience in the clashes over rules, especially as the Israeli state and its place in overall rule making took form.

The *state* component in the state-in-society approach has two distinct, sometimes clashing, sometimes reinforcing, sides to it—*the image of the state* and the state's actual *practices*. The first side leads us to think of the state as yet one more grouping or organization in society, vying in a coherent, unified manner for supremacy of its rules, its laws and regulations, against those of other social groups. It differs from practically all the others, to be sure, in its mass—in the sheer extent and quantity of the sanctions and rewards at its disposal—and the (unreachable) aims of its officials to make it the ultimate rule maker, either devising all the rules itself or determining who else might make some of them in society.

In this sense, its leaders work to create the image of the state as the monolithic, ultimate rule giver, making both the most nitty-gritty sorts of rules, such as which side of the street to drive on, as well as foundational rules, refereeing through its courts and bureaucracy which of society's rules apply when they are in conflict. The state, especially the democratic state, can be strengthened by vociferous conflict in civil society as long as that conflict is contained within the state's foundational rules. But, if the image of the state—the premise that it provides the framework for resolving conflict—is challenged, as I indicate in chapter 5, then conflict can weaken even the democratic state, as it has in Israel.[4]

For all their aspirations, state leaders' goals of making everyday rules and foundational rules, of creating the indisputable image of the state, can never be, in fact, achieved. Nonetheless, that image of the state is itself very powerful[5] and involves distinguishing the singular state in two ways: 1) by drawing a social boundary between it (as the ultimate rule maker) and the rest of society, that is, the state-society divide, and 2) by drawing a territorial boundary between the physical space where it claims to make rules and the space beyond its so-called sovereign control. Other states (and the organizations that they create, such as the United Nations) thus end up legitimating and reinforcing the image of the state as the centralized, unified organization establishing preeminence over the population in a given territorial space.

It seems to me that the issues of territoriality and boundaries have received far too little scholarly attention during the last half-century, in part because of the unusual, temporary stability that the Cold War gave to political boundaries, making them seem almost unproblematic.[6] And, if the issue of boundaries was not ignored altogether, scholars often assumed that societies shape boundaries, not, as I argue in chapters 6 and 7, that boundaries play critical roles in defining the society. In this sense, Israel, as an important exception to this Cold War boundary stability, serves as an important corrective. Its borders were problematic from the beginning, and they changed radically in midstream. The 1967 war and its reconstitution of the area's territorial boundaries give special insight into the relationship of borders and the strength and coherence of the state in rule making. One key element that the Israeli case suggests is that unstable boundaries create a pervasive sense of insecurity that may push societies into ethnic self-definitions and increased ethnic conflict.

In chapter 7, I discuss how Israel's uncertain and changing boundaries have complicated the efforts of its political leaders to establish and maintain the preeminent image of the state, especially in the wake of the 1967 war, which opened the question of the ultimate shape of those boundaries to endless debate. Indeed, one strain of Israeli social science, from Baruch Kimmerling's classic work on the frontier to Adriana Kemp's recent dissertation on borders in the postindependence era, has put the question of boundaries at the center of understanding state power and its limitations in the case of Israel (as has, too, the important work of Ian Lustick).[7]

The second side of the state moves from what its officials profess, the image of the state, to its actual practices. The move induces the observer to shift from speaking about the state in the singular form, as if it were coherent and unitary in purpose and action, to the plural form, recognizing the state's multiple faces. Here, the fragments of the huge state, the many bureaus and other organs—and the people who make them up—face resistance from other rule-making groups, as well as all sorts of lures from those in other groups to modify the state's singular set of rules represented in the image of the state. In other words, this side of the state involves the practices of its parts in the ongoing struggle among multiple groups over whose rules will prevail. The resulting networks, alliances, and crony relations that are part of the struggle serve to devalue and blur precisely those two boundaries that the image of the state seeks to consecrate—between state and society, and between the state and territory outside its claimed borders. Parts of the state become partners in creating alternative, competing sets of rules that recognize neither the division between state and society nor the sovereign sanctity of the territorial boundaries.

To my mind, the two dimensions of the state, the image of it as well as its actual practices, are distinguishable analytically, but both serve as powerful effects on everyday behavior and forms of domination. The tangible expression of the image of the state in such institutions as the Rule of Law, even in the face of contradictory practices by police and judges and other state officials, acts both synergetically and dialectically with actual state practices. These dynamics have powerful effects on the overall struggle over which rules will prevail and under what conditions. Indeed, the practices of the state cannot be seen as generated independently of the image of the state. As the Friday night Jewish liturgy notes, "*Sof ma'aseh b'mahashava tehilah,*" the final deed (or practice) has its beginnings in the idea.

Why do I think of this state-in-society approach as unorthodox for Israel? As with many newly minted twentieth-century states, maybe even more than for most others, the attempts to understand the distinctive character of state and society in Israel have suffered from what I call heroic-style scholarship. By this, I mean an emphasis by scholars in explaining structure and change in terms of key figures who have a blueprint for what they want and act tirelessly to make that design into a reality. Heroic-style scholarship sees social and political outcomes—how society is structured, who dominates, the path of change—in terms of the intentionality of particular groups or figures; they get what they want. Ironically, this style of scholarship has been as characteristic of the recent, critical scholarship that blossomed in Israel in the 1990s as it was for research in the decades following Independence.

In the early years of Israeli statehood, the heroes found in the dominant scholarship were the *halutzim*, the pioneers and leaders from a variety of sectors, who, for all their petty differences, shared key Zionist values and norms. The study of Israeli society and politics for most of the half-century after the creation of the state cleaved closely to the conventional social science theories that emerged in the post–World War II period, especially those coming out of the United States. As American political scientists and political sociologists, for example, delved into behaviorism and electoral studies, displacing the older concerns with formal institutions, so too did Israeli scholars follow suit.[8] Both in the United States and Israel, no scholarly approach was more important than social-systems theory developed by Talcott Parsons and applied to the new states by Parsons's collaborator, Edward Shils.[9] And, for Israel, social-systems theory provided a way to enshrine in scholarship the role of the heroic *halutzim*.

Far and away, S. N. Eisenstadt towered over the study of Israeli society and politics during the country's first half-century, and he was a key figure in developing this systems-oriented approach internationally. He was strongly influenced by Parsons and, particularly, by Shils's concept of a dominant center transforming divergent normative orders. The seminar on social change that I took with Eisenstadt at Harvard in the late 1960s during my second year of graduate school was the most stimulating and mesmerizing of any I have ever attended. It was not hard for me to understand in later years why he had such a marked effect on several generations of Israeli social scientists. I became a very big fan of his and have remained one to this day, even as I have departed from his type of interpretation of Israel and of social change generally.

The key to Eisenstadt's analysis and to those of his disciples was the integrated character of the Israeli center. This followed Parsons's argument that "the core of a society, as a system, is the patterned normative order through which the life of a population is collectively organized."[10] Criticism of this approach has come from a number of directions, focusing on its functionalism, its insensitivity to conflict in society, and its misbegotten hopes of creating an overarching theory of society. My concern here is with its tendency to overlook critical dynamics of society, imparting a *deus ex machina* quality to social and political change, through its heroic-style scholarship. For Eisenstadt and other early heroic-style scholars, Parsons's patterned normative order was the "Zionist normative consensus" forged by the *halutzim*.[11] That consensus was the glue for an active center, in precisely the terms put forth by Shils, bent on creating a modern society. Eisenstadt wrote,

> Perhaps the most outstanding characteristic of the Yishuv [the pre-state Jewish society in Palestine] was that its centre developed first. Its central institutions and symbols crystallized before the emergence of the "periphery" made up of broader, less creative social groups and strata.

This centre—built up through the élitist and future orientations of the pioneering sects—was envisaged as being capable of permeating and absorbing the periphery which (it was hoped) would develop through continuous migration.[12]

This perspective was adopted by Eisenstadt's followers, as well. The most important of these in the study of Israel were Dan Horowitz and Moshe Lissak, professors at the Hebrew University of Jerusalem, which was also Eisenstadt's academic home. Their first joint work, *Origins of the Israeli Polity,* in particular, proved to be among the handful of truly influential books on Israel in the twentieth century. It emphasized how the center in the *yishuv* coordinated and regulated "the relationships between the subcenters . . . and also cultivated certain values that served as the common normative basis of the subcenters."[13] This statement is almost a classic representation of the social-systems approach and its use of the center-periphery model to outline the process of change in new states.

A number of Eisenstadt's students rebelled against his macrohistorical approach and went on to study for their doctorates under the famous British anthropologist, Max Gluckman. In some ways, Gluckman was the polar opposite of Eisenstadt, magnifying the smallest details of social relations in the African societies he studied, rather than seeking the broad brush strokes for which Eisenstadt was famous in his macrohistorical accounts. Gluckman's students were frustrated by the highly abstract nature of prevailing Israeli sociology. Still, key analytic elements of the social-systems approach present in the writings of Parsons, Shils, and Eisenstadt could be found in Gluckman's work and in that of his students who studied Israel, as well. In Gluckman's words, "The search for the systematic interdependence of customs remains a hallmark of social and other kinds of anthropology. . . ."[14] This was a page taken directly out of the social-systems theory book.

Gluckman and his students saw the direct connection between their anthropology and Eisenstadt's sociology. "It seems to me," Gluckman wrote in the foreword to a book by one of his students who went on to great success in Israeli academia, Shlomo Deshen, "that in the nature of their trade our sociological confrères are concerned to analyse the structure of social systems in terms of certain abstract variables, which have proved to be significant, in determining the interdependence of social roles, groups and categories in an external environment, both physical and politico-economic. . . . They have in this way greatly deepened our understanding of social action, of how people live in societies. . . ."[15]

Anthropologists, he felt, added a distinctive methodology, a highly detailed, nuanced look at structures, to the work of the sociologists. They also contributed a close study of culture, customs, and beliefs. It is not surprising, then, that Gluckman tended to focus on the same sort of systemic integration that characterized the work of Eisenstadt, and, like social-systems theorists, he sometimes did this at the expense of seeing deep structural conflicts. Note his idyllic account of what he describes as Israel's national dance in one village: "The *hora*—in which I have seen colonels and majors embrace the shoulders of privates, ashkenazi and sephardi—with its whirling circle was the appropriate symbol of the achievement of a new national unity."[16] As was the case for Eisenstadt, Horowitz, Lissak, and others, the heroism of the pioneers, for Gluckman, was in creating the normative consensus that underlay that "national unity."

For all of the serious problems and pitfalls that social-systems analysts found in Israeli society, their approach was one that fell victim to its own assumptions about the inexorable march of social integration. Hidden teleological assumptions ran through the approach. It was the *hora,* more than, for example, the deep resentment of *ashkenazi* domination expressed by a *sephardi,* cited by Gluckman, that overall symbolized Israeli society and foretold its future.

While the social-systems approach dominated much of Israeli scholarship for the first three decades of the country's history, critics and dissidents certainly did emerge, especially from the 1980s on. Again, as in the United States, one strain of criticism came from so-called state theorists who took aim at social-systems (and Marxist) theorists for their failure to take seriously enough the distinction between the state and other parts of society. They were particularly critical of the functionalism of social-systems theories. Stressing the awesome power and autonomy of the state, this approach emphasized its special place in rule making and overall social domination.

A second, and sometimes overlapping brand of criticism, came from so-called critical or "new" historians. Here, fault was found not so much in the theoretical shortcomings of social-systems theory as in the uncritical stance taken toward the founders of Israel and their myths. Ironically, both the state-centered theorists and the new historians developed their own brands of heroic-style scholarship, theoretically reminiscent of the literature they were roundly criticizing. Additionally, a third group of critical sociologists and political scientists, the so-called "new" sociologists (a label pinned on me on more than one occasion), leveled a series of diverse salvos at Eisenstadt and his students. While some of these also reproduced heroic-style scholarship, others opened new, exciting paths in the study of state and society in Israel.

No one was more important among the state-centered critics than political sociologist Yonathan Shapiro of Tel-Aviv University. He truly was a leading light in the study of Israel. Shapiro took sharp aim at the functionalism of the social-systems theorists, hitting at their inclination to focus on stability and integration, rather than change and conflict. But, in Shapiro and his disciples' elite-driven theories, the heroes simply narrowed from the *halutzim* and their normative order in general to the state founders and leaders specifically.[17] In fairness to Shapiro, his treatment of his "heroes" was much less hagiography than a critical (sometimes, very critical) assessment of their actions. Still, the analysis centered on these men (with a rare woman thrown in), as the molders of the state, and on the state, as the molder of society.

In Israel, the "bringing-the-state-back-in" literature popular in the United States had special resonance.[18] As Shapiro pointed out, Israeli founders brought both the ideology of state socialism and the practices of Bolshevism to the development of the Yishuv. They thus created a top-heavy society in which the top was the institutions that would eventually become the state.[19] Also, the disruption to other social institutions that came through immigration of Jews to the country and the difficulty of piecing together the diverse streams of immigration in effective and powerful social institutions gave the state an unusually privileged status. Lev Luis Grinberg in his critique of the state-centered approach presents its key elements:

> The new Israeli state created in 1948 became a strong institution with a significant potential for autonomous action. The state concentrated in its hands tremendous material resources: all capital inflows from abroad and all property "abandoned" by the Palestinian refugees (this included both land and private homes). The state also unified and centralized the authority of the military forces that had recently defeated the Arab armies, and created a large apparatus to absorb the mass of immigrants requiring state assistance.[20]

The state in Israel, and not the vague conception of a normative Zionist consensus put forth by the social-systems theorists, now became the starting point for numerous analyses of social change and social domination. It was not that the origins of the state itself were not explored—as a new state those could hardly be taken for granted. Indeed, it was precisely the question of origins that engaged Shapiro in his best-known book.[21] Rather, in focusing on the precursors of the state and then on the state itself, many studies minimized or ignored any sources of authority other than the state as progenitors of sustained, meaningful social change. They tended to focus on the state as a tightly coiled organization that totally dominated the other sectors of society. It imposed order on society and was the source of society's consequential rules. Understanding social action in Israel, this approach maintained, demanded studying the state first and foremost. The particular character and structure of Israeli society, in this view, came out of the intentionality with which state policies were invested.

One ironic aspect of state-centered theories is that they came into prominence in the 1980s, at the very moment that observers began to note that global forces were challenging state dominance and even sovereignty everywhere. And, in Israel, all sorts of domestic factors (discussed in chapters 5 and 7) combined in the period after the 1967 war with these international forces to diminish the impact of state on society. For these reasons, the impact of Shapiro's state-centered sociology on Israel studies had a relatively short heyday.

Besides the state-centered type of research, the 1990s also brought a second (sometimes overlapping) set of critical works aimed at the earlier research dominated by social-systems theory. Many of these, too, promoted scholarship that tended to attribute Israel's distinctive rules to the intentionality of a powerful group, just as the heroic-style scholarship it so bitterly attacked had. The twist was that the critical works turned the heroes into villains. They did not see the central characters as forging national unity, as the social-systems theorists had earlier, but as a cabal imposing odious structures of domination on weak internal groups and on Israel's neighbors.

The fierce battles over Israeli historiography that developed in the 1990s between the new and old historians, especially regarding the history of the Yishuv and the 1948 war, stemmed in good part from the convergence of academic studies in the early decades of Israel's history with the national myths constructed by actual political and social leaders.[22] Works that, wittingly or unwittingly, accepted the teleology of an integrated center and social system suited the purposes of leaders eager for acceptance of their own version of society's "consensus," in Israel's case, the Zionist normative consensus. Heroic-style leadership, after all, made them into heroes. And, in Israel for someone like Ben-Gurion, being a hero could have even a messianic quality to it. The critical sociologist Michael Shalev put it this way: "According to this image," he writes, "the seeds of Israeli society were planted by the vision of the Second Aliyah [the wave of immigration in the early twentieth century] pioneers and their translation of this vision into both individual sacrifice and collective action. . . . This account is profoundly conservative. It echoes the official version of history and self-image of the founding fathers."[23]

The new historians, then, attacked the old studies as much for their uncritical acceptance of Israel's dominant political myths—for their anointment of these leaders—as for the theoretical inadequacy of the social-systems approach. And, in that regard I would have to place myself among these new critics and their rejection of the old way of doing history and social science in and on Israel.[24] Where I part ways with many of the new historians is in the continued use of conceptions of integrated centers and great leaders found in many of their works.

This deficiency of the critical literature is pronounced in books such as Avi Shlaim's *The Iron Wall* and Joel Beinin's *Was the Red Flag Flying There?*[25] For all its professions to revisionism and new history, Shlaim's much-touted book is the most conventional (and tired) form of foreign policy analysis, the representation of the entire state and society in particular, single-minded figures. From Ben-Gurion all the way to Netanyahu, and others in between, the story of Israel's relations with its neighbors is the sad tale of the misbegotten designs of single leaders. The revisionism or "*new* history," I suppose, is in the fact that Shlaim does not like these leaders or their policies. The old hagiography is gone, and we are left with diabolical, calculating leaders. The old hero-worshipping myths are certainly put to rest. But the kind of layered complexity to explain foreign policy in analytic terms that one finds in the works, say, of Aharon Klieman or Michael Barnett, which are far more innovative and imaginative, is wholly absent here.[26] The construction and reconstruction of foreign policy goals through the roiling events of Israel's history of international relations and through the interaction of state and society, and parts of the state with each other, are nowhere to be found in Shlaim's oddly staid account.

Beinin is much more willing than Shlaim to depart from old-style high politics in his analysis, moving from a focus on individual leaders to a more class-based account. He asks why Marxist movements were marginalized in Israel in the years surrounding the creation of the state (and in Egypt under President Gamal Abdul Nasser). The answer for the Israeli case takes on an odd resemblance to "pulling-yourself-up-by-your-bootstraps" analytic quality of the mythic-style scholarship. That is, Beinin's answer tends to bore in on the Zionist and state leadership and its deliberate policies as the principal factor explaining the Left's failure. The dynamic of interaction of that leadership with the Marxists is present but attenuated. But the dynamic interaction of the Zionists, both of centrist Labor and the left-wing Mapam Party, with the Palestinians (and the British)—the Zionists and Palestinians were, after all, at war for nearly two years and lived side by side long before that—is entirely analytically absent. Somehow, the redefinition of goals, tactics, and strategy and the restructuring of the parties themselves through the process of Arab-Zionist interaction, in war and in other settings, finds no place in Beinin's analytic construct. It is that sort of redefinition and restructuring that a state-in-society approach homes in on. And, without it, Beinin's story ends up sounding more like a morality tale than a rich explanation of why left-wing parties, such as Mapam, ended so far from their original Marxist principles. Beinin's readers are left with a shopworn account of the bad guys who undermined class solidarity, rather than a close analysis of how Arab-Jewish interaction reshaped the Jewish left. Indeed, Beinin's work is no less a morality play than the works of the old historians, such as Shabtai Teveth, writing of Ben-Gurion and his heroic exploits.[27]

Besides state-centered theories and the works of the new historians, a third stream of criticism directed at the old-style scholarship came from the critical or new sociologists. Their critiques have led to vituperative debates in Israel's newspapers, scholarly journals, and academic conferences.[28] Unlike the attacks from the new historians, the barbs from the new sociologists have been directed, not only at the chummy relationship between the "establishment" figures and the Zionist leadership, but also at the theoretical underpinnings of the old theories. It is difficult to cast these critics as part of a single group because their theoretical points of view differ substantially.[29]

To take one important example, Shalev employs the tools of political economy to tell a very different story about the Yishuv (and the state) from that of Horowitz and Lissak. Shalev's innovative account of Israel's labor history treats the founders much more critically than earlier works and, at the same time, employs theoretically sophisticated tools. Still, he fails to make problematic the relationship between what these founders intended and what actually occurred. In his account, Ben-Gurion and others maintain their mythically powerful qualities, even as they operate in a complex and constraining environment. These leaders, according to Shalev, had a single-minded goal and achieved it, even if they did have to experiment with various means to do that. A political economy in which the dominant labor group, for instance, both co-opted and discriminated against Arab workers was explained by Shalev in terms of the overall goals of the state (or Yishuv labor) leadership.[30] To be sure, Shalev wrote about a period in which the labor and political institutions were perched on the top of the social hierarchy. Still, his reliance on the notion of state autonomy provides too easy answers, it seems to me, to questions about complex processes of domination. He tends to miss the most interesting problems by focusing on the strategic goals of the political leaders and their supposed ability to have their way with others who might have leaned toward Arab-Jewish worker class solidarity.

Some of the intricacy and originality of Shalev's valuable book are thus blunted by an approach that tends to see a straight line between state leaders' intentions and the social results, rather than one that takes the process of state-society interaction as important in determining final outcomes. Like some of the other leading books among the new critics, his account has a disturbingly conspiratorial air about it, in which powerful leaders plot what they want and then achieve those aims. For all the originality of Shalev's valuable study, the characters in his story of labor in the Israeli political economy are static, stick figures who maintain fixed goals even in the process of tumultuous interaction over the course of decades. The shortcomings of his work stem less from an ideologically oriented approach (of which Lissak accuses him and other new sociologists)[31] than from the weaknesses inherent in the political economy theory that he embraces.

For all the problems in a work such as Shalev's, it brought new vigor to the study of Israel. Other new sociologists, with different theoretical perspectives, have also breathed new life into research on Israeli society and politics at the turn of the century. They have taken aim at both the social-systems and state-centered theories of previous decades. They no longer dismiss society as putty in the hands of the state, as an undifferentiated passive periphery shaped by the center or as sectors or subcenters dominated by the state. Works such as Uri Ben-Eliezer's wonderful research on civil-military relations have disaggregated the state in useful ways.[32] Among the first and most important figures looking at the interactive effects of state and society was Baruch Kimmerling, my collaborator for chapter 8. His innovative political sociology took the interaction of state and society quite seriously in topics ranging from civil-military relations to competing forms of social and political identity. He was one of the first Israeli sociologists to look carefully at the impact of Israel's domestic Arab-Palestinian population and the conflict with Arabs more broadly on the structure of Israeli state and society.[33] Gershon Shafir, Gad Barzilai, and others followed in his footsteps, opening up the study of Israeli society in new and exciting ways.[34]

Even among those who do not identify, as such, as new sociologists, one finds exciting accounts of new Israeli voices resisting, combating, or usurping the heroic state. Efraim Ben-Zadok, for example, began his edited collection on the growing power of local communities as follows: "The chapters in this book shed light on a new trend which is likely to change social relations and the distribution of power in Israel in the years to come. Since the early 1970s, local communities and regions began to demand their share of power from the central government and gained importance in the politics of the country."[35] Yael Yishai and Gadi Wolfsfeld echoed similar sentiments regarding the growing power of interest and protest groups.[36] As in the U.S. and European cases, a new emphasis was put on Israel's state as one in retreat from its previous dominating role.[37] It is interesting that even among these new studies of society, analyses often begin with an explanation of how the *old* pattern of state domination no longer holds (implying that, before then, it had stood up quite well).

The state-in-society approach suggests a framework for understanding Israel's history and society that embraces the important steps some of these social scientists have taken in recent years. Its unorthodox character comes in its focus on more than the construction and reconstruction of society, which could be seen even in works such as those by Eisentstadt and, in more compelling fashion, by the new generation of social scientists. State-in-society's innovation is in the mutual constitutive relationship of society and state—a state understood in terms of the tension between its larger image and its diverse practices. My approach's emphasis is not on the imagined linear relationship between actors' designs (or policies) and outcomes. Its theoretical focus is *on the process of becoming*—the continuing reconstruction of state and society—and on the lack of coherence among the state's practices.[38] The remaining essays in this book are not a finished product as much as themselves a theory that is becoming. As such they rely heavily on the recent innovative research by social scientists who have rejected some of the old myths that had shackled inquiry into Israeli society.

WHY STUDY ISRAEL?

The chapters in this book serve a dual purpose. On one side, they tell an alternative, or unorthodox, story about Israel's history, one that avoids simplistic mythic-style scholarship, with its larger-than-life heroes and villains. My story grounds its explanations, instead, in the processes of interaction of state and society. The aim here is not, as has been the case with some followers of Foucault,[39] to remove "agency" from the analysis. I believe that it is important to withhold credit from individuals when it is warranted and assign personal blame when that is necessary. But my approach does not see a straight line between leaders' designs and actual outcomes; rather, social outcomes are the result of the interaction of several agents, some far more powerful than others.

The starting point is how the engagement of those who had differing designs for how life should be ordered—powerful Zionist leaders, new immigrants, various elements of Palestinian society, neighboring states, great powers, and others—resulted in outcomes not fully intended by any one of these parties. It means taking seriously, for example, the notion that Zionism was not simply a normative system devised by key East European Jews, for good or for evil, but was shaped, in part, by Palestinians and other Arabs through their interaction with it. Similarly, for all the posturing among Zionists that they built the Israeli state despite the barriers the British posed, chapter 3 demonstrates that British actions and decisions were key components in Israeli state formation. On the other side, the essays in this book, especially chapter 6, implicitly (sometimes explicitly) argue that Israel is an excellent case through which to analyze comparative issues of state and society and to develop general social and political theory.

The selection of any case by a researcher is shot through with both personal considerations, involving all sorts of serendipity, and methodological judgments about the usefulness and appropriateness of the case in comparative terms. My writing on Israel is no exception. Methodologically, I will not belabor the point here of why I think Israel presents a useful lens for viewing general social and political phenomena and theorizing about them. I deal with portions of that argument extensively in chapters 2 and 6, and I touch on it in a number of the other essays. Also, I think that both Kimmerling in *The Israeli State and Society: Boundaries and Frontiers* and Barnett in *Israel in Comparative Perspective: Challenging the Conventional Wisdom* have already made that point quite convincingly.[40] In brief, my central methodological argument is that Israel actually is a very useful case to build theory for comparative purposes because of the transparency of its processes of state formation and society formation. Because all states and other social groupings are continuously being formed and re-formed, constructed and reconstructed, it is very instructive to have cases such as that of Israel in which those processes are clearly open, self-conscious, and immediately visible.[41]

I would like also to address the issue of personal considerations in using Israel as "my" case, since this is no less important in my choice than issues of strict methodology. The connection of my family's history to Israel's traces back to the closing years of the nineteenth century, and that history has had an undeniable effect on me and how I have viewed Israel academically. Living in what is now Belarus, in a *shtetl* outside the town of Slutsk, my mother's parents became devout admirers of Theodor Herzl, the founder of Zionism. At great risk to him and his family, my grandfather, Shmuel Dov Marshak, squirreled away a picture of Herzl in the house, taught his eight children to speak and write modern Hebrew, and initiated them (and any others who would listen) into the tenets of Zionism. While he, a *shohet* (ritual slaughterer) and rabbi, ended up in the Orthodox Zionist movement, Mizrahi, most of his children became committed socialist Zionists in the secular, left-wing Shomer Ha'Zair. When the family finally was able to solicit help from a branch of the family in the United States to make its way out of Russia in 1924, by then the Soviet Union, the two oldest children had to be left behind. One had been imprisoned for Zionist activities, and the other's boyfriend and future husband had been incarcerated for teaching Jewish history to children.

Later, both miraculously managed to make their way out of the country. The oldest, Shimeon, migrated directly to Palestine a bit more than a year after the rest of the family had left. His name eventually came to be branded into the heads of generations of Israeli high school students, all of whom used the notorious Marshak math book that he authored.

Kreine, the second oldest, was far less fortunate. She was compelled to stay with her husband, Shabtai, and their four children (one of whom died, probably from malnutrition) in the Soviet Union through the purges and terror of Stalinism. Shabtai's vivid descriptions to me of day-to-day life under Stalin's reign, especially the breakdown of all trust among family and even the closest of friends, literally made the hair on the back of my neck stand up. His accounts inculcated in me the power of the idea of Israel as a refuge for Jews from persecution, as the viable answer to the Jewish Question.

Only after World War II were Shabtai, Kreine, and their children able to surreptitiously hook onto a wending convoy of returning Polish refugees leaving the Soviet Union and march out of the country, finally landing up in a Displaced Persons camp. Their only son was killed in the 1948 Independence War almost immediately after the family's immigration to the newly created State of Israel.

Kreine and especially Shabtai, who took on the family name Beit-Zvi (the house of Zvi) in memory of their fallen son, had their entire world view recast by the Stalin years, the horror of their flight, and their son's death. Shabtai abandoned anything smacking of socialism, joining the right-wing revisionists led by Menachem Begin. He became highly active in the Soviet Jewry movement, which eventually led him, a science teacher in a vocational high school, to write a self-published book that improbably became an underground sensation in Israel.[42] Believing that the leftist political leadership of Israel was using the plight of Soviet Jews for its own immediate purposes, he investigated the earlier role of that leadership during the Holocaust to see if the same had occurred previously. The book that resulted from his years of research severely castigated Ben-Gurion and other Labor-Zionist leaders for consciously passing up viable opportunities to save Jews during World War II when the plans did not figure to further the goal of establishing a Jewish state. Ironically enough, the book became an inspiration to the leftist new historians and sociologists who were also so critical of the labor leadership.

Of my grandparents' six children who accompanied them to the United States, half eventually settled in Palestine and spent their lives in Israel. Zipporah was a founder of Kibbutz Ein HaShofet; and Avraham, of Kibbutz Kfar Menachem. Ruchama lived outside Tel-Aviv and wrote English-language textbooks for Israeli schools. My mother as the oldest of those in the United States began working immediately after the family's immigration to the United States, mostly in New York's garment industry. But that did not stop her own Zionist activities. In fact, she met my father in 1927 while handing out leaflets in Brooklyn's Prospect Park for a trip to Bear Mountain sponsored by the Zionist youth organization, *Zeire Zion*.

In the 1930s and 1940s, my parents' lives were tied up in the desperate struggle of trying to make ends meet for their young family as sometimes employed, sometimes not, garment factory workers. But, even in those grueling years, they found time for their passion, Zionism. I remember their evening Farband (Labor Zionist) and Pioneer Women meetings. When the UN voted in 1947 to authorize the creation of a Jewish state, they and their neighbors poured into the street to dance nothing other than the *hora*. In the 1960s, when they finally were able to take short vacations, they went to Unser Camp, the Farband summer resort in the Catskills, where for his entertainment my father spent mornings and afternoons soaking up lectures in Yiddish and English on Zionism and Israel. For my part, I spent summers in high school and college working as a busboy and waiter in Unser Camp, serving the Yiddish-speaking immigrants who came to the Catskills.

It is not surprising, then, that the idea of Israel was as strong an element in my childhood as any that I can remember. As soon as I scraped together enough money from my summer tips, I took a trip to Israel, working and studying on a kibbutz and traveling around the country. That 1964 journey, when I was nineteen, only intensified my love affair with the country and the people. And it fed all the heroic myths in the literature on Israel that I read.

But the society puzzled me, too, and these quandaries began to bring the old myths into question in my mind. The Arabs who made up about 15 percent of the total population at that time were all but invisible, still largely rural and governed by military administration. Jews from Middle Eastern countries were often far off the beaten track, too, in desultory towns such as dusty Ofakim. Rickety shacks, *tsrifim*, housing poor immigrants, again mostly from Arabic-speaking countries still surrounded Tel-Aviv. Jewish immigrants from India, the B'nai Israel, decried the religious leaders, who were folded into the state structure and who exercised tremendous power in such issues as marriage, for not recognizing the authenticity of their Judaism. For all the talk of national unity and absorption of the new immigrants, for all the allure of people dancing the *hora*, Israel was a country rife with largely hidden social tensions, with clear forms of social privilege, and with deep anger about the distribution of social and material rewards.

My feelings about these anomalies were largely inchoate and unarticulated at the time. But, by the time I returned for a much longer stint in the country for most of the first half of the 1970s, the unrest that had boiled over in the United States in race riots and antiwar protests, had sensitized me to look beyond rosy myths. Also, many of the stresses that had been barely visible in 1964 had now surfaced in Israel. The newspapers catalogued the daily wildcat strikes in boxes on the front page, and the vaunted labor organization, the Histradrut, seemed to have lost control of its membership. Black Panthers, modeled at least in name after the infamous Black American activists, expressed a new militancy of *mizrahi* Jews whose parents had come mostly from Arabic-speaking countries. Tens of thousands of low-level Arab laborers from the newly conquered West Bank and Gaza became the foundation for a restructured economy, which created all sorts of mobility opportunities for almost everyone other than these Palestinian workers themselves. The political leadership seemed confused, almost clueless, about the social and economic changes overtaking the country, and then it was hit with the blow from which it would not recover: the surprise attack of Syria and Egypt on Yom Kippur, 1973.

In my first job after receiving my Ph.D., a lecturer position at Tel-Aviv University, I found the academic establishment as bemused as the political leadership. Many economists and sociologists seemed oblivious as to how the addition of over 100,000 Arabs to the workforce, doing the most menial forms of labor, was turning social life, including that of Jews, topsy-turvy. I began to travel to villages in the West Bank to talk to Palestinians about how Israeli rule was affecting their daily lives. But I also began to think about how their presence was creating a society and a state in Israel that did not fit the images I had developed through my love affair with the country or the academic models touting a "normative Zionist consensus."

The new social mobility of *mizrahi* Jews was spurred by the injection of Palestinian workers into the economy occupying the lowest rungs of the occupational ladder, precisely those rungs previously held by these Jews from Middle Eastern and North African backgrounds. Their upward mobility, ironically, fueled loud political expression of their discontent. I marveled at how the new activism of young *mizrahi* Jews was dismissed by the politicians as the doings of "bad boys," in the words of Golda Meir, and how academics faltered initially in incorporating this activism into scholarly models or relating it to the addition of Palestinians to the workforce.

And I began to wonder, too, which was the *real* state in Israel? Was it the progressive Rule of Law that guaranteed all its citizens equal access to individual rights and state services? Or was it the bureau that served the Western Jew sitting in the waiting room ahead of the Middle

Eastern Jew and the Arab who had arrived earlier? The answer, of course, is that the Israeli state was and is both of these. Probably nothing influenced me more in my thinking about the concept of the state than viewing these co-existing, but highly contradictory, images of the same state. Increasingly, I felt that Max Weber's understanding of the state seemed to miss the mark. I began, as Kenneth Lawson wrote about the U.S. state, "to walk a tenuous line that avoids the scholarly tendency to accept uncritically the ontological status of the state (and thus replicates it), yet one that also recognizes the state as created and recreated by human agency."[43]

THE UNCERTAIN PATH TO A STATE-IN-SOCIETY MODEL

It is difficult to shed one's cloak of old myths. For me, that is true for both myths about Israel that grew out of my (continuing) love affair with it as well as for those theoretical myths about states generally that were inculcated in seminars and through years of academic reading. In the years that the following essays were written, from the latter half of the 1980s to the end of the 1990s, my state-in-society model was very much a work in progress, and the old myths pop up in them far too often. In fact, as I re-read them, I blanched at how often I fell back so readily into what Lawson referred to as the ontological status of the state. Indeed, Lawson noted that "Migdal himself struggles against (and I would argue sometimes capitulates to) the inclination to assign a single overarching purpose of the state to dominate society, pitting the state against, rather than within, society."[44]

This tendency to lionize the state and thus to overlook the extent to which even the early Israeli state was constituted and re-constituted through its interactions with elements of Jewish society, as well as with various groups of Arab and other actors, is particularly evident in part II, which contains the earliest written essays in this book. Grinberg quite correctly criticized chapter 3 on precisely this basis.[45] And Ben Smith wrote of chapter 2, "The framework is heavily focused on the inceptions of states. It seems a bit deterministic to me, as though the inception or original period of state-building sets a course from which no, or little, divergence can take place. . . . The beginnings of institutions are an important predictor of their subsequent capacities, but so too are later junctures."[46] Similarly, chapter 4, seeks overzealously to establish a stark contrast between Ben-Gurion and leaders of Egypt and Mexico, Gamal Abdul Nasser and Lázaro Cárdenas. The result is that the essay too readily accepts the pervasiveness and dire effects on the latter two leaders of social dislocation and local strongmen and, in Ben-Gurion's case, too eagerly dismisses the limitations posed on him by social forces and other political forces. Ben-Gurion emerges, I think, looking more invincible than he should, and the staying power of local strongmen in Egypt and Mexico as the cause of the failure of Nasser and Cárdenas is not sufficiently supported.

For all these difficulties, these three essays were important vehicles for me to break out of the box imposed by dominant, European models of so-called state-building and to begin to venture beyond the long theoretical shadow cast by Max Weber. They present a portrait of state formation in which the Europeans serve as actors and participants (in the case of Israel, the British), rather than as theoretical models. Additionally, these three essays take the process of the construction and reconstruction of states from the ahistorical realm to one in which world historical forces play a key role. Finally, they inject potential state-makers into a sociological milieu in which they must contend with other potential rule-makers, inside and outside the state organization, and in which the struggle itself transforms the participants.

In part III, the emphasis shifts from state formation to what I call society formation. Here, my focus is on the emergence of countless groups, associations, and movements in society making all sorts of demands on the state and on the changing balance of Israelis' self-understanding of their society—who is to be included and who, excluded from central participation in the nation. These essays were written later than those in part II and reflect my attempt to move away from a purely linear explanation of the character of societies or the capacity of states. Instead, the articles focus on the on-going struggles in which groups have been engaged over the question of rules. Chapter 6 analyzes the vexing changes that have occurred in Israeli society in the process of the continuing struggle over rules and who makes them, as ethnic bonds have moved to overshadow civic ones.

For the Israeli state, chapter 5 argues, these struggles may have led to diminished internal coherence and capacity. This chapter, like those in part II, falls into the trap that I criticized others of earlier, of assuming that the Israeli state before the 1967 War was overbearing and seemingly immune to influence from an enfeebled society. Again, I was too anxious to create a contrast, this time between the state of the 1950s and 1960s with the more beleaguered one from the 1970s on. The earlier state did have remarkable capacity for a new state; circumstances, as I show in chapter 2, made it far more formidable than other new states. Still, it is important to qualify its strengths and indicate the factors that limited it.[47] Also, in an effort to demonstrate the challenges to the state, especially to its leaders' efforts to present it as the maker of foundational rules that mediate among competing sets of everyday rules, I underplay an important dimension of civil society that emerged in later decades. The mushrooming of women's groups, environmental associations, civil rights movements, and more have frequently empowered the state as a whole or a part of the state against other parts. This mutually constitutive relationship between fragments of the state and fragments of society is an important dimension of Israel's recent history that is slighted in the essay.

Part IV aims to explore further the mutually constitutive and transformative relationships of social groups and the state (and its fragments). Chapter 7 argues that exogenous factors, especially ones as disruptive as war, can have momentous effects on the struggle over rules. Here, I examine how the 1967 War and the territorial changes it brought about led to changes in Israelis' understanding of both their state and society. The silent actor in the changes analyzed in this chapter, as well as in other essays in the book, is the Palestinian population of Israel. Chapter 8 brings that group to the fore.

Chapter 8 differs from all the articles that precede it. The others all grapple with the interaction between theory and Israel's history and society explicitly, attempting to understand the phenomenon of state-in-society through the particular experience of Israel. Chapter 8, which I wrote jointly with Baruch Kimmerling as a part of *Palestinians: The Making of a People*, uses the state-in-society approach implicitly, but the model does not drive the logic as it does in the other chapters.[48] Still, I thought the issue of Israel's Arab population important enough to warrant an extended discussion in this book, even if it has a somewhat different feel from the others.

In sum, my journey in developing the state-in-society approach has been an exciting, if uncertain, one. My encounter with Israel, and with my own preconceived notions about Israel, has been a crucial element in advancing theoretically, but that encounter has entrapped me more times than I would like to count. The progress of the articles below, from the earliest to the latest ones, attest to that.

PART II

State Making

CHAPTER 2

The Crystallization of the State and the Struggles Over Rule Making: Israel in Comparative Perspective

BUILDING A COMPARATIVE FRAMEWORK TO ANALYZE THE HISTORICAL EMERGENCE OF STATES

Much of the recent literature on the concept of the state and its role in social change has centered around the experiences of Europe. Authors such as Dyson[1] and Badie and Birnbaum[2] have gone so far as to rule out explicitly from their consideration "stateless societies," ones lacking a long historical and intellectual tradition of the state as an institution that embodies public power. They have argued—wrongly, I think—that the "idea of the state" is as important as the organization and functions of the state, and consequently European states, which have long intellectual traditions concerning the state itself, stand apart from practically all others.

The near-exclusion of other cases from the lively debate on the role of the state in society is a pity. The "idea of the state"—whatever the differences in the length of its tradition from society to society—has quite simply demolished all other conceptions of large-scale political rule. In no previous period of recorded history do we find the homogeneity of political organizational types that we do currently. Throughout the world, agreement now abounds among political elites that the state is the proper way to organize politics and that the state organization should provide the predominant (if not exclusive) set of "rules of the game" in each society. And, in cases where states do not make some of the rules, it is still they that should authorize other organizations (e.g., families, markets) to do so in particular realms of social interaction.

These rules of the game that state officials have sought to impose on their societies have involved much more than broad constitutional principles. They have included the written and unwritten laws, regulations, decrees, and the like, which officials have indicated they are willing to enforce through the coercive means at their disposal. Rules have spanned the entire gamut of social life, from registering births and deaths to designating classes of acceptable and unacceptable sexual partners. They have involved the entire array of property rights as well as the boundaries of acceptable personal behavior. Fueled in this century by the notion of self-determination and by the sanctification of the state form as well as the specification of its purposes by the United Nations, the conception of the state has emerged as a kind of inviolable canon of contemporary political discourse. This homogeneity in the image of what states should be lends a strong basis for comparative analysis beyond the European cases.

This chapter takes this notion that there is a rationale for comparative analysis of all contemporary states one step farther by asking if and how we can compare the historical emergence, or crystallization, of states. Must the histories of states be written, as has most often been done, only in individual "national" terms, mining the evidence in each case as if its circumstances were unique? Strong national myths, such as that found in Israel or almost any other society for that matter, have subtly and not so subtly supported accounts of the founding of the state that emphasize its "differentness," the special experiences and values of the culture group that shaped its unique character. In the academic study of the emergence of the state of Israel, as with most other new states in Asia and Africa, one finds only a smattering of works that transcend the assumption of a unique national history and historiography. Among the exceptions are Kimmerling's[3] use of the concept of frontier and Horowitz's[4] use of the notion of deeply divided societies.

My purpose here is not to attack the celebration or analysis of national distinctiveness. A viable approach to the *comparative* analysis of the historical emergence of states, however, is sorely needed to enhance and complement other studies in important ways. At the very least, it would provide a set of questions drawn from a variety of experiences that might give insights into specific cases. On a more ambitious level, such an approach might also offer explanations about critical differences among contemporary states by using an analytical framework that can compare the historical roots of these states.

One of those crucial differences—the one to be singled out in the discussion that follows—concerns the varying capabilities of states. Although agreement abounds among political elites worldwide that states are the proper way to organize politics and that state organizations should provide the predominant rules of the game, there has been wide variation in the actual capabilities of states to make such rules and have them stick. Badie and Birnbaum[5] allude to the varying capacities of states, comparing them in their ability to impose ways of behavior on their societies (what they call the autonomy and capacity of states):

The progress of state building can be measured by the degree of development of certain instrumentalities whose purpose is to make the action of the state effective: bureaucracy, courts, and the military, for example. Clearly, the more complex and highly developed these instrumentalities are, the greater the capacity of the state to act on its environment and to automatically impose collective goals distinct from the private goals generated within the social system itself. In this situation, the state's autonomy corresponds to a tangible reality.

The aim of this chapter is to present a preliminary outline of a comparative historical approach to state crystallization. This approach can suggest explanations about the important differences in the capacity of states to initiate and enforce the rules of the game in their societies. Israel presents an excellent case study for outlining such an approach for several reasons. First, on almost any overall scale measuring state capabilities, Israel falls among the very highest of the new states and even fairly high among all contemporary states. As an exceptional case, it can help shed light on the general process of the consolidation of state power in the post–World War II era. Second, an anomaly in Israel's capabilities helps point to different aspects of state capabilities, which can vary even within a single state. The anomaly lies in Israel's impressive ability in having new rules it makes stick while having grave difficulty in formulating and initiating such new rules in many social realms—quite the opposite phenomenon from most other new states. That is, the Israeli state is much better at getting people to obey its rules once they are made than in making rules in the first place. This variation can be instructive in disaggregating, or taking apart, the process in which states achieve higher capabilities.

In attempting to develop a comparative approach to the historical crystallization of states that can illuminate key differences in their present-day capabilities, I am not treading on a terribly well-worn path. Certainly, at least from the time of Marx, some scholars have attempted to relate general historical phenomena (e.g., the development of capitalism or industrialization) to the character of the modern state. But the concern of Marx and many others was much more to explain the appearance of a certain genus or sort of political organization—the modern capitalist state—than to understand the important differences between such states. One of the first—and still best—efforts at explaining variation between modern states was Moore's *Social Origins of Dictatorship and Democracy*.[6] Moore's emphasis, however, was on the historical roots of different forms of the state, dictatorship and democracy, rather than on state capabilities or what Nettl[7] called the degree of "stateness."

Practically all other serious efforts at building a comparative framework for studying the historical emergence of states have been done within the European context. For the most part, these valuable works[8] have stressed the internal factors leading to the sorts of institutions (courts, police, army, revenue-collecting agencies) that constitute a modern state—what Badie and Birnbaum called the instrumentalities of the state. Once again, the variations in "stateness" have been slighted in many of these works in favor of several explanations of the modern state as a unique form of political organization. Many authors also have overemphasized the internal causes for change while underestimating the international factors that played a critical role in state crystallization. Wallerstein[9] redressed the balance in differentiating states according to their strength and in emphasizing the world-systemic factors, but he went too far in the opposite direction. In his schema, states turn out to be little more than functions of capitalist development, and important internal dynamics in the creation of state institutions and their capabilities are underrepresented in his analysis.

The approach developed here is designed to use the commonalities of all contemporary states as a basis for comparison, while highlighting key events in the historical process of consolidating power that will point to why states have turned out so differently in their actual capabilities. Our focus will be on the struggles that are necessarily implied in a definition of the state as institutional—an organization enforcing a certain set of rules. If the accepted conception among political elites is that states should make the rules to govern even the minute details of people's lives, then the emergence of the state connotes possible struggles with at least three sorts of opponents:

1. *old rule makers*—those who had made and maintained other sets of rules for all or part of the population claimed by the state;
2. *potential rule makers*—those who at the moment of state expansion sought to make different rules, within or outside a state organization, in all or part of the territory claimed by the state;
3. *potential state breakers*—those who did not seek to make the rules themselves in any part of the territory claimed by the state but nonetheless maintained an interest in keeping the state from making and enforcing the rules of society.

The crystallization of states has reflected the preparation by leaders of states or states-to-be (through institution building, political mobilization, coalition making, and so on) to encounter those opposing the implementation of state rules and the actual engagement with these forces (the struggle for social control of the population). Our comparative approach, then, involves an analysis of the degree of opposition states have encountered from these three types of groups having interests in thwarting the formulation and application of rules. It suggests the hypothesis that the current aggregate capabilities of a state are inversely proportional to the overall strength of these three sorts of actors during the historical struggles to extend the state's rule-making domain. A second hypothesis is that the distinctive character of a state derives, at least partially, from particular defeats, compromises, and accommodations, which depended on the varying strength of opponents in the three categories of old rule makers, potential rule makers, and potential state breakers. The particular strength of oppositional forces in one of our three categories will later reflect itself in state weakness in a particular realm of rule making and rule application.

In short, we can better understand the variation between states in capabilities by comparing them in the overall level of opposition they faced in making and applying rules from forces in the three categories. And we can better understand the variation in capabilities in different spheres within states (i.e., the character of states) by comparing the varying degree and kind of opposition they encountered from the forces of the three categories. These forces resisting the designs of the leaders of the state organization, as we shall see, have come from both inside and outside the territory claimed by the state. Thus, both domestic and international patterns of stratification have affected the process of the crystallization of states and their current capabilities.

SOCIAL CONTROL AND STRATEGIES OF SURVIVAL: HOW TIED IS THE POPULATION TO EXISTING RULES?

In our framework, then, the critical processes for understanding the historical emergence of states and the current capabilities of these states are struggles with domestic and outside groups that can be classified through the categories of old rule makers, potential rule makers, and potential state breakers. Before looking more closely at the relationship of these groups to state crystallization, we will ask a prior question: What are their struggles with the state over? As noted above, the conflicts concern rule making and application, or social control. State social control means subordination of people's own inclinations of social behavior, or their obedience to other social organizations, in favor of the behavior proscribed by the rules of the state. What does social control entail? How is it achieved? All sorts of organizations in society, ranging from small families and neighborhood groups to mammoth foreign-owned companies, have used a variety of sanctions, rewards, and symbols to induce people to behave in their interactions according to certain rules or norms, whether those interactions have been between father and son, employer and employee, landlord and tenant, priest and parishioner, or any other.

Social organizations, including states, have combined symbolic configurations with material rewards and sanctions (means to solve mundane needs of food, housing, and the like as well as to avoid physical punishment, ostracism, etc.) to offer people the wherewithal to devise strategies of survival—roadmaps for effective and acceptable behavior for individuals in a world that hovers on the brink of a Hobbesian state of nature. As roadmaps, these strategies of survival guide one through the maze of daily life, ensuring one's existence and, possibly, pointing the way toward upward mobility. They also provide a link for the individual between the realm of personal identity and self-serving action, and the sphere of group identity and collective action, including solidarity built through kinship, religion, ethnicity, or citizenship.

From the perspective of the state, social control stems from its offering the components to the population for viable, effective strategies of survival. The more successful states are in selective use of material rewards and sanctions and the more meaningful the myths or symbols they present, the more they can demand obedience and even garner legitimacy from the population. The components for strategies of survival and social control are the basic elements of the exchange between subjects and states, and it is from this exchange that states generate power, which can be used both within the society and outside.

Through most of human history, however, there have been legions of strategies of survival at work in areas that are today claimed by single states. Territories have hosted a potpourri of different rules for personal behavior. Political leaders have generally found it exceedingly difficult to dislodge rival strategies of survival, particularly among risk-averse poor peasants.

One key factor in determining the success of states in their struggle against other groups pressing different rules upon the population has been how tightly those old rules have bound the population. Social control is not a constant but varies in different times and circumstances. Strategies of survival that are binding and convincing at one moment may become unbearably burdensome or irrelevant with changing conditions. These changing circumstances that strengthen or weaken the hold of existing rules have often been exogenous to any efforts by leaders to use the state organization for making new rules in society. That is, it may be sheer chance whether the struggle by the states against old rules is launched at a moment when existing strategies of survival are strong throughout the society or at a time when a great many have been battered by exogenous forces.

What sorts of exogenous forces have weakened existing strategies of survival through vast portions of a society simultaneously, thus opening new opportunities for aggrandizing state leaders? These have had to be forces powerful enough to cause widespread social dislocation among the population. Factors such as war in tandem with destructive plagues or revolution have upset man-land ratios, undermined resource bases, and made old strategies of survival irrelevant in the conditions of social disruption. Aside from these fairly rare circumstances, the existence of working strategies of survival among the potential clients or subjects of the state has posed stiff resistance to the attempts of political leaders to increase vastly the social control of the state.

The present-day Israeli state, with its relatively high capabilities, benefited greatly from historical circumstances that presented it with a population whose strategies of survival had been greatly weakened. Its powerful ally that caused vast social dislocation was migration. Migration—especially massive migration—can be as effective a force as war, plague, and revolution in weakening existing strategies of survival. The generation of the Mandate, leading up to the creation of the state in 1948, witnessed a nearly tenfold increase in Jewish population. The number of Jews grew from less than 80,000 after World War I to nearly three-quarters of a million on the eve of Independence. Old strategies of survival simply could not endure the uprooting of migration. The inability to replicate old social organizations and their functions was true even of families and clans seeking to maintain as much of their old strategies as they could. Among the young (many unmarried) migrants to Palestine, especially those consciously rejecting the dominant symbols of the East and Central European Jewish society from which they came, one was even less likely to find entrenched strategies of survival.

The sort of resistance to the designs of aggrandizing new states found among potential subjects in old societies of Asia and Africa, clinging to tried and tested ways, did not exist in the case of Jewish society in Palestine. Much more to the point, new Jewish immigrants desperately sought new strategies to deal with the immediate mundane, and more long-range transcendental, problems that they encountered in the process of physical relocation. Leaders of the Yishuv had to address those needs on the symbolic as well as the material level. It is not surprising that aspiring state leaders looked to commonly held symbols, especially "the continued Jewish identity of the vast majority of the population . . . ,"[10] for use in the strategies of survival they proffered. But even the endurance of such unifying symbols could not mask the deep differences in what and how Jewish traditions should be fit into comprehensive strategies and the continuing desperate search for new strategies to overcome the severe dislocation so many had suffered.

In sum, a state's capacities in making and enforcing new rules—gaining social control among its population—have depended on its ability to have the strategies of survival that it offered accepted by the population. Serendipity played a major role in determining the state's success in pressing its strategies on the society. Where people were tied tightly to their existing strategies of survival, state officials found the going very difficult. But where exogenous forces widely disrupted social life and made existing strategies unbearable or irrelevant—as vast social changes in Europe coupled with the trauma of migration had for the Jewish population in mandatory Palestine—those states (or prospective states) faced much more promising circumstances for having their own strategies accepted.

THE STRUGGLES FOR STATE SOCIAL CONTROL: OLD RULE MAKERS

The strength or weakness of old strategies of survival among those in the territory claimed by the state, how tied in people were to the old rules, relates most directly to the struggles of the state against old rule makers. It was these old rule makers, after all, who proffered the strategies and rules, which either still stood as the established codes for the population or had suffered through the battering of exogenous forces. Leaders attempting to consolidate power in a newly organized state may have confronted two sorts of old rule makers: 1) those whose power was limited to a local domain, such as the European feudal lord and his demesne, and 2) the ancien régime itself, which sought to make at least some rules over the entire territory now claimed by the newly organized state (or its organizational predecessor).

On the level of actual rule making and application—governing the details of people's lives—the more important of these two sorts of old rule makers in many societies may very well have been the figures with limited domains. Social control was most often highly fragmented, with many different strategies of survival and different organizations offering the elements for those strategies in a country. In various times and places, these figures were called *caciques*, *effendis*, *zamindars*, chiefs, lords, *sheikhs*, *kulaks*, and more. We can simply label them strongmen. These strongmen used their ability to regulate access to key resources to build organizations with significant social control in local areas. Their organizations typically employed a mix of sanctions (including physical violence) and material rewards (especially land, water, and credit in peasant societies) to increase social control. Many strongmen built or strengthened their organizations by controlling key bottlenecks in the flow of capital, goods, and labor during the period of the rapid advancement of capitalism out of Europe in the latter half of the nineteenth century. Although the patron-client ties that have constituted the backbone of these strongmen's organizations have often been considered "traditional," in fact many have been intimately tied to the spread of the modern world economy.

Where such old rule makers were strong, officials attempting to expand the jurisdiction of the state encountered stiff resistance in a particular realm—the actual implementation or application of the state's rules. The results of these struggles only infrequently resulted in the elimination of strongmen's social control. In a number of cases of state crystallization, the struggle, involved on-again, off-again campaigns by the state against strongmen, leading to some state success in dislodging particular strongmen or even particular groups of strongmen but with others quickly filling the gap. This pattern typified Egypt under the rule of Gamel Abdul Nasser, with its nationalization of large landholdings, Campaign against Feudalism, and the like. In other cases of state crystallization, the strong social control of strongmen led to somewhat different results. The struggle in states such as Mexico resulted in accommodations in which strongmen managed to employ state resources to strengthen their own social control over clients. They have thus undermined the ability of the state to direct the behavior of that portion of the population through state rules and strategies. These strongmen have openly used state funds, offices, and so on to build strategies of survival inimical to those developed in the state's capital city. The rules and strategies proffered to the population at the local level, then, reflect a historical, unwritten *compact* between state organizations and local strongmen, sometimes fairly longlasting (as in Mexico since the 1930s) and sometimes fairly unstable with different groups moving in and out of the strongman roles (as in Egypt since its revolution in 1952).

Only where there have been strong forces causing widespread social dislocation and weakening of the ties of the population to the old rules did states make major advances in their own capacities at the expense of such strongmen. In a number of such cases, states triumphed sufficiently in their struggles that they could avoid such compacts. The states in Vietnam, Yugoslavia, China, the Soviet Union, and several other selected cases were able to take advantage of weakening social control on the part of the old rule makers caused by the devastating combination of war and revolution to increase vastly their own capabilities in applying their rules.

The institutions in Palestine that eventually came to be the core of the Israeli state—the unusual mix of the Jewish Agency, the Histadrut, the *Va'ad Leumi* (National Council), and the leading party, Mapai—had particularly good fortune in the struggle against old rule makers. First, the constituency of these new institutions was limited to the Jews of Palestine. Fortunately for the Zionist leaders it was only among the Arab population that such strongmen played any real role in the attempts at consolidation of power (we shall return to this point below). Among the Jews, such strongmen were limited mainly to a portion of the religious community. Some religious organizations, in fact, did work against the Zionist parastatal institutions and the attempts to proffer new strategies of survival, but the numbers of Jews these religious strongmen influenced were fairly limited. For the rest of the Jewish population, few strongmen of any sort survived the process of migration and social change. In short, the struggle with old rule makers at the local level that so affected the eventual capabilities of many states was much less significant in the case of Jewish Palestine. The Jewish parastatal institutions in Palestine never had to face the same sort of difficult struggle against fragmented centers of social control that so many other states did in their process of crystallization. Powerful forces did not enforce different rules and present different strategies effectively among most of the Jews of Palestine. The entry of the Zionist institutions into this breach resulted in their developing unusual capabilities in the application or implementation of rules at the local and personal levels.

Opposition to would-be states with new leaders eager to consolidate power came from a second sort of old rule makers as well, the ancien régime. The old political organization claiming the entire territory presented important opportunities in addition to obvious obstacles to leaders seeking to replace it with a newly organized state. Whether a foreign-dominated regime, as in the case of colonial states, or an indigenously ruled one, the old political organization had important assets—bureaus, politically and bureaucratically experienced personnel, capital, symbols, legitimacy—that could be of great use in the establishment of the newly organized state. On the other hand, these old regimes most often had severely limited social control themselves, ruling as they did through the strongmen of society rather than through direct application of rules to the population. Simply appropriating their assets did not necessarily create a stronger, more capable state for the new leaders. The amicable handing over of the assets of the state—as occurred, for example, when the British presented the reins of power to the new indigenous leaders of Sierra Leone in 1961—could lead to a weak state as reliant on its strongmen as was the colonial regime that preceded it.

Two sorts of circumstances in the historical crystallization of states seem to have led to enhanced capabilities. First, where the ancien régime, particularly colonial states, limited its active, direct promotion of strongmen through material resources and other favors, newly organized states had a better chance of developing direct links to the population through their strategies of survival. Second, where leaders seeking a newly consolidated state had to engage in a prolonged conflict with the ancien régime, they were more likely to develop increased capabilities as they sought to mobilize materials and personnel directly from the population in service of their struggle.

In Palestine, the British Mandatory state that preceded Israel could have posed one or the other of two sorts of barriers to increased capabilities for the Zionist political institutions. In fact, they did neither. The British could have promoted strongmen in Jewish society, channeling resources selectively to those creating strategies in local domains. The success of the central Yishuv institutions, especially the Histadrut, in devising new strategies of survival for the immigrants preempted the creation of other effective organizations run by strongmen along ethnic or other lines, which could have provided such strategies. Zionist success, in no small part, resulted from British policy. British early encouragement and later sufferance of the building of central Jewish institutions contrasted sharply with their policies in most of the empire. Elsewhere, as in Sierra Leone prior to so graciously handing over power, the British behaved quite differently. They actively promoted tribal chiefs, giving them the authority to tax the population, make their own regulations, and adjudicate cases based on those rules. These strongmen, endowed with resources and authority garnered from the colonial rulers, remained important obstacles to state leaders seeking social control even after independence was granted.

British rulers also could have posed a serious obstacle to the creation of central Jewish institutions in a manner other than by encouraging ethnic strongmen and organizations. They might have attempted to build in Palestine a strong Mandatory state, itself capable of achieving social control among the population. Certainly Britain had the resources and administrative abilities to offer directly the components for viable strategies of survival to Palestinian Jews and Arabs. Once British rulers realized the difficulty of reconciling Jews and Arabs, however, they quickly gave up on the idea of a strong, unified Mandatory state. Powers in the territory, they concluded in the early 1920s, should be devolved to separate communal institutions of the Arabs and Jews.[11]

Despite the often discordant relations between British rulers and Zionist leaders, almost from the outset of the Mandate, the Jews came to reap tremendous benefits from the collaboration that stemmed from Britain's willingness to devolve authority to the two communal groups. Wasserstein wrote,

> Towards the Jewish National Home in Palestine [High Commissioner Herbert] Samuel pursued a deliberately passive policy: the task of the

Government of Palestine in relation to Zionism was merely to create the conditions, political, legal, and (to a lesser extent) economic, necessary for the Zionists themselves to carry on their work; the government would facilitate rather than encourage or direct Jewish immigration and settlement. This had the advantage for the government of precluding the diversion of state revenue to investment in Zionist development.

British despair early-on of creating a viable unified political framework for Palestine worked to the Zionists' advantage, allowing them to create a basis for an autonomous Jewish community with relatively consolidated social control. The British, while posing all sorts of obstacles in the path of the Zionists in the 1930s and 1940s, nevertheless removed themselves from any struggle with the Zionists over the exercising of social control among the Jewish population. In addition, those obstacles the British did put before the Zionists, together with their encouragement of the Arab cause from the late 1930s on, helped induce the Zionists to redouble their efforts at mobilization of Jews and Jewish resources for their struggle. This mobilization also increased Zionist capabilities in rule application.

The British, then, presented the Zionists with a near optimal mix of positive and negative policies to help increase the capabilities of parastatal organizations. On the one hand, they devolved considerable authority and channeled some material resources to the Zionist central institutions, rather than fragmenting power by promoting numerous strongmen as they had done in so many colonies. By the time of the issuance of the 1939 White Paper, on the other hand, they had effectively abandoned the Balfour Declaration in favor of an eventual Arab-dominated state in Palestine, thus precipitating mobilization efforts by the Zionists that strengthened the central Jewish leaders' ties to the Jewish population.

In sum, state capabilities—especially in the implementation of rules at the local level that comes through direct, close ties with the population—were shaped in great part in the struggles against old rule makers during the process of state crystallization. The greater the efficacy of strategies of survival supported by strongmen in local areas, the more difficult did newly organized states find it to apply their own rules. The old rule makers in the ancien régime could strengthen these strongmen even further through policies to channel resources and authority that enhanced the strongmen's rule. Where such strongmen were weakened, however, newly organized states had a much greater chance of establishing social control. The capabilities of new state leaders, ironically, could be further enhanced by the opposition of the ancien régime, forcing the new leaders to mobilize resources and personnel directly from the population in support of their struggle. In Palestine, the Zionist institutions benefited from an unusual array of circumstances. These conditions left them with only marginal opposition from strongmen, thus opening the way for direct access to the Jewish population, but with growing opposition from the British (and, as we shall see, Arab nationalists), which provided strong incentives to redouble that access to the Jewish population in order to mobilize personnel and material resources for the struggle.

POTENTIAL RULE MAKERS

Those aspiring to consolidate new power in the state faced not only the challenge of established social control in the society by old rule makers but also that of other powerful figures and their organizations vying for future control. Three sorts of groups could fall into this category: 1) those seeking to set up an alternative state organization, 2) those supporting the existence of the newly organized state (or the major goals of the parastatal institutions for control of the territory) but with fundamental dissension about who should form its leadership and what its rules should be, and 3) the potential recruits to the state organization who would implement the state's rules.

As in the case of the ancien régime, those seeking to establish an alternative state provided opportunities as well as obvious liabilities to the leadership of the crystallizing state. The nationalist Arab movement presented the Zionist leadership with clear challenges, as both sought control of all of Palestine, and with subtle opportunities for increasing Zionist capabilities.

The opposition by the Arab nationalists to any sort of Jewish autonomy was total and unrelenting. Despite all the drawbacks they encountered—including the British commitment to a Jewish national home, their own factionalism, and the difficulty of unifying a heterogeneous people in circumstances of rapid social change—they remained consistent and unified in their demand throughout the Mandate for an Arab-controlled state in the entire territory. For reasons that I have elaborated elsewhere,[12] however, that leadership did not work toward the development of the "instrumentalities" that Badie and Birnbaum wrote about, whose effect would have been to lay the basis for an effective state. They did not conceive of the struggle to create an Arab state in Palestine as one that involved proffering the elements for strategies of survival through central institutions among their potential clients, the Arab population. As a result, Arab strongmen whose bases of control were local drained the nationalist movement of its hope of establishing a strong

countrywide base of power. This enfeeblement of the national movement occurred even as these strongmen participated directly in the struggle against the British and the Zionists.

The lack of social control by any central Arab institutions visited
upon them two related disasters. The first was loss of the struggle
against the Zionists and the British. Initiative on the Arab side fell to the
heads of the surrounding Arab states, not the Palestinians. The second,
of course, was their inability to meet the challenge of civil war and then
of international war against the Zionists in 1948. The fact that they
could not make the rules of the game among the Arab population in
Palestine during this critical period meant a glaring inability to mobilize
and organize for war. The tack they had taken to establish a state served
them adequately as long as the British dealt with only a thin elite layer
of each communal group, Arabs and Jews. With British withdrawal
from Palestine, however, the Arab leaders' conception of the state
proved wholly inadequate. The Zionists had developed strong social
control among their constituency and the ability to field a regular army.
The Arabs had not. Their leaders did not prove to be effective rivals for
control over the territory.

While the Zionists benefited in their attempt to establish their own
social control throughout Palestine from the weaknesses among Palestinian Arabs, they also increased such control as a result of their perception and fear that a future war with the Arabs could destroy the
Zionist enterprise altogether. During the last two years of the Mandate after aborted attempts to step up active opposition against the
British, Ben-Gurion began to dwell more on possible war with the
Arabs than on the immediacy of British rule. He contemplated seriously, for the first time, the real short-term likelihood of British withdrawal from Palestine. Ben-Gurion focused Jewish preparations on the
possibility of an attack on the Jews by Palestinian Arabs and the regular armies of the neighboring Arab countries following British withdrawal. Political and military leaders in the Yishuv needed to plan, not
only the tactical changes demanded by regular warfare, but also the
creation of mobilizational capabilities to support such an effort. The
Yishuv leaders, then, felt a strong imperative—induced by their concern for the coming war—to increase the capabilities and control of
the organizations that would constitute the basis of the future state.
Some of these efforts met with success; others, such as the attempt to
unify all Jewish armed forces under the Yishuv political institutions,
failed. The overall result, however, was increased social control for the
Zionist parastatal institutions as a result of their leaders' fear of the
potential of alternative rule makers, the Arabs.

During the War of Independence itself, Ben-Gurion pursued his internal struggle for increased state control. The refusal of Menachem Begin to turn over all the arms on the ship *Altalena* to the state army precipitated Ben-Gurion's decision to fire on and sink the ship. Similarly, the autonomy of the commanders of the prestate Jewish fighting units and the lack of organizational suitability to the war at hand led Ben-Gurion to reorganize the leadership of the new army, inducing the resignation of the High Command. Amid charges and countercharges of revolt against the state and imposition of a dictatorship, Ben-Gurion, weighing the grave risks stemming from war with the Arabs, extended the struggle of the state against internal Jewish forces attempting to assert their own rules of the game.

In brief, as potential rule makers seeking to establish an alternative state organization, Palestinian Arabs and their allies failed organizationally to establish the social control necessary to displace the Zionists, opening the way for Zionists to develop significant control in the boundaries of Palestine. At the same time, Palestinian threats further motivated the Zionists to enhance their social control among the Jewish population. Threat of war influenced Zionist leaders' calculations about how far to push the internal struggle; that is, war affected their willingness to risk incurring the dangers of internal instability and even of loss of limited support from certain domestic groups. The dangers in not extending internal social control, and with it mobilizational capabilities, in the face of the threat of war induced leaders to take risks against other domestic Jewish forces pressing their own rules of the game, which they might not have taken otherwise.

A second dimension of the struggle that Ben-Gurion and his cohorts undertook against potential rule makers involved other Zionists who supported the idea of a Jewish state but harbored some very different ideas from Ben-Gurion's about how to achieve and organize it. A variety of streams existed within the Zionist movement, each with its own conception of how to lay the basis for an autonomous Jewish community. Although most of these streams did not openly articulate their conception of what a state should or would be, at least until the Biltmore Program in the 1940s, their actions and attitudes toward the Jewish Agency (the foundation of any possible state in the future) indicated widely different ideas about the nature of a future state.

Chaim Weizmann, for example, worked incessantly to build a broad worldwide consensus of all sorts of Jews, including non-Zionists, as the basis for Jewish political autonomy. His concern with the future state was much less directed toward its organizational aspects—and the control implied in such organization—than toward the development of a set of broad operating principles that could serve as a common denominator to unite Jewish elites. Justice Louis Brandeis, to take another prominent example, hinted at a different conception of a future Jewish state, one drawn from liberal America. He foresaw strong Jewish control within private self-sustaining enterprises. A state, in his view, must establish a basic framework of justice within which such organizations can flourish, and it must protect individual rights, but the direct social control to be exercised by the state should be minimal. Neither of these conceptions of the state—nor that of Vladmir Jabotinsky, leader of yet another Zionist stream—served as a blueprint for building a state with a high degree of "stateness." They did not propose a state that would or could address the needs of potential clients in Palestine directly. Their lack of attention to creating mobilizational capabilities through increased social control of the Jewish population in Palestine left them fairly weak in the struggle to define and lead the institutions that would eventually become the state.

It was the labor Zionists who recognized the importance of establishing firm social control among potential clients as the basis for a future state. As one of several streams within the larger movement, labor's position within the World Zionist Organization (WZO) was at first fairly weak. It gained only about 20 percent of the votes for delegates during the 1920s. Rather than focusing on coalition building among world Jewry to increase influence in the WZO, labor leader David Ben-Gurion used the early 1920s to spin workable strategies of survival for the small but growing Yishuv population. Institution building focused on the worker federation, the Histadrut, which claimed the membership of 70 percent of Jewish workers in Palestine by 1926. By offering such services and institutions as health care, labor exchanges, trade unions, education, workers' kitchens, and a bureau of public works, labor leaders created a tap of rewards and sanctions that could be turned on and off to regulate the exchange of social control for the components going into new strategies of survival. They also elaborated a set of myths drawn from nationalist doctrines, socialism, and Jewish history to give transcendental meaning to these strategies.

The tactics of the labor movement to focus its efforts on the mundane needs of future clients in Palestine created for it a near-monopoly of social control among the Jews of Palestine. Other Zionist streams, for both ideological and tactical reasons, chose not to challenge Ben-Gurion for social control. The result was that the labor-dominated institutions did not encounter a difficult struggle in the post-Independence era against subjects already harboring other strategies of survival. Social control in Palestine also gave labor leaders an advantage during the 1930s in taking control of the worldwide Zionist movement because of the tremendous organizational advantage they had over other streams, especially in Palestine itself. WZO leaders "soon realized they could not build a bureaucratic organization of their own to handle all of the necessary functions—especially since most of the members were foreign Jews. . . ."[13]

The preoccupation of World Zionist Organization leaders, especially Weizmann, with the international mobilization of support may have had an added benefit for labor leaders building social control in the Yishuv itself. Although they had to be on guard against occasional attempts by WZO personnel to demand accountability for the material aid that the world organization channeled to the labor groups, labor leaders had a relatively free hand in using outside funds to build the sorts of strategies of survival they wanted. The WZO served to build a consensus among world Jews for the Zionist enterprise; it mobilized funds for Zionism; and it worked to gain support of important states. It left the question of social control largely to the labor leaders of the Yishuv. With the external preoccupation of the organization, it found itself increasingly dependent on the leaders in Palestine. As Arthur Ruppin put it,

> Experience had taught us that, the settlements of ours go to pieces as the result of inner division, where there does not exist at least a kernel of individuals with a more or less unified outlook to give the tone, and to assimilate to their unified outlook, the other members of the groups.[14]

The disinterest of Weizmann and other WZO leaders in the actual organization of strategies of survival enabled labor leaders to play the core role, garnering outside resources while paying minimal costs in terms of their own social control. Even the sporadic efforts within the WZO to demand self-sufficiency of Zionist institutions in Palestine, however, made labor leaders wary enough of possible outside control to work for dominance within the world organization as well as within Palestine. Ben-Gurion thus compromised his adamant opposition to alliances with capitalist Jews in his famous change in the late 1920s "from class to nation"[15]—a change that served as the prelude to labor's domination of the entire Zionist movement, both inside and outside Palestine.

The informal division of labor among the Zionist streams in recruiting and applying outside support worked to the advantage of the labor leaders, who were building the organizational basis for social control in the Yishuv. They benefited from the international achievements of Weizmann and others in countering the forces opposing the creation of a Jewish state and from the material support, mostly from world Jewry, that the WZO attracted. At the same time, they were able to use such support to build strategies of survival without an undue amount of external interference and with only fairly limited changes in the conception of the state.

Besides the opposition of potential rule makers such as Weizmann, Brandeis, and Jabotinsky representing secular Zionist ideologies, labor leaders encountered serious dissent from ultra-Orthodox Jews, as well, some of whom denied altogether the national basis for Jewish society. The ability of the ultra-Orthodox Jews to affect the very conception of a possible future state or possibly to block the emergence of a state altogether stemmed from several factors. First was their sheer size and moral standing within the world Jewish community. Second was their domination of the existing Jewish society in Palestine that the Zionists first encountered in the late nineteenth century. Ultra-Orthodox Jews controlled many important aspects of life in the Old Yishuv. Third, and perhaps what is most important, British policy during the Mandate gave an important institutional foothold to the ultra-Orthodox Jews, allowing them to force compromises in the main leadership's conception of the state.

Although the Balfour Declaration referred to a *national* home and Winston Churchill expanded the national conception in a speech in the early 1920s, British policy at least from the mid-1920s on rested on a religious definition of the Jewish community in Palestine. Moreover, the British sanctioned the creation of authoritative religious institutions with significant control over aspects of Jewish life. The rabbinical courts and the Chief Rabbinate were creations of British rule in Palestine. These institutions were incorporated into the self-governing structures of the Yishuv.

In addition, in order to gain British acceptance of the Yishuv's representative body, Knesset Israel, and its executive arm, the Va'ad Leumi, the new Yishuv leaders allowed for as inclusive participation of various Jewish streams as possible, including even anti-Zionist groups. Parties with radically different notions of the proper agencies to govern Jewish society thus became an important part of the new central political institutions of the Yishuv. Later, with the voluntary withdrawal of some ultra-Orthodox Jews from these institutions, partly over the issue of women's suffrage, labor leaders made significant ideological compromises in order to maintain at least the pro-Zionist portion of the Orthodox stream within the labor-led political institutions.

As a result, in 1948 the new State of Israel inherited "an established religion and a tax-supported rabbinic establishment exercising judicial powers, as well as a religious trend as part of the public school system."[16] It also maintained its inclusive (proportional) electoral system that guaranteed important representation to the small Orthodox political parties in the Knesset. The proportional electoral system made it less likely that any party could achieve an absolute majority, thus increasing the chances of small religious parties to become integral parts of government coalitions. The continuing presence of these parties in Israel's cabinets has cut deeply into the unity of purpose of the state and the ability of the central leadership to apply many aspects of its conception of the state during the period of state crystallization.

If there was one struggle in which the labor Zionists faltered in their efforts to establish effective social control in Palestine, it was in this area of interaction with the Orthodox institutions. Labor leaders confronted Orthodox organizations that had well-defined constituencies with functioning strategies of survival. In addition, the British policies to channel authority and resources to Orthodox-dominated institutions coupled with the labor Zionists' efforts to portray the institutions they headed as broadly representative induced Ben-Gurion and his associates to accommodate and compromise with Orthodox leaders. The first effect of the accommodations was to narrow the range of issues of governance in which the state could establish an autonomous position. Many matters of personal status, including marriage and divorce, for example, came under the jurisdiction of religious law, leaving no room for autonomous state initiatives.

A longer-term effect of the compromises was to limit the state's ability to take initiatives in nonreligious issues as well. The labor Zionists agreed to an inclusive legislative system through proportional representation in order to portray the Zionist institutions as community-wide rather than as ones that were narrowly based or sectarian. This system not only gave the Orthodox parties, with less than 15 percent of the vote, the leverage to maintain the status quo in religious issues or more recently to extend religious jurisdiction, it also has been the basis for coalition governments that have severely limited the power of the largest party. The system generally has made it difficult for the state to take policy initiatives or speak with a single voice on major social issues. It has injected groups with marginal vote-getting ability into a position where they could obstruct state initiatives. Whereas single-district voting systems usually give the largest party an agenda-setting role during its term of power, in Israel the accommodations in the struggle with potential rule makers among the Orthodox Jews resulted in precariously balanced governments that have had difficulty in creating a coherent agenda at all. Rule making has been the weak link in the Israeli state.

States are large and complex organizations. Although a handful of people and their particular conceptions have in many cases been the driving forces behind the crystallization of the state, they have had to attract numerous others into the organization in order to make it work. Those recruits into the agencies dealing with the application side of the rule-making process have had interests of their own and distinctive conceptions about what the state should be. These recruits constitute a third group of potential rule makers with which state leaders struggle, after those seeking to establish an alternative state and those who support the state but with fundamental dissension about its rules and leaders. That struggle is based on two ill-fitting needs: satisfying the interests and conceptions of these potential members of the rule-applying agencies of the state organization while still maintaining the unity of purpose of state founders or leaders.

The task of preserving some semblance of the leaders' conception of the state, especially the central myths or symbols that they propound, and of instilling a unity of purpose in state agencies is perhaps as difficult as dealing with out-and-out rivals to the entire state organization. All states have been wracked from within by tremendous centrifugal forces. The question that Horowitz[17] asked about Palestinian Jewish politics involves an issue that applies to other states and states-in-the-making as well: "How did the 'centripetal' propensities in the Yishuv overcome the 'centrifugal' propensities . . . ?" Ben-Gurion reflected his fear of these centrifugal forces within the agencies sponsored by the central political institutions. Such agencies, he noted, "pursue their own interest instead of being guided by an overall national plan" and each could end up "ruled by itself and for itself."[18]

Ben-Gurion's fear, however, was tempered by his need for the cadres who would eventually staff state offices. The cadres were the critical elements who actually applied or implemented the new rules of the game and made strategies of survival attractive to the population. In all cases, these cadres or bureaucrats have had interests of their own. In fact, Kraus and Vanneman[19] have argued that it is worthwhile regarding bureaucrats as one of many groups in society seeking its own interests.

In those cases where tradeoffs have maximized both the interests of such groups and the autonomy of states, cadres have been relatively independent of existing bases of social control in the society's nonstate organizations and have been skillful enough to execute the grand designs of state leaders. They have identified their own survival and mobility—their careers in society—with the success of the state as an autonomous organization. Where social differentiation has produced such individuals, whose primary interests and loyalties have not been with existing civil social organizations competing with the state for social control, the possibility has existed for forging the interests of state rulers and state officials. The struggle to build effective implementation machinery has been less forbidding when social groups have existed whose loyalties to parochial groups have been weakened and whose status could be enhanced through the crystallization of an autonomous state.

Shapiro[20] has reviewed some of these early struggles in the Yishuv in the 1920s. He has focused on the tension between those who turned out to be the major leaders of the future state, especially the Second Aliyah leadership of the Ahdut Ha'avodah Party (later, Mapai) with its major personality, Ben-Gurion, and the core of their future cadres. These cadres were part of a younger generation that immigrated to Palestine in the Third and Fourth Aliyot. Many were *Zeire Zion*-Socialists, who had received important political education during the Russian Revolution and the subsequent Russian civil war.

By 1922, the Soviet regime had turned against Zionism, and these young, politically capable socialists found themselves in Palestine, devoid of their former ties to the Bolshevik enterprise. Many of these immigrants had middle-class backgrounds and had some sort of higher education. They did not seek laborer positions but saw their mobility in paid party or Histadrut posts. As they joined the Ben-Gurion-led Ahdut Ha'avoda Party, new tensions emerged. Shapiro reports how in 1924–1925, Ben-Gurion seemed to shy away from expanding the party, fearing "to invest too much power in a party apparatus manned by newcomers, not his old associates." Eventually he found, however, that his control of the party was put in jeopardy without the support of these newcomers, who were so adept at organizational tasks. Ben-Gurion ultimately entrusted the building of the party apparatus, which was to control the Yishuv's central institutions, to these young cadres.

> These encounters in Ahdut Ha'avodah between the veteran leaders and the younger ZS [*Zeire Zion*-Socialist] organizers who had just escaped the Bolshevik dictatorship, resulted in close cooperation between the two. . . . The veterans needed a party apparatus and the newcomers were willing and able to build it. The newcomers, at the same time, were willing to follow the lead of the older leaders. Their arrival as refugees from Soviet Russia may have contributed to their deference to the veteran leaders. . . . The newcomers accepted Ahdut Ha'avodah's socialist-Zionist orientation and supported Ben-Gurion's idea of class democracy within the Histadrut. . . . These two groups—the top leaders at the helm of the party and the Histadrut, and the apparatus builders—in cooperation managed to organize and direct the masses.[21]

The price that these cadres exacted from the top leadership was not ideological for the most part. They demanded, instead, an opportunity to assume organizational posts without first paying their dues as agricultural laborers. Ben-Gurion was thus able to build the infrastructural prerequisites to deliver viable strategies of survival to the Jewish population and to expand social control without unending struggles with his cadres about the purposes or modes of administration of the future state. Unlike those potential rule makers who were incorporated into the Knesset and the Government itself—the ultra-Orthodox politicians who harbored such fundamentally different views—the new cadres did not exact a price for inclusion that would dilute either the rule-making or implementation abilities of the future state.

POTENTIAL STATE BREAKERS

The most direct and often the most formidable struggles for those attempting to build social control through a state or future state organization have been with the old rule makers and potential rule makers. As we have seen in the case of Israel, a number of important exogenous forces, including high rates of migration, the structure of the Arab national movement, and the availability of unencumbered cadres, all served to weaken the possible opponents to the increasing control of the parastatal institutions led by the labor Zionists. The result has been that the current aggregate capabilities of the Israeli state have been exceptionally high, especially relative to those of other new states. The difficulties the state has had in the areas of rule making have stemmed in part from the specific accommodations made in the pre-state period to the relatively important and central groups of Orthodox Jews.

Struggles for state supremacy have involved more than those already making the rules and those who wished to do so. State consolidation in a highly interdependent world has been an issue of concern to those who did not want to be rule makers at all but nevertheless saw their interests deeply affected by the possible rise of a state with significant domestic social control. The most important of these actors have been outsiders, other states or powerful transnational forces. Struggles that have constituted the formative historical experiences for the creation of control and power by states have by no means been limited to internal conflicts.

Outside enemies, of course, can have the most devastating impact on the ability of leaders to achieve their goals of state predominance within a given territory. In the worst of circumstances, they can militarily defeat the state and its leaders and demand the most drastic sorts of changes. Even in less severe circumstances, they can cripple the state's domestic control through war, economic sanctions, and more. They can also aid directly those internal groups that are struggling with the state for social control.

Ironically, potential enemies in war can unwittingly lead to enhanced social control by the state organization. The aims of the neighboring Arab states to destroy the Israeli state in 1948 and in subsequent wars failed, but their sustained hostility has been an incentive to the

Israeli leaders to maintain the highest mobilizational capabilities possible. In an odd fashion, then, the threat of Arab attack has led to enhanced social control by the Israeli state. In short, the actual wars with the Arab states have had very little impact in impeding rule making and application by the Israeli state, and the perceived dangers inherent in the struggle have even been motivating factors for Israeli leaders to extend state control through high tax rates, universal conscription, immigrant absorption policies, and the like.

The Israeli state similarly avoided the negative impact of possible state breaking by any of the world's powers. Because no single power could establish the sort of hegemony in the Middle East in the post–World War II period that Britain maintained prior to the war, Israeli leaders could use the competition among states, especially the Cold War, to its advantage. From the UN vote to create the state in November 1947, to its reliance on U.S. support to deter unrestrained state breaking by the Soviet Union, the Israeli state has managed to avoid the sort of interference in its consolidation experienced by such states as Hungary or the Dominican Republic.

International stratification, then, can be as important in shaping the process of state crystallization and ultimately the capabilities of particular states as patterns of domestic stratification. Counterintuitively, states crystallizing in a nonhostile environment or under the wing of a major world power may find circumstances less favorable for developing state capabilities than those emerging in a hostile environment or one marked by power competition. Israel's state took great domestic risks in its mobilization in order to counter the threats of Arab states and, at the same time, avoided the potentially stifling effects of single-power dominance (at least until the late 1960s).

CONCLUSION

State crystallization has not simply been a function of the will and commitment of a particular people and its leaders to realize their distinct national goals and values. Potential obstructions to the emergence of a capable state—one able to offer viable strategies of survival to its population and establish firm social control—have littered both the domestic and international settings. State capabilities have risen or fallen as a result of the struggles with three sorts of actors that have been concerned (as has been the state) with the rulemaking process, the formulation and implementation of norms for social behavior. The following chart indicates the struggles with these actors that have deeply affected the historical crystallization of states.

TABLE 2.1
Struggles in the Historical Crystallization of States

1. Old Rule Makers	local strongmen
	ancien régime
2. Potential Rule Makers	rivals for the entire territory
	ideological dissenters
	cadres
3. Potential State Breakers	neighboring states
	world powers

The above framework provides a basis for comparative analysis of the historical experiences important in the crystallization of states. Internal and external struggles, often shaped by how exogenous factors have affected various groups (e.g., the impact of migration on existing strategies of survival, the effect of the Russian Revolution on cadres for the Yishuv), have in large part determined the ultimate "stateness" of states. Of course, each state's struggles have differed, but the above schema provides a basis for comparing those varying experiences.

Our hypothesis has been that the overall capabilities of contemporary states stem in great part from the degree of opposition state leaders faced in the process of state crystallization. Where the overall level of opposition by the three sets of actors has been high during the crystallization process, the state's ability to formulate and implement rules for the population has remained low. And where exogenous factors have weakened or neutralized these actors, states have been much more likely to develop high levels of social control and capabilities. We have also argued that the distinctive character of states comes in part from the accommodations and compromises state leaders have made with particular actors in their struggle for domination. The strength of a particular opponent brings about modifications and compromises in parts of the process of formulating and implementing policies. Variation in the strength of different actors struggling to make and apply rules helps explain the unique set of bargains, compromises, and coalitions into which different states enter with forces inside and outside their societies.

In the case of Israel, an unusual number of exogenous factors neutralized and weakened the negative effects of old rule makers, potential new rule makers, and possible state breakers on state consolidation. The overall weakness of actors in these three categories in actually challenging for social control coupled with the labor Zionists' fear of the potential damage some of these actors could do resulted in an unusual opportunity for the Israeli state to build a relatively high level of social control and capabilities. These factors include:

1. the weakening impact of migration on old strategies of survival among Jews;
2. the weaknesses of potential local and all Palestine rivals, both among the Jews and Arabs;
3. the willingness of British leaders of the Mandatory state to grant significant autonomy;
4. the availability of skillful cadres, who did not exact a high ideological price for their participation in the state-in-the-making;
5. the willingness of elements in the World Zionist movement to work for diplomatic support and to channel significant material support to the Yishuv without exacting a high ideological or organizational price;
6. the relatively limited negative effects of the destruction of war on the ability to offer strategies of survival and the positive effects of the threat of war on inducing increased mobilization;
7. the existence of a power balance in the Middle East, which impeded the emergence of a state-breaking hegemony in the region.

The one struggle in which labor leaders had to cede considerable ground as they worked for state predominance helps explain a peculiar feature of the Israeli state. That struggle was with ideological rivals in the Yishuv, especially Orthodox religious groups. The concessions made in order to include broad sectors of the Jewish population of Palestine in the new political organizations have had a long-term impact on the nature of the Israeli state: they have helped make Israel a strong state with a weak government. That is, the state has had high relative success in implementing the social and fiscal policies, the rules, that it has adopted,[22] but it has had increasing difficulty in coming to decisions about which rules of the game should obtain in society. As the state's environment has changed, its leaders have found the mechanisms of the state ill-suited to facilitate their adoption of initiatives to meet the new circumstances.

CHAPTER 3

Laying the Basis for a Strong State: The British and Zionists in Palestine

While chapter 2 surveyed a number of key factors that facilitated the consolidation of a strong Israeli state, this chapter hones in on one factor, the unusual effect of British rule in Palestine. Zionist history prefers to portray its early leaders as succeeding despite British rule. In fact, the British facilitated the attempts to consolidate power and avoid the fragmentation that overtook ex-colonies in Africa and elsewhere.

VARIATION IN THE RECREATION OF SOCIAL CONTROL

The recreation of social control following the tremendous expansion of the world market and of European state power starting in the mid-nineteenth century took on different hues in various societies of Asia, Africa, and Latin America. Centralized control of Zionists in Palestine contrasted sharply with the fragmentation in, for instance, Sierra Leone. Fragmentation of social control and the eventual creation of an extremely weak state were not necessary outcomes of colonialism, even in already heterogeneous societies. Direct colonial rule, such as that of French or Portuguese colonialism, channeled resources somewhat differently from British techniques, leading to different distributions or amounts of social control in the indigenous societies. Even within the British empire, the type of rule varied considerably with wildly different results.

Although a now deeply fragmented state such as Sierra Leone may be a prototype for many former British colonies, all former colonies have by no means shared its experiences of continuing fragmentation of social control. Different types of collaboration yielded varying results. States of different strengths do exist, even some emerging from British *imperium*, and some are much stronger with respect to their populations than that of Sierra Leone. These variations in strength should be explicable, in no small measure, by differences in outside influence on the organization of society during that historic window of opportunity when so many societies' old strategies of survival failed.

In India, for example, British actions had a much more contradictory effect than in Sierra Leone, sometimes tending toward fragmentation and other times toward consolidated control. Creation of the vaunted Indian Civil Service led the list of actions that spurred the creation of an all-Indian, unified elite. Civil servants, as Rothermund indicated, were in a position to act as "umpires" for a unified set of rules.[1] British influence in establishing a cohesive Indian army and a new legal system (with the proliferation of Indian career officers, as well as lawyers and judges, respectively) also created strong institutional and human bases for a formidable state after independence. The new educational system did much the same. At the same time, the diversion of British authority and resources first to various *rajas*, *zamindars*, and other lords and later to rich peasants recreated a foundation for numerous strongmen to exercize fragmented social control throughout the country. Much of the essence of Indian state-society relations since 1947 has been the accommodation and struggle between a state with significant mobilizational capacity and the rich peasantry with its tenacious hold over aspects of rural life.[2]

The Israeli state offers a case at the opposite end of the spectrum from Sierra Leone's, a case in which strongmen with fragmented social control did not at all become a major part of the state-society relations. Israeli society—even only the Jewish portion of Israeli society—was extremely heterogeneous. Yet, the state's ability through social policies to change its population's daily habits and to preempt and delegitimize contending social organizations from exercising autonomous social control has placed it among a handful of new strong states.

BACKGROUND TO CREATION OF
JEWISH SOCIETY IN PALESTINE

The world system's forces that so drastically changed the face of Palestine in the twentieth century first took root far from that country. The Jews of Europe, especially Eastern Europe, faced head-on the unsettling political and economic winds that buffeted the European continent throughout the nineteenth century. New symbols, which cemented the revised strategies of survival among the peoples of Europe, left the Jews open to grave dangers. The latter part of the nineteenth century witnessed rapid growth in the importance of these symbols, particularly those contained in new aggressive nationalist ideologies, which effectively excluded the Jews. The strategies of the Gentiles now put the differentness of the Jews in a new light. In Romania, to take one example, "Jews *as such* were denied citizenship even where their families had lived in the Principalities for centuries."[3] Vital quoted a Romanian court decision of 1877, which stated that "the Jews do not have a country of their own and therefore do not belong to any state."[4]

The growth of a world economy based in Europe and the consolidation of new states on that continent upset the Jews' bases of social control and existing strategies of survival as much as any group's. What became known as the "Jewish problem" was the combination of this internal dislocation with the exclusion of the Jews from participation in the new strategies that took hold in the countries of Europe. Jews faced growing antisemitic sentiments, open attacks, and hostile state policies at the very moment in their history when many of them considered the elements of their old strategies of survival—adherence to rabbinic codes, communal organization, alliances with princes, and more—irrelevant to their new needs.

Jews responded to the Jewish problem with a tremendous burst of creativity in at least four sorts of solutions. They tried, where possible, to assimilate into Christian European societies, assuming the mores and habits of their non-Jewish neighbors with unbridled enthusiasm. Second, they created new Jewish institutions, such as Reform temples, which could change Jews sufficiently to fit into new European societies, without losing their identity as Jews. Third, they left Europe in massive numbers, mainly for the United States but also for many other countries. Finally, they proposed radical transformations of society—either general society or Jewish society or both—to eliminate altogether the bases for the Jewish problem. Anarchists, communists, socialists, Bundists, and others set out the schematic contours of future societies in which the underpinnings for any sort of Jewish problem would be entirely absent; they participated in movements and organizations, heavily populated by Jews, to work toward their goals.

Zionism was one such proposal to transform society radically. Its creators, led by the stately Viennese Jew, Theodor Herzl, envisioned a social transformation in which Jews no longer would occupy selected, vulnerable niches in other societies. Instead, they would fill the whole range of "normal" social roles in their own Jewish society located in their own territory. Herzl wrote:

> We have sincerely tried everywhere to merge with the national communities in which we live, seeking only to preserve the faith of our fathers. It is not permitted us. In vain we are loyal patriots, sometimes superloyal; in vain do we make the same sacrifices of life and property as our fellow citizens; in vain do we strive to enhance the fame of our native lands in the arts and sciences or their wealth by trade and commerce. In our native lands where we have lived for centuries we are still decried as aliens, often by men whose ancestors had not yet come at a

time when Jewish sighs had long been heard in the country. The majority decide who the "alien" is; this, and all else in the relations between peoples, is a matter of power.[5]

After some arguing within Herzl's movement, by the early twentieth century the Zionists agreed that the territory of the Jews would be Eretz Israel, Palestine. No other place had the symbolic overtones for the socially dislocated Jews, whom the Zionists so desperately sought to recruit to their cause. In addition, Palestine had always maintained a Jewish population, and after the 1880s the settlement grew fairly quickly. Its numbers swelled from about 23,000 in 1881 to 85,000 by the outbreak of World War I; however, this was still considerably less than 20 percent of the country's total population. Probably close to 100,000 Jews immigrated to Palestine in those years, but more than half left shortly after their arrival in that desolate Asian outpost.

Zionism certainly did not yet offer sufficient components for strategies of survival for a society of Jews in Palestine. By 1914, it did little more than propose a set of symbols—or more accurately, a number of competing sets of symbols from its various factions—which could eventually be incorporated into such strategies. Zionist organizations lacked the rewards and sanctions and the symbols that could tie together and provide the material base for effective strategies of survival. Jewish society, growing alongside the more established Muslim and Christian Arab society in Turkish-ruled Palestine, was still very much in the making. What sorts of social control would be created at this historical moment when Jews were migrating into the country seeking viable strategies of survival was an open question.

Jewish experience in reconstituting social control in Palestine was clearly an exceptional case. After all, the demise of their old strategies included transplantation to a faraway land. Such migration, however, has many analytic similarities to the spread of the world market in the late nineteenth century. Migration is one of the most powerful means of shattering old forms of social control. Together with the effects of the new world economy on the Jews as well as the aggressive nationalism in Eastern Europe, migration had a severely dislocating impact on Jewish society. Breaking old patterns of social control among Jews was not terribly different from destroying existing forms of social control among other societies.

Other aspects of the Jewish case were also exceptional. Most of the original Jewish settlers, for example, were from Europe, not the Third World. Jewish society in Palestine, the Yishuv, grew in a bicommunal setting in the midst of established Arab society, and the two were deeply divided. Also, among many new Jewish settlers, there were both high motivation to achieve a unified political entity and deep commitment to certain shared symbols derived from Jewish history and religion. In these and other important ways, the Yishuv was a singular experience.

Nonetheless, it has been argued quite convincingly, both generally and in the particular instance of the Yishuv, that the exceptional case can shed light on the general phenomenon.[6] In the matter of the reconstitution of social control in the wake of socially dislocating forces, the Yishuv and later Israeli society provide some stark lessons about the impact of outside forces on this process and the ultimate creation of a strong state. Dan Horowitz, who felt the Yishuv could be very instructive in understanding some general issues of social change, posed the question before us in this way: "Despite these cultural and ideological splits and despite the great potential for conflict embodied in them, how did the 'centripetal' propensities in the Yishuv overcome the 'centrifugal' propensities; for the history of the Yishuv during the Mandate can be portrayed as an almost continuous process of growth, integration, and deepening of communal autonomy."[7] The battle between centripetal and centrifugal forces lies at the heart of the political process throughout the Third World. Israel's experience in how these forces confronted each other is illuminating for understanding other countries whose histories have differed considerably in other ways from those of Israel.

THE BRITISH PROPOSE A JEWISH AGENCY

The Ottoman Empire's defeat in World War I and the British succession to power in some of the Ottomans' former Middle Eastern provinces sent shockwaves through the local populations, especially in Palestine. For Palestinian Arabs, the new status of Palestine as a united country, separate from the rest of the Arab and Muslim world and ruled by an alien Christian power, raised even farther the level of anxiety many felt due to the emerging threat of Zionism.[8] Jews in the country faced seemingly more sanguine prospects, a ruling power committed to promoting in Palestine the establishment of a Jewish national home where the Zionists could realize their dream of an autonomous Jewish society.

Even before the British marched into Palestine in 1918, their Secretary of State for Foreign Affairs Balfour wrote to Lord Rothschild, on November 2, 1917, that "His Majesty's Government view with favour the establishment in Palestine of a national home for the Jewish people, and will use their best endeavors to facilitate the achievement of this object." This simple statement turned the Middle East topsy-turvy: Jews rejoiced; Arabs have mourned and demonstrated each November 2, until this very day. The Balfour Declaration became a cornerstone for the subsequent establishment of British rule in Palestine.[9] In fact, the preamble to the Mandate for Palestine, approved by the Council of the League of Nations, stated that the Allies "agreed that the Mandatory should be responsible for putting into effect the declaration originally made on November 2nd, 1917."

The new system of mandates resembled colonialism because it involved the direct appropriation of the highest formal decision-making posts in the society by the outside power. Unlike the building of empires in Africa, however, the new mandates were not intended to establish the hegemonic power's rule into the indefinite future. Article 22 of the Covenant of the League of Nations recognized explicitly the temporary and provisional character of all mandates. The antiimperial legacy of World War I, in fact, initiated a half-century of what has been called "Imperial sunset."[10] The mandatory powers sought ways to build local forces that could secure their interest in the region without a permanent colonial presence.

In Palestine, the Mandate was unusually specific about the need for the ruling British to share power with local Jewish forces: "Article 4. An appropriate Jewish Agency shall be recognized as a public body for the purpose of advising and cooperating with the Administration of Palestine in such economic, social and other matters as may affect the establishment of the Jewish National Home and the interests of the Jewish population in Palestine."[11]

The British decision in the early 1920s to encourage the creation of a Jewish Agency, with an active role in the economic and social affairs of the Yishuv, was a critical element in shaping the nature of Jewish society and the entire future of Palestine. It also had much greater repercussions than the British foresaw or with which they could cope. When the British attempted to include the Arabs of Palestine as local forces participating in ruling, they found the Arabs simply unwilling to accept power sharing based on the premises of the Balfour Declaration. In fact, Arab leaders rejected any official participation in the administration of the Mandate, including the option of an "Arab Agency" alongside the Jewish Agency, because it included the Balfour Declaration with its promise of a national home in Palestine for the Jews. Britain's inability from the start to reconcile the growing animus between Arabs and Jews—so painfully obvious with the first outbreak of anti-Jewish Arab rioting in April 1920—led the British officials to conclude that a unified political framework in Palestine was unattainable. Although they continued to speak officially about the goal of unity through the 1930s, they basically lost hope in such a framework by the early 1920s.

For the British, this realization constituted a profound disappointment. From the strategic view of London-based Foreign Office civil servants, control of Palestine and other parts of the fertile crescent had been extremely important at the end of World War I. It gave the British unimpeded access to the northern overland route to the Persian Gulf and from there to India, in addition to their control of the southern waterway route to the Indian Ocean through the Suez Canal. Fear of spreading Bolshevism magnified Foreign Office concerns at the end of World War I. Alarm over the possibility of a Turco-Bolshevik threat to India through the Middle East only increased the strategic value the British placed on the region and their hold on Palestine.[12]

Prior to actually setting foot in Palestine, they had believed that a unified Mandatory state working toward a Jewish national home and protecting the rights of the Arabs could provide a British strategic presence in Palestine. Through power sharing they felt they could avoid the high costs of governing the territory directly. The arrangement could also lead to a stable regime even after a formal end to the Mandate, ensuring British interests. These hopes evaporated quickly after the implementation of the Mandate. As early as 1920, former Foreign Secretary Balfour, who after all had authored the very document that had fired Jewish hopes, spoke of Palestine as "no great catch."[13] In 1922, debates were held in parliament on the question of abandoning the Mandate altogether.[14] With the growing tension between Arabs and Jews in the 1920s and 1930s, the Foreign Office became less and less convinced of the strategic importance of Palestine and of the viability of an autonomous Jewish national home.[15]

Left with the responsibility of actually governing the territory and realizing there would be no reconciliation of Jews and Arabs within a unified Mandatory state, Colonial Office civil servants sought some new political framework. Many powers in the territory, they concluded in the early 1920s, should be devolved to separate communal institutions of those Arabs and Jews, although some functions such as security and public works stayed within the Mandatory state.[16] The implications for the reconstitution of social control among the local forces in Palestine were profound. Even though some of these implications, such as the growing British penchant to play Arabs and Jews off one another in classic divide-and-rule form, were ominous, there were also clear advantages to be gained.

For the Jews, the benefits reaped from the distribution of British resources did not stem from warm personal ties to Mandatory officials. In fact, Jewish leaders' relations with these civil servants ranged from outright antagonism, as in the case of the military administration in 1919, to strong suspicions and recurring tensions, as in the case of High Commissioner Herbert Samuel's regime from 1920 to 1925. The British habit of periodically restricting Jewish immigration and land buying in order to deal with Arab sensibilities and violent outbursts undermined for the entire Mandate period the basis for a harmonious collaboration between British officials and Jewish representatives. Jews claimed such restrictions constituted a retreat from the promises in the Balfour Declaration and the Mandate itself. However, it is important to stress that, although the collaboration between the British and the Jews was not harmonious, it was still collaboration.

The benefits the Jews reaped came from the authority the British allowed them in spite of, perhaps even partly because of, the existing tensions and antagonisms. Bernard Wasserstein wrote:

> Towards the Jewish National Home in Palestine Samuel pursued a deliberately passive policy: the task of the Government of Palestine in relation to Zionism was merely to create the conditions, political, legal, and (to a lesser extent) economic, necessary for the Zionists themselves to carry on their work; the government would facilitate rather than encourage or direct Jewish immigration and settlement. This had the advantage for the government of precluding the diversion of state revenue to investment in Zionist development.[17]

British despair of creating a viable unified political framework for Palestine worked to the Zionists' advantage, allowing them to create a basis for an autonomous Jewish community with relatively consolidated social control. Even British restrictions, such as those on immigration, assisted the central Zionist leadership to a degree when it controlled the distribution of the limited numbers of certificates for immigration. For the Arabs, the effect of British rule was precisely the opposite. By refusing on principle to collaborate with the Mandatory power, the Arabs lost the opportunity to use British authority and resources to succor fledgling, countrywide Arab institutions. Arab-British collaboration existed, to be sure; no colonial rule was possible without it. Its bases, however, were personal (Arabs, for example, who worked as policemen, magistrates, or clerks) or local organizational (for example, village councils, which established official relations with the Mandatory power). This sort of collaboration limited the amount of resources and authority the British supplied to the Arab population and directed that limited quantity to reinforce fragmented control.[18]

In short, the resources the British proffered were not so much material as the authority to undertake tasks, which in Europe would normally have been performed by state agencies. Arabs intent on building national power hardly benefited from the offers of British authority because they refused to deal officially with the Mandate that included the Balfour Declaration. For the Zionists, British policy contained disadvantages, mostly concerning their shortage of capital, but it also held great potential. The Zionists' assumption of statelike tasks was, at least in part, a sign of their slackening confidence in the Mandatory government, but in the end it gave them the foundation to establish consolidated social control in the country. We will look at how the Jews seized the opportunity presented by the particular way the British chose to collaborate and offer resources. For the moment, we must still answer the question of which Jews benefited. Who were those who collaborated with the British, thereby garnering the resources essential for the establishment of effective social control?

THE STRUGGLE AMONG THE JEWS

Britain's proposal to recognize "an appropriate Jewish Agency" focused the struggles among the Jews to create social control in the Yishuv. The Jewish Agency, by the very latitude the British were willing to allow it, was to become the centerpiece of all Jewish communal institutions. The struggles to control it molded the character and capabilities of Jewish political organization, including the ability to resist British designs after 1939, when Zionist leaders felt the British had finally annuled the legitimacy of the Mandate. This agency that the Mandate singled out as the basis for British-Jewish collaboration, was the forerunner of a strong Jewish state, the state of Israel.

Article 4 of the Mandate for Palestine, had obliquely answered who would lead the Jewish Agency: "The Zionist organisation, so long as its organisation and constitution are in the opinion of the Mandatory appropriate, shall be recognized as such agency." The explicit recognition of the World Zionist Organization (WZO) in the Mandate gave that organization the League of Nations' stamp of approval, enhancing its claims among Jews as the proper representative body to solve the Jewish problem. Article 4 took cognizance of two sorts of Jews. It spoke of both the Jewish population in Palestine (the Yishuv) and, implicitly, of the larger worldwide Jewish population for whom the Jewish national home would be a refuge. As it turned out, both Jews of the Yishuv and Jewish leaders from abroad constituted part of the struggle for dominance. Numerous groups and coalitions formed among Jews in Palestine and in the Diaspora in order to gain control of the Jewish Agency. They were led by some of the great names of Jewish life of that time: Louis Brandeis, Nahum Goldmann, Vladimir Jabotinsky, and others. The two coalitions led by Chaim Weizmann and David Ben-Gurion stood out. Their strategies differed markedly, although there was also close cooperation between the two coalitions at many important junctures. We can label Weizmann's tactics, the external strategy, and Ben-Gurion's, the internal strategy.[19]

WEIZMANN'S EXTERNAL STRATEGY:
BUILDING A GLOBAL CONSENSUS

In some ways, the very constitution in 1929, at long last, of a Jewish Agency, broadly accepted by Zionist and non-Zionist Jews, by Palestinian and Diaspora Jews alike, was the personal achievement of Weizmann. In 1904, he had immigrated to England at age thirty from Eastern Europe. Later, as a well-known scientist and Zionist, he had cajoled the British into issuing the Balfour Declaration, catapulting him to the head of the Zionist movement. His eyes were most often turned toward the international movers and doers of his age—the Lloyd Georges, Arthur Balfours, and Jews of great wealth and influence. His strategy involved endless statesmanship of cultivating British politicians and influential non-Zionist Jews in Europe and North America. Through his tireless negotiations, he laid the basis for his leadership of an autonomous Jewish community in Palestine, directed by a broadly based Jewish Agency.

Even before the Mandate was officially in place, while the British military still ruled Palestine through its administration, the Weizmann-dominated WZO urged the British to allow it to form a quasi-government in the territory of Palestine. As early as December 1918, the very month in which the British assumed actual rule in Palestine, these Jews had produced an "Outline for the Provisional Government of Palestine." In some ways, the British had encouraged such initiative. They had sent the Zionist Commission, what Wasserstein called the embryo of the future government of Israel, to Palestine in March 1918.[20] With Weizmann at its helm, the commission, consisting of Jews from several countries, was to carry out steps to help establish the national home and act as an interlocutor between British authorities and the Yishuv. The commission, however, went even further; it proposed that it would have to agree beforehand to every implementation of policy, a suggestion not received kindly by the British military administrators. And, throughout the 1920s, while Weizmann kept up his continuous dialogue with the British urging full implementation of the Balfour Declaration, he also hammered out the compromises necessary to win support from non-Zionist Jews for the entire Jewish enterprise in Palestine and especially the proposed role of the Jewish Agency.

The Zionist Commission was indeed the kernel of a future autonomous Jewish community. Weizmann took personal charge of it in 1918, but his interests were much wider than the commission's principal concern with day-to-day affairs in Palestine. By the time the commission had instituted departments to deal with education, technical matters, and agriculture and settlement in the Yishuv, Weizmann had handed over its leadership to others in order to pursue his global lobbying. His style was simply not attuned to the nuances of building strategies of survival and mobilizational capabilities in the Yishuv; his principal interests were not in using selectively the resources funneled through the Zionist Commission as a base for his social control in Palestine. This sort of organizational work held little attraction for him; rather, his passion was achieving compromises in principle and language in order to reach a broad consensus among world Jewish leaders. His time was spent shuttling among them. Weizmann wrote:

> During all those years I spent the bulk of my time traveling, sometimes accompanied by my wife, sometimes alone. . . . I was actually at home only for short intervals between trips to America, Palestine, Germany, France, Holland and Belgium, not to speak of my attendance at various international conferences. I was trying to build up the movement, making contacts with governments and Jewish communities, and in the process acquiring a good many friendships in political, literary and scientific circles in different countries. I came to feel almost equally at home in Brussels or Paris or San Francisco.[21]

Weizmann, as president of the WZO, worked relentlessly through the 1920s to create an extended Jewish Agency. He beat off opposition from American Zionists, led by Brandeis, and from East European factions. Weizmann then forged alliances with non-Zionist Jewish groups, which could supply badly needed capital and technical expertise in building the national home, and with Zionists, who would supply the ideological motivation behind the drive for sovereignty. His initiative led to the establishment of a basic fund, Keren Hayesod, which could attract the money of Jews personally unwilling to join the World Zionist Organization. In 1923, the congress of the WZO gave Weizmann the authorization to implement his plan for the extended Jewish Agency. It then took him six years to cultivate the non-Zionist leaders in the United States, Britain, and elsewhere and to work out the minute details in constituting it.

BEN-GURION'S INTERNAL STRATEGY: BUILDING SOCIAL CONTROL IN THE YISHUV

Ben-Gurion's internal strategy for dominance of the Jewish Agency contrasted with Weizmann's external strategy. In the first few years after the British put forth the idea of the Jewish Agency, Ben-Gurion and other socialists were heavily dependent on WZO capital for their activities in Palestine.[22] Very few of their enterprises were even close to being self-supporting. Ironically, Weizmann's defeat of Brandeis, who had demanded that the WZO devote funds on a businesslike basis only to profitable investments in Palestine, ensured an open tap to the enterprises initiated by Ben-Gurion and his colleagues. They undertook those enterprises for a number of reasons, most of which had little to do with sound economic criteria. The financial dependence came even as the labor parties could muster only about 20 percent of the vote for delegates of the WZO during the 1920s. They wielded very little influence in that organization.

Ben-Gurion's tactics for dealing with these financial and political weaknesses at first may seem a bit odd. Instead of spending his time on international lobbying, he focused his efforts principally on building the labor parties in Palestine and expanding their scope of control in the Yishuv itself. Peter Medding wrote: "From the very beginning of the resettlement in Palestine, these parties, in keeping with their all-encompassing ideological view of life, sought to cater to the needs and interests of their members in many spheres. They produced separate journals and organized separate labour exchanges, soup kitchens, loan funds, cultural activities and agricultural collectives."[23]

At first, the parties had competed among themselves to offer the components for viable strategies of survival for the tens of thousands of Jewish workers in Palestine, but the competition prior to the 1920s had involved small stakes, since the parties had so few material resources with which people could construct meaningful strategies. The only part of a strategy of survival the parties offered in abundance was symbols, and under such circumstances factions had developed over fine shadings of ideological meaning. All parties in Palestine prior to 1920 had been fairly unstable entities, with party membership and lists changing from year to year. The labor parties had been ahead of others in the beginnings of the development of a stable party leadership, but they, too, were more centers of hot rhetoric than much else.

Conditions did not change immediately after the British takeover. The military administrators, in the fine tradition of colonial rulers, did little that might enhance the creation of a consolidated Jewish leadership. They opposed London's policy of promoting a Jewish national home and refused, therefore, to promote the idea. By the 1920s, when the civilian administration had assumed power and High Commissioner Herbert Samuel's civilian regime had failed to create the basis of a unified political framework for Jews and Arabs, British rulers allowed the Jews an assertive role in taking on functions of public service themselves. It was to this British sufferance that Ben-Gurion and his party, Ahdut Ha'avodah, addressed themselves.

The Ahdut Ha'avodah party (forerunner of Mapai and later the Israel Labor Party), formed in 1918–1919, finally achieved preeminence among all the competing parties. It became the dominant indigenous Palestinian element in the incipient Jewish state. Even though its ideology was not widely accepted within the Jewish society in Palestine during that crucial decade following World War I, it triumphed in Palestine because of its brilliant use of the resources and opportunities offered by both the British and the WZO. The party offered the components for workable strategies of survival for many of the small but growing Yishuv population in the 1920s and 1930s by concentrating on two internal spheres.

The first, and far less important, was a representative political structure for the Yishuv alone, autonomous of the worldwide representative political structure embodied in the WZO. Without British opposition, Yishuv leaders established a set of national institutions referred to as Knesset Israel.[24] The first elected assembly of the Yishuv was constituted in 1920, with almost 80 percent of the eligible electorate voting. Despite some splintering on a religious and communal basis within the Palestinian Jewish community, Knesset Israel made strides in bringing the Yishuv's political life under a single umbrella. The Ahdut Ha'avodah party was at the center of this process, as the largest party in the assembly, and came to hold the key positions in Knesset Israel's working arm, the National Council (Vaad Leumi). The mandatory government aided greatly by granting legal recognition to Knesset Israel based on the Religious Communities Ordinance of 1926.

Yishuv leaders, particularly those in the secular socialist parties led by Ahdut Ha'avodah, bridled at the British conception of Jewish society as primarily religious (as the 1926 ordinance implied). They viewed the Yishuv as a national political community. Also, they resented the British policies of allowing individuals to withdraw from Knesset Israel's registry and of recognizing separatist groups, such as sections of the Jewish Orthodox community, as autonomous religious communities. Nonetheless, legal recognition of Knesset Israel constituted an important step in Ben-Gurion's campaign to achieve increased autonomy for the Yishuv through his party's leadership.

Still missing were the material resources upon which people would build strategies of survival, so important because the Palestinian economy was so poor. A small part of this problem was solved in the 1930s when the British allowed Yishuv authorities and local community councils to collect their own taxes. But for the most part, Knesset Israel and its National Council were sideshows in the 1920s because they contributed so little revenue to the enterprises that constituted the backbone of Ahdut Ha'avodah's efforts to create viable strategies of survival. The inducement to control the Jewish Agency with its connection to wealthy Diaspora Jews, then, was quite high.

Besides the comprehensive Yishuv political structure of Knesset Israel, the other internal sphere upon which Ben-Gurion and Ahdut Ha'avodah concentrated their efforts in creating strategies of survival was the socioeconomic arena. Here, they sought not a comprehensive structure but an institution for their main potential constituents, the Jewish workers. The General Federation of Labor, commonly known as the Histadrut, was created by labor parties in Palestine in 1920. By 1926, 70 percent of Jewish workers in Palestine belonged to the Histadrut.[25] In the Histadrut elections in the 1920s, Ahdut Ha'avodah won more than half the votes and gained control over the labor federation's executive bodies.

This dominance in the labor federation was very important because of the wide-ranging functions the Histadrut performed. The British regarded the Histadrut with suspicion but nonetheless did little to impede it. In fact, the British gave wide latitude to the central Jewish leadership to provide services through the Histadrut to the Jewish population. The services offered by the Histadrut included health care, labor exchanges, trade unions, education, workers' kitchens, and a bureau of public works. By the end of the 1920s, the Histadrut, under the direction of Ahdut Ha'avodah's leaders, created bonds of dependency with a large part of the Jewish population in Palestine. New Jewish immigrants found in the Histadrut the primary basis for strategies of survival, including jobs, housing, and schools for their children. Ben-Gurion and his compatriots' initial tactic, then, was to enhance the labor leadership's social control in the Yishuv by using their limited resources carefully and selectively, in close conjunction with the symbols their Zionist socialist ideology provided, to offer viable strategies of survival. Their success was outstanding. As Howard Sachar wrote, "Nearly all phases of a man's life, and the life of his family, were embraced by the vast canopy of the workers' organization. By the eve of World War II, the Histadrut had become much more than a powerful institution in Jewish Palestine. For a majority of the Yishuv, the Histadrut was all but synonymous with Jewish Palestine itself."[26]

The Histadrut probably could not have blossomed without the WZO. There was, of course, the flow of revenues from the WZO to the labor federation to undertake the latter's social and economic tasks. In addition, the Histadrut gained by the recognition the British accorded the WZO, first through Article 4 of the Mandate and later through actions by Samuel and subsequent high commissioners. British recognition of the WZO allowed the Histadrut to expand its services as a direct beneficiary of the Zionist organization. To be sure, tensions abounded on all sides. The British often rued their decision to include Article 4. One British official wrote, "An exception has been made in this country for which, I think, there is no precedent elsewhere, of associating with us in the administration of the country another body, the Zionist Commission." He went on to note "that H.M.G. was bound hand and foot to the Zionists."[27]

There were tensions, too, between members of the Zionist Executive (before 1920, called the Zionist Commission), which represented the world body, and the local Histadrut leadership. Histadrut representatives felt continually hamstrung by the limited funds they received from WZO. Zionist Executive members, for their part, uneasy with the independent social control being built by Ben-Gurion and other labor leaders, attempted to use their subsidies to the Histadrut to gain control over its operations in Palestine by demanding economic accountability on the part of Histadrut enterprises. Ben-Gurion countered by arguing that Zionism per se, not narrow economic criteria, should direct the flow of funds and, since the interests of labor expressed the true national interests, discretionary spending should be left in labor's hands. To a surprising degree, this argument won the day, even though workers were far from constituting a majority of the Yishuv population.

Formally, the labor leaders depended on the Zionist Executive for both revenues and access to the British. The fact that the Histadrut had created such effective social control in the Yishuv, however, actually made the Zionist Executive, and later the Jewish Agency itself, dependent on the labor leaders. To further their goal of enhancing the autonomy of the national home, WZO representatives had to rely on Histadrut leaders, who had so effectively established social control in the Yishuv, and accept their argument that the interests of labor best expressed Jewish national interests. The labor organizations stood head and shoulders above other organizations in their ability to mobilize the Jewish population for common purposes.

The effectiveness of the Histadrut made the Zionist Executive into a conduit for revenues. The executive's Department of Colonization, which absorbed one-third of its budget, mainly channeled revenues for the Histadrut agricultural settlements; its Department of Labor supported all other Histadrut enterprises.[28] The WZO oversaw the actual distribution of funds in only the most minimal fashion and then only in the face of vigorous protests by Yishuv labor leaders. As Shapiro notes, the WZO leaders "soon realized that they could not build a bureaucratic organization of their own to handle all of the necessary functions—especially since most of the members of the Executive were foreign Jews."[29] WZO leader Arthur Ruppin explained the abdication of responsibility in favor of the Histadrut in this way: "Experience had taught us that, the settlements of ours go to pieces as the result of inner division, where there does not exist at least a kernel of individuals with a more or less

unified outlook to give the tone, and to assimilate to their unified outlook the other members of the group."[30]

Direct control of the Jewish Agency by the Yishuv labor leaders did
not come until the 1930s, grounded in the firm internal social control
they had established in Palestine. It also came only after Ben-Gurion
took a new approach toward coalition building in the WZO. In the first
years of British rule, the socialist Ahdut Ha'avodah leaders viewed the
Zionist Executive as the perpetrator of "a sinister design by the mon-
eyed class abroad to control the laborers in Palestine."[31] The Yishuv
leaders declined to enter into any political coalitions with these bour-
geois elements, refusing to join the Zionist Executive and consigning
themselves to a marginal role in the running of the WZO.

Only in the latter half of the 1920s did the Ahdut Ha'avodah leaders change tactics and enter into political coalitions with middle-class
leaders in the Yishuv and abroad. By that time, they had built the tools
to create social control in the Yishuv. Ben-Gurion paraphrased the
change in tactics as "from class to nation."[32] The first step was to gain
representation on the Zionist Executive. WZO leaders, for the most
part, welcomed the labor leaders' new role since "they had become convinced that only the laborers had an organized force in Palestine which
could reach the Zionist goals."[33]

Next, the labor leaders used their firm base in the Yishuv to mobilize support for WZO elections. Ben-Gurion spent months in cities in
Europe and North America in a major organizational effort. In 1933 at
the Zionist Congress held in Prague the Palestinian labor parties made
their major gains. They won 138 of 318 seats and, what is even more
important, an absolute majority on the Jewish Agency Executive. By
1935, Ben-Gurion was chairman of the Jewish Agency Executive and his
lieutenants ran the key "ministries."

Ben-Gurion was now in an ideal situation: control of the World
Zionist Organization placed him in an indisputable position to be recognized by the British as the national leader of the Jews. Not only did
his party control the Histadrut with its strong social control, it led the
very Jewish Agency the British themselves had proposed. In short, Ben-
Gurion's internal strategy had paid off handsomely. The keys to his success lay first in the exploitation of the opportunities presented by the
British; these included the proposal for a Jewish Agency and the subsequent British inclination to devolve communal responsibility to that
agency upon their failure to reconcile Jewish-Arab differences within the
context of the Mandatory regime.

Ben-Gurion's rise to the status of preeminent leader of the Zionist
movement in place of Weizmann and, ultimately to the post of prime
minister of Israel, stemmed directly from his tactics exploiting the

opportunities the British presented for the consolidated control of the national home through a single agency. Those tactics were to concentrate initially on building the organizational bases for offering components for workable strategies of survival to the immigrant population. Until the latter years of the 1920s, he largely eschewed Weizmann's globetrotting, especially after one unproductive episode in London.

Instead, he stayed at home in Palestine, combining his unusual organizational talents with the energies of a group of young immigrants from Russia. For them, Ben-Gurion was the prince, whose vision and plan of action could shape the very essence of this new society with them as the point men in execution. Their rebellion against the old construction of Jewish society, especially in Eastern Europe, put them in a perfect position to support the preeminence of the party and its allied organizations without conflicting loyalties to specific groups in Jewish society. They strengthened the labor party and then, with Ben-Gurion as general secretary of the Histadrut, offered workers a set of comprehensive services. Only once control in the Yishuv was secure did he use that base in a worldwide effort to gain direct control of the Jewish Agency.

Weizmann's strategy successfully mobilized capital for the national home, but it failed to build the means to use that capital to increase control in Palestine for his WZO. His talents were in mediation and conciliation, not in organization. He neglected to use the new talent pouring into the Yishuv in the early 1920s; he ignored those young men freed from the moorings of the old world and willing to build frameworks that transcended the ethnic and language differences differentiating the Jews of Palestine.

A fortuitous factor that aided Ben-Gurion in his campaign to gain control over the Jewish Agency stemmed from a British decision. The London-based WZO lobbied British officials constantly throughout the 1920s, pushing for full implementation of the national home. To escape this pressure, the Colonial Office decided at the beginning of the 1930s to transfer the locale of Jewish-British negotiation from Britain to Palestine. At that time High Commissioner Arthur Wauchope became the key link for the Zionists instead of the London-based Colonial Office. Just as the labor leaders' activities in Knesset Israel, the Histadrut, and the WZO were beginning to pay handsome organizational dividends among the Jews, these Yishuv leaders were now also much more strategically located than the non-Palestinian Jewish leadership to deal with the British on issues of importance and to influence British policy.

In the two decades of British rule until 1939, the labor leaders and foremost the indomitable Ben-Gurion exploited every activity the British sanctioned, from distributing certificates of immigration to collecting taxes. One of the activities that the British intermittently put restrictions on, Jewish land purchases, became the most important of all in consolidating the Zionist leadership's control in the Yishuv. As Kimmerling has pointed out in his innovative book, *Zionism and Territory*, the existence of a very limited frontier became a tool in the hands of Ben-Gurion and his fellow Yishuv leaders.[34] As the Jews drove up the price of land, the Zionist organization came to control more than 50 percent of all Jewish-owned land through its arm, the Jewish National Fund. The JNF bought lands with resources raised almost exclusively among Diaspora Jews. The distribution of the land in long-term leases to selected Jewish groups and individual Jews was critical in the establishment of central social control. The marshaling of resources from the British along with those from world Jewry enabled Zionist leaders in the Yishuv to create a pattern of social control among Jews already in Palestine and, later, among European Jewish refugees in the 1930s who constituted the largest wave of Jewish immigration to that point.

Colonial forces could push in precisely the opposite direction from that in their African colonies such as Sierra Leone. In Palestine, the reconstitution of social control—putting Humpty Dumpty together again—involved consolidation much more than fragmentation. Article 4 and the British decision to devolve an unusual amount of responsibility for delivering public services to the Jews allowed the labor leaders to use the British-proposed Jewish Agency as a springboard for centralized social control. Consolidation of the incipient state was truly impressive. Among the branches of the Jewish Agency were Labor, Financial, Trade and Industry, Agricultural Settlement, Organization, Statistics, and Political departments. The latter even served as a kind of Foreign Office. Labor leaders controlled the most important of these departments. As J. C. Hurewitz commented, these bureaus were providing valuable experience in self-rule as well as a core of trained civil servants.[35] Probably most important were the bonds of dependency, the social control, that grew from the new organizations. Medding wrote:

> The Jewish community thus enjoyed fairly wide self-governing functions: the Elected Assembly [Knesset Israel] and the National Council (its executive body) represented the Jews of Palestine before the British government in matters of civil and legal rights, and were responsible for economic activities, health facilities and, after 1931, education. The Jewish Agency Executive in Jerusalem, the local representative of the World Zionist Organization, was given charge of all settlement activities, immigration, foreign affairs, education (until 1931), and defence. By 1935, Mapai [the labor party] led all the main bodies of Palestinian Jewry.[36]

WEIZMANN ENSURES BEN-GURION'S SUCCESS

The success of Ben-Gurion's strategy depended on skillfully using the opportunities presented by Article 4 and the nature of British rule. It was not determined simply by the world conditions that created the Jewish problem and the severe social dislocation of Jews in the late nineteenth and early twentieth centuries. Weizmann, too, understood the importance of Article 4, but his strategy failed finally because he paid more attention to the Jewish problem than to the Jews with problems. With his lack of social control plaguing him and his party, the General Zionists, and his position in the WZO slipping, Weizmann had to make a fateful choice at the seventeenth Zionist Congress in 1931. Two other blocs existed to which he could throw his support after a vote of no confidence in his policies had effectively removed him from the WZO presidency: one, of course, was labor; the other was the Jabotinsky-led Revisionists.

In substance, Weizmann may actually have been closer to the Revisionists. He was not a socialist, after all. Also, the Revisionists put much greater stock in international diplomacy and paid much less attention to the organization of daily life in Palestine. But, in the end, Weizmann cast his lot with labor. In part, that may have come about because differences in tone are frequently as important as differences in substance. Jabotinsky's militancy, as eloquent as he was, grated against Weizmann's most basic instincts. Weizmann, too, was deeply wounded by Jabotinsky's charges that he was not forceful enough in his dealings with the British. His support of labor, however, also came from an understanding that the Revisionists had exceeded even his own failing of not taking advantage of the opportunity the British gave the Jews in Article 4. The Revisionists had steadfastly maintained during the pre-state era that it was the Mandatory government's responsibility to provide the Jews with services. They scorned the opportunity for Jewish autonomy within the framework of the Mandate. The position of the Revisionists left them without access to a tap controlling the rewards and sanctions that made labor's strength possible.

Shaken by the WZO's rejection of him—"the feeling came over me that here and now the tablets of the law should be broken," he wrote without undue modesty—Weizmann understood the importance of Ben-Gurion's success in the Yishuv.[37] Surveying the choice before him, Weizmann wrote,

> It was the conflict between those who believed that Palestine can be built up only the hard way, by meticulous attention to every object, who believed that in this slow and difficult struggle with the marshes and rocks of Palestine lies the great challenge to the creative forces of

the Jewish people, its redemption from the abnormalities of exile, and those who yielded to those very abnormalities, seeking to live by a sort of continuous miracle. . . . I felt that all these political formulas would be no use to us. . . . It was not lack of respect for governments and parties, nor an underrating of the value of political pronouncements. But to me a pronouncement is real only if it is matched by performance in Palestine. . . . If there is any other way of building a house save brick by brick, I do not know it. If there is another way of building up a country save dunam by dunam, man by man, and farmstead by farmstead, again I do not know it.[38]

With Weizmann's support, the labor bloc went on to become the dominant force in the WZO and Zionism.

JEWISH AUTONOMY AND BRITISH COMPLICITY

The autonomy that the Jewish Agency and Histadrut achieved was remarkable for a colonial-type situation. Britain's role in this extraordinary consolidation of the means of social control by Ben-Gurion and his cronies was more in what it permitted than in what it gave or did. The mandatory government allowed the growth of social services and political functions under a central Jewish leadership because of its own unwillingness to assume those tasks.

In cases, such as India, where certain policies on the part of the colonial state did push toward consolidation of control, they took place in the face of other, even stronger policies pushing toward fragmentation. Also, even those forces pushing toward consolidation in India took place either within the context of the colonial state itself, especially creating a small army of civil servants trained in British techniques, or within organizations directly opposed to the colonial state, most important of which was the Congress Party. In fact, Gandhi dubbed the Congress Party a parallel state.

In Palestine, there were such Jewish civil servants working directly for the Mandatory state, but they were a negligible factor in the ultimate struggle over social control. The Jewish Agency, although frequently in conflict with the British, essentially grew as an organization promoted and sanctioned by the colonialists and used by them to lessen their own burdens of ruling. Thus, the disadvantages of multiple loyalties, which Indians in the British civil service frequently felt, or of building autonomy under difficult, clandestine circumstances, which plagued many nationalist movements, were not as serious impediments to Ben-Gurion and his cohorts.

The Zionists certainly had other important advantages, too, in working toward consolidated social control. For many Jewish immigrants, especially those who chose Palestine over other options (after 1930 or so, refugees often landed in Palestine because of lack of other choices), Zionist myths and symbols were already well assimilated. Many came to Palestine because of their deep-seated belief in the Zionist solution to the Jewish problem. Establishing social control under these conditions was easier than "selling" Zionist symbols to a skeptical public. Even for Jews whose understanding of those symbols differed from that of the labor leaders, the shared attachment to Jewish religious symbols, even when used in new contexts of a secular civic religion, gave a common ground to those seeking social control and those piecing together strategies of survival. Also, the Zionist leaders benefited in their drive for consolidated social control by the devastating effect immigration had on the viability of people's old strategies.

With the first outbreak of widespread Arab rioting in Palestine in 1920–1921 and with every major incident thereafter, especially those in 1929 and 1936–1939, the British reexamined their policy of creating a Jewish national home. As the first British illusions about the viability of a unified political framework for Palestine shattered, important differences in the conception of Britain's role opened up among British officials. As in Sierra Leone, policy was not of a cloth, the product of a single accepted understanding of British interests, nor did policy always have the effects its implementors intended.

The actual governing of Palestine was the responsibility of the Colonial Office. It adopted its familiar pattern of devolving much of the actual day-to-day local control into the hands of its officials placed in Palestine, especially after 1931 during the term of Wauchope.[39] Not surprisingly, the various high commissioners and their staffs had a penchant for ruling as securely and cheaply as possible. And, obeying the universal cardinal rule of bureaucrats, they did everything in their power to prevent ruckuses from reaching upward to London. They set about devising scheme after scheme to contain Jewish-Arab tensions without jeopardizing security. In the end, those schemes took much of the actual governing from them. Authoritative positions in the central government and in districts, to be sure, remained in their hands, but they devolved many administrative responsibilities to the two communities; they gave more to the Jews, who accepted them readily.

Unfortunately, despite their schemes, the high commissioners were incapable of containing disturbances sufficiently to keep London officials from willy-nilly becoming involved in Palestinian events. The 1929 Arab riots brought one commission, and the 1936 Arab general strike and revolt brought another, the latter at the initiative of an exasperated Wauchope. It is not startling to find contempt for Wauchope in London once he admitted defeat and placed the unpleasant issues in the hands of

London officials. The War Office concluded "that the method adopted by the High Commissioner was entirely ineffective."[40] The head of the Colonial Office, W. G. A. Ormsby-Gore, spoke of Wauchope as "a dear little man, admirable while the going is good, but hardly the character to ride out a storm."[41] Another superior noted, "Sir Arthur Wauchope loves greatly, administers with knowledge and imagination, but he does not rule."[42]

The Colonial Office in London, though, had scarcely more success than Wauchope and its other civil servants in Palestine. Its officials in London continued to search for some plan that would satisfy both of its irreconcilable clients, the Zionists and the Palestinian Arabs. The plan they finally came to back was based on the 1937 proposals of the Royal Commission, the so-called Peel Commission Report, which recommended the partitioning of Palestine. Colonial Office civil servants, led by Ormsby-Gore, supported the idea of partition, while the Foreign Office, under the direction of the formidable Anthony Eden, was loath to see the plan implemented.

The Foreign Office's opposition to the partition of Palestine between Arabs and Jews grew out of its particular vision of British interests. Unlike Colonial Office personnel, whose field of vision had narrowed in this period of the sunset of empire to the tragedy of Palestine itself, Foreign Office officials regarded Palestine as only one part of their global strategic concerns. With the emergence of independent Arab states in the Middle East, Foreign Office officials feared that continued support for a Jewish national home, even in a partitioned Palestine, would gravely affect Britain's interests and standing in the region. As Aaron Klieman wrote,

> The lines could not possibly have been drawn any clearer: the eastern department [of the Foreign Office] saw partition as a betrayal of the Arabs; the Middle East department [of the Colonial Office] saw its cancellation as betrayal towards the Jewish people. Of interest for bureaucratic politics in general is the fact that both perceived of each other's position as damaging British national and imperial interests.[43]

In the end, the Foreign Office and Eden simply outweighed their competitor. Ormsby-Gore and the whole idea of partition supported by the Colonial Office could not stand up in the government to the more powerful sister ministry, the Foreign Office. In 1939, the British issued its renowned White Paper on Palestine. It outlined a new policy, which the Zionists considered formal abdication of the Balfour Declaration and its support for a Jewish national home by the British. The White Paper indicated the British intention to create an independent Palestine state with an Arab majority within ten years, limit Jewish immigration to a trickle for five years and then to prohibit it entirely without Arab consent, and to forbid all land sales to Jews. This document, not surprisingly, led to a rapid deterioration in British-Jewish relations and to open animosity, much still neither forgotten nor forgiven.

The British rediscovered in the 1940s what had become apparent in the early 1930s, namely, that they had created something of a Frankenstein. In the 1930s, too, the British had attempted on a smaller scale to hamper Jewish activities in areas where the Jewish Agency or its allied institutions had dominated, such as agricultural settlement, land purchases, and immigration. Just as then, British officials found Jewish leaders, strengthened by their control over activities that had been bequeathed to them by the British themselves, able to circumvent many British regulations and restrictions.[44] Even after the White Paper was issued the Mandatory state refrained from excessive meddling into the social services and political functions the Jews had assumed. As in the early 1930s, British officials felt that their own performance of such tasks among the Jews might only further harm their relationship with the Arabs.[45] Moreover, the Mandatory state simply lacked the capabilities at that point to provide those services.

It would have taken an extraordinary effort by the British, who were by late 1939 concerned primarily with European affairs, to reverse the social control the Jewish labor leaders had consolidated in Palestine. Even earlier in the 1930s, there were moments when the existence of a consolidated Jewish leadership had been so loathsome that the British had adopted some subtle and not-so-subtle policies to weaken labor's control. The voting regulations for Knesset Israel's Elected Assembly in 1932, for example, provided for separate ethnic groupings. Jewish parties then had proposed candidates for three groupings, Sephardic, Yemenite, and Ashkenazic.[46]

Even with the shared hopes that many immigrants harbored due to their belief in the Zionist program as a solution to the Jewish problem, the potential for social and political organization of the Yishuv along ethnic lines or, for that matter, according to language groupings, countries of origin, or religious differences was certainly always very much present. Jews from every continent converged in Palestine with almost no organizational ties among them. Even cultural affinity—their very Jewishness—paled next to the differences in dress, language, forms of worship, and more.

The remarkable result, however, was that Britain had not been able to exploit these differences: they did not become highly politicized. Social groupings with the ability to enforce their own rules of the game did not achieve any notable success among the Jews. For the most part, the labor leaders channeled the very real tensions among the diverse

Jews into the political and social institutions they themselves dominated. The labor leaders dictated the rules of the game. When the Sephardim, along with the Revisionists, boycotted the 1944 elections, they found their basis for opposition undermined by the turnout that labor and the other parties could generate.

In the 1920s and early 1930s British policy had opened the doors too wide to the Jewish Agency for the British now to destroy the agency's control and refashion the society. Hundreds of thousands of Jews had already settled onto Zionist-owned land and bought into the educational, health, and other services that labor leaders had spun into strategies of survival. Perhaps a wholesale withdrawal of authority from the Jewish institutions and a move to assume the provision of these services by the Mandatory state itself could have undone the social control built by Ben-Gurion and his fellow labor leaders. But even this drastic an action probably would not have been effective at this point given the growing strength of labor's symbols among the Jews. Such a withdrawal, however, is but idle speculation because the British were unwilling. Even when labor undertook armed resistance against British rule after World War II, the Jewish Agency and its affiliated organizations continued in many spheres to work as collaborators with the British in ruling the Yishuv.

Only in one area did Jewish autonomy in Palestine develop mostly outside the sphere of British complicity—security and defense. Jewish self-defense units, called Hashomer (The Watchman), had existed as far back as the beginning of the century in Palestine, but the British put a firm clamp on their reemergence in the immediate aftermath of World War I. The Arab riots of 1920–1921, however, posed the strongest sort of threat to Jewish settlement in Palestine. British intervention against the rioters proved so paltry that the labor Zionists opted to develop a clandestine force, the Haganah. The labor Zionists were not the only Jews attempting to organize defense. Jabotinsky tried to activate units during the riots of 1920, but he met with little success. In fact, control of defense and security policy and forces became a major source of struggle for social control in the Yishuv throughout the Mandatory period.

From the time of the founding of the Histadrut, labor leaders sought to add defense to the host of services they offered Jewish immigrants. The threat of Arab violence was perceived as all too real to trust what the labor leaders considered an indifferent British administration or to leave security issues to Jewish organizations outside their control. Labor leaders put the Haganah under Histadrut political auspices and then set out to attract Hashomer members into both the new Haganah and their political party, Ahdut Ha'avodah. Various new ploys were then used to control former Hashomer personnel.

At times, the Haganah was an underground force, operating illegally and, at other times, it was a semilegal organization allowed by the British to perform tasks they were unwilling or unable to undertake. For example, for much of the period the Haganah illegally imported arms and, after World War II, even mounted raids against British installations. In 1936, however, the British created and armed Jewish guards, whose actual membership in the Haganah the British accepted.

Challenges to labor's control of the Haganah came within the Jewish community, too. The WZO, for a time, was reluctant to fund a defense organization intended for the entire Jewish community but so completely dominated by one segment, labor. One Yishuv party wanted the Haganah under the control of the National Council and not the labor federation, the Histadrut. Jabotinsky successfully organized an additional armed group, the Irgun (Irgun Zvai Leumi), which broke labor's monopoly on control of violent means among those in the Yishuv. Another group, Lehi (the Stern Gang), undertook terrorist acts and daring raids against the British. As in no other area, labor faced intense competition. Even within the Haganah itself, there were indications of military leaders smarting under the control of Histadrut leaders.

The labor leaders, for their part, felt their social control could be imperiled by allowing independent military forces to organize in the Yishuv.[47] At times, they coordinated efforts with the Irgun and Lehi, and, in other instances, actually turned members of these forces over to the British when they felt these groups were working contrary to the best interests of the Yishuv. Ben-Gurion, probably more than any other leader, was guided by a central principle: the potential of Arab violence was so great as to make control of defense, no matter what the costs he might have to pay in maintaining Jewish consensus, something labor simply could not give up if the Yishuv was to survive and labor was to maintain its social control.

ISRAEL AS A STRONG STATE

Despite the repeated blasts to the conception of a self-governing Jewish national home—culminating in the most forceful blow of all, the White Paper of 1939—the earlier actions of the British proved to have the longest and deepest impact on the Yishuv's social and political organization. The early recognition of a single Jewish Agency and the appropriation of broad responsibilities to it provided the outlines for the new distribution of social control in Palestinian Jewish society. An irony of the entire situation was that the policies of the Colonial Office devolving so much autonomy to the Jews, though they eventually were rejected by the government, were able to have the most enduring effect on the future of Jewish society and, indeed, the entire Middle East. With the continuing fragmentation of Palestinian Arab society during the Mandate, the central Jewish organization came to be far and away the strongest local base for social control in the entire country.

The test of the strength of the Israeli state, which grew out of the Jewish Agency, came immediately upon the declaration of independence in May 1948. By that time, events had long since overtaken the policy of the White Paper. Palestine's future was decided by a UN resolution and the outcome of war, not by the British, who found themselves increasingly powerless to control events after 1945.

For the new state, the test in 1948 was twofold. The first was the Arab-Jewish civil war for control of Palestine and the accompanying interstate war between Israel and its Arab neighbors. Innumerable popular and scholarly accounts have documented the 1948 war. Of interest here is that despite the vast population that the Arab states and Palestinian Arab leadership had to draw upon, the Israeli state leaders, ruling a society of considerably less than a million people, were able to use the social control they had garnered in a tremendous mobilizational effort. Their forces tripled from 30,000 soldiers in May to more than 90,000 in October. By that time, they had accomplished an astounding defeat of the combined Arab armies. The advantage in mobilization that the Jews had in the 1948 war grew directly out of the painstaking social control they had developed in delivering mundane services such as housing, jobs, and education.

The second threat to the Israeli state came in the internal Jewish challenges to Ben-Gurion's leadership and organizations. The social control built in the 1920s and 1930s created the basis for a state able to withstand challenges from disaffected military leaders in the Haganah and from Menachem Begin's autonomous military force, the Irgun.

The British had divided their collaborative efforts between the two competing communities of Arabs and Jews. Arab rejection of a British offer to back a counterpart to the Jewish Agency was at the center of a number of factors fragmenting social control. Elsewhere, I have discussed that fragmentation of control among the Palestinian Arabs that resulted from British rule.[48] In the ultimate test of war against the Zionists, Arab fragmentation led to disaster. Arab political institutions collapsed, the Israeli forces advanced, and Palestinian Arabs fled or were driven from their villages and cities. Only slightly more than 10 percent of the Arab population of Palestine remained within the territory controlled by the Israeli state at the end of the war. What had started as organizations to establish social control exclusively among the Jews of Palestine now became the basis of a state exercising such control over Jews and the Arab remnant population alike.[49]

Since the tumultuous events of 1948, Israelis have survived from crisis to crisis. Much of the social control built in Yishuv institutions has, with some fits and starts, been shifted to the agencies of the state.[50] On many indicators reflecting the relative strength of states in respect to their societies, the Israeli state is very high, especially for a new state. In 1979–1980, it collected 36 percent of GDP in taxes, higher than any OECD state; it offered nearly universal education through elementary school and high school; it devoted almost one-quarter of GDP to defense expenditures; it demanded universal military service for Jewish males, service from a high percentage of Jewish females, and service from some Arab males; it adopted a housing policy so that virtually no Jewish family lived more than four to a room.[51] The Israeli state has created extensive policy networks, simultaneously making it one of the most militarized states in the world and among the most extensive welfare states.

The legacy of labor's rule—the Israel Labor Party was turned out of office only in 1977—also contains some elements that have eroded the consolidated social control of the state. The primacy of politics over economics has led to a tendency for the state to promise far more than it can deliver, especially with the severe resource limitations faced in Israel. Even after the creation of the state, the Jewish Agency and Histadrut continued to exist, with modified functions, making policy coordination difficult. Labor leaders' concern with building a constituency among former East European Jewish workers left other groups, by the 1980s the clear majority of the population, open to disaffection and other parties' recruitment. Deepening social cleavages and a near-electoral stalemate in Israeli politics have resulted. With the shift from "class to nation" came broad coalitions and concessions to small parties, diluting ideology (effective symbols) and creating numerous ministries to accommodate all. Again, policy coordination has been a victim.

Despite all these factors, the Israeli state's strength relative to other new states is impressive. Waves of immigration helped swell the numbers of Jews in Palestine from about fifty thousand at the beginning of the century to about five million today, introducing forces with tremendous divisive potential. Immigrants came with vastly different backgrounds and needs. Labor leaders seized the opportunity the British afforded to develop central political and social institutions through the Jewish Agency. The vast array of services monopolized by the incipient state, and later the state itself, made it extremely difficult for localistic social organizations to offer meaningful rewards, sanctions, and symbols to the individual. Attempts to this day to build political organization on a different basis have met with little success.

THE CONDITIONS FOR CREATING A STRONG STATE

Let us return to Horowitz's question quoted earlier in this chapter, how did the "centripetal" propensities in the Yishuv overcome the "centrifugal" tendencies? Among the most important factors are:

1. The emerging Jewish society in the Yishuv until the end of World War I was weak. Economic dislocation in Europe, the growth of the "Jewish problem," and migration itself produced a society in search of new strategies of survival. Old social control had crumbled.

2. The Mandate for Palestine created the opportunity for consolidated social control through the latitude given to the Jewish Agency and allied organizations.

3. There existed a skillful leadership. Weizmann and Jabotinsky had faced the same challenge as Ben-Gurion, but they failed to see the advantages in concentrating on the building of viable strategies of survival through an artful blend of rewards, sanctions, and symbols. Not only must that leadership discern the proper path, but it must also have strong organizational capabilities. Weizmann's talents simply did not run in that direction. Ben-Gurion's colleagues prized him as an exceptional organizer, as much as thirty years before he became prime minister of Israel.

4. The top labor leaders had available a group of talented young "pioneers," as they were called in Palestine, freed from the moorings of the old world. They saw their personal fulfillment in the successful implementation of the top leaders' visions and plans. And they were willing and able to build an autonomous set of organizations that transcended parochial ethnic and language ties among the Jews. Their strength lay in implementing the policies that would create strategies of survival for the population, not in devising those strategies from scratch.

5. The military threat posed by the Arabs made Ben-Gurion and his colleagues accept the risks of challenging any fragmented power bases, such as the Irgun, that had arisen. It was too risky not to consolidate social control; the very survival of the leader and his carefully nurtured organizations, the new state, depended on it.

The emergence of a strong, autonomous state is by no means a natural outcome of the social transformations associated with the modern era. The empirical question is, who could take advantage of the new circumstances and reestablish social control? In this regard, the role of the leader is paramount, as will be discussed in the next chapter. But leaders are not unfettered. There are two necessary conditions for the success of those about to consolidate social control, eventually in a strong state. One is rapid and universal dislocation. The other, relevant to societies that experienced direct, outside hegemonic rule, is the channeling of resources to indigenous organizations capable of extending social control throughout the society. African countries such as Sierra Leone fit the first condition but not the second; Jewish society in Palestine fit both. Ethnic identities there did not disappear altogether, but for most of the history of Palestine and Israel since World War I, they have been irrelevant among the Jews to the exercising of social control. Primary identity for Jews came to be Israeli, not Moroccan or Sephardi or Orthodox. For most, although certainly not for all Jews in Israel, the state's social control has reached the level of legitimacy. They not only comply with state rules to an impressive degree, but they also accept the rightness of the state's making the rules of the game. As chapter 8 will show, for Arab citizens of Israel (nearly one-fifth of the population), social control has mostly been at the level of mere participation, not legitimacy. They take part in the education, health, and other systems of services, but they have not accepted the major myths the state has propounded. Those symbols have mostly been irrelevant to their identities and strategies of survival.[52]

CHAPTER 4

Vision and Practice:
The Leader, the State, and the
Transformation of Society

In the last of the three chapters on state making, I step beyond the surrounding, contingent factors that impede or facilitate the consolidation of the state. Here, the focus is on how these environmental factors can be used by a skilled leader. In Israel's case, the presence of David Ben-Gurion was key to the emergence of a consolidated state.

What makes a visionary leader visionary? A major part of the answer to that question lies in the leader's ability to have his followers or potential followers picture a world radically different from their own. And he must convince them that their present world somehow can be transformed into the one in their mind's eye. That transformation may focus principally on the religious, social, or political realms of their lives. Each realm suggests a major reformulation of the strategies that people adopt to get through the vagaries and uncertainties they face daily.

Consciously or unconsciously all people build strategies of survival. These relate people's goals—gaining material sustenance, shelter, physical protection, respect love, salvation, and the like—to the means of achieving them. In these strategies, people also seek codes for making sense of their daily experiences and look for systems of meaning to give their lives transcendental significance. Their codes and systems of meaning—whether in the form of religious beliefs, secular nationalism, scientific dogma, or any other system—are entwined with the more material and mundane aspects of survival strategies. The drudgery of work, for example, may be linked to some transcendental goal such as glorifying God or building the nation.

Visionary leaders, then, aim at nothing less than offering new strategies of survival for masses of people. In some cases, they have sought such change by emphasizing the symbolic side only, new systems of meaning, and then have hoped to attract followers through the glimpse of the future that their words and symbols convey. More often than not, however, their tactics in offering new strategies of survival have involved also an institutional dimension. Visionary leaders have become as much organizers as orators, building institutions that can become the means for individuals to achieve their goals. These institutions have changed people's daily behavior, and thereby have not only given a glimpse into the future but also have helped bring about the heavenly or worldly city of the vision.

In the twentieth century, possibly in the last half millennium, no type of visionary leader stood out more than the political one, and no organization distinguished itself as more transformative than the state.[1] That distinctive cultural artifact of the modern era, the idea of progress,[1] came to be inseparably linked to the organization of society by the state. From Hobbes's premise that there could be no civil society without a state, to the more recent notion that "development" could occur only through proper public policies, the state has emerged as the transformative organization par excellence.

This chapter explores why some leaders have been able to use the state as a transformative mechanism to realize their visions, while others have been unable to reshape the strategies of survival of their populations through state initiatives. First, I discuss the state as a transformative organization and look at the nature of the opposition it encounters in pressing for fundamental social change. I then analyze some environmental circumstances, what I call "world historical conditions," that have affected the chances of realizing such leaders' visions. Finally, I examine the lives of three men—Cárdenas of Mexico, Nasser of Egypt, and Ben-Gurion of Israel—and the influence of world historical conditions in specific contexts.

THE STATE AS A TRANSFORMATIVE ORGANIZATION

Since the beginning of the contemporary state system in Europe about five hundred years ago, an international norm has evolved (not without tremendous resistance) that states should be the predominant organizations in their societies. That is, states should establish and enforce the rules of the game for human interaction within given territories, or in some spheres authorize other organizations, such as families, churches, and markets, to set those rules. Through its monopoly of coercive means, the state should back up its rules and those of the other organizations that it authorizes. Poggi noted the centrality of rule making to the purposes of states when he wrote: "One can visualize the whole state as a legally arranged set of organs for the framing, application, and enforcement of laws."[2] Of course, countercurrents have opposed such predominance by the state or have aimed to temper it. One thinks immediately of the notion of a "higher law," for example. In the last 25 years, the conception of a universal set of human rights has gained popularity as a means to limit state prerogatives. Probably the most effective resistance to state predominance has come from much less assuming quarters. Within societies, all sorts of formal and informal organizations, from feudal manors, to churches, to clans, have not accepted automatically the state's rule-making hegemony and predominance. In the absence of comprehensive, viable strategies of survival proferred by states—the situation of practically all of human history—other organizations devised such strategies and set the rules or norms for people's daily behavior. Those who led and benefited most from these organizations resisted the attempts by state personnel to strip them of their prerogatives by consolidating rule making in the single organization of the state. All these organizations—all the clans, clubs, and communities—have used a variety of sanctions, rewards, and symbols to induce people to behave according to their rules and not the state's, whether people's behavior involved interactions between father and son, employer and employee, landlord and tenant, priest and parishioner, or others. These rules have included at what age to marry, what crop to grow, what language to speak, and much more.

Practically all notable visionary leaders in this century have sought to break the resistance of these organizations. Leaders have aimed to transform the fragmented rules set by heterogeneous organizations by creating inclusive state organizations. Their goal has been to create states that could make a set of universal rules, a common law, to govern the details of all people's (citizens') lives throughout a given territory. To do so, leaders have had to go beyond mere rhetoric. They have had to build state organizations to meet the needs until then addressed by the other, fragmented organizations. The state itself has had to satisfy the needs of the populace for everything from sustenance to salvation, or authorize other organizations to do so. In short, visionary leaders in the modern era who have sought to transform society through politics have come to see the state as the organization that could be complex and strong enough to devise new strategies of survival for the populace, new rules of behavior governing human interaction, and the means to enforce those rules.

States, however, have not necessarily been strong and complex enough to change people's behavior and transform vision into reality simply by their very being. "Real" states—those recognized juridically within the modern system of states through diplomatic representation, membership of international bodies, and the like—have varied considerably in their "degree of stateness."[3] That is, actual states have been closer to or farther from an ideal type of state, an organization with a monopoly over the principal means of coercion, autonomy from existing social groups in what rules to make, and the ability to get its population to follow those rules. Under what circumstances have visionary leaders been able to create states with a high degree of stateness, ones capable of building effective new strategies of survival and of transforming society?

Although part of the answer lies in the resources available and the talents of the leaders themselves—their ability to recruit and organize state cadres, to develop evocative and convincing systems of meaning (e.g., national myths)—their success has depended also on world historical forces beyond their immediate control. In certain instances, those forces can reduce drastically the dangers and difficulties the leader faces in attacking the prerogatives of existing organizations in society. Likewise, they can increase significantly the risks in not clashing with other such centers of power. There are three sorts of influence that world historical forces have had on leaders and their proclivity and ability to consolidate power in the state.

A Convergence of Socially Dislocating Forces

World historical forces have had widespread and deep impact on the abilities of fragmented social organizations, those resisting state predominance, to provide viable strategies of survival and maintain effective rule-making capabilities. Since the sixteenth century, states have emerged in clusters, almost exclusively in the wake of highly disruptive world forces that have rapidly, deeply, and universally weakened existing control by fragmented social organizations in a given territory. These forces reduced opposition as well as the risks for leaders bent on stripping other organizations of their autonomous rule-making capabilities and consolidating power in the state.

Forces sufficiently strong to batter the moorings of so many social organizations most often consisted of a convergence of elements. The initiatives by European princes, starting about 1430–1600, to enforce tax collection, maintain standing armies, and build effective courts and police forces came in the wake of such a convergence of factors during the calamitous fourteenth century. Nothing caused more dislocation at that time than the Black Death, which claimed the lives of as much as 40 percent of the population. As if that were not enough, the Hundred Years War devastated sections of western and northern Europe, where the new states made their headway. Old strategies of survival suddenly became irrelevant in the new circumstances. The two pillars of basic exchange within feudal life—the lord's protection for the serfs' production—crumbled. Lords' abilities to defend their manors and organize their serfs for battle suffered badly through the plagues and wars. The high death rate also drastically changed the man-to-land ratio, making serfs' labor much dearer and more competitively sought after. Rents diminished, the amount of cultivated land declined, and wages rose. In some areas, the changes ruined entire landowning classes. The old strategies of survival simply did not work in such radically changed circumstances.

Similar dislocation preceded the further consolidation of state power in Europe that occurred in the Age of Absolutism. Severe economic crises, internecine wars of unrest in European countries, the Thirty Years War, recurring outbreaks of the plague, and splits in the Church all weakened existing strategies of survival in the early seventeenth century. The one realm of life that seems to have emerged reinvigorated from this so-called crisis of Europe was the political one. Even given the internal political instability in seventeenth-century England, France, and The Netherlands, state power increased dramatically. State leaders used the opportunities presented by the weakening of old social arrangements to increase the state's rule-making powers.

In the twentieth century, too, a convergence of factors led to the rapid consolidation of state power in a few cases. Commonly, international war and civil war (or revolution) on the heels of one another have preceded the emergence of stronger states. For Russia, the devastation of World War I plus the aftershocks of the Bolshevik Revolution and revolts predated Lenin's and Stalin's major drive at state consolidation. In Yugoslavia, Vietnam, and China, the havoc of destruction and occupation in World War II, coupled with internal battles and drives against foreign forces led by Tito, Ho Chi Minh, and Mao Zedong, battered existing strategies of survival and the fragmented social organizations that maintained them. Landowners fled, man-to-land ratios diminished, and production suffered badly in all these countries. Old social organizations were weakened, reducing the barriers to new consolidation of these states in the 1950s. Some weakening of the fragmented social organizations stemmed directly from the initiatives of the visionary leaders themselves, principally through their revolutionary wars. Their success, however, came as much from their exploitation of converging forces over which they had little or no control. These forces raised the prospects of success for the visionary leaders by diminishing the capabilities of their domestic rivals. The initial hypothesis is, then, that the greater the social dislocation preceding a leader's drive for directed social transformation, the greater the chance to overcome resistance and achieve his goals.

Outside Threats to the Survival of the Leader and the State

War can play another role besides that of directly weakening the sources of internal resistance to a leader's attempts to consolidate power in the state. War or the threat of imminent war, of course, also increases risks to the leader and the state. These risks can be a major impetus for leaders to confront the fragmented rule-making organizations in their society. Leaders' own fears about war may motivate them to attack the prerogatives of other domestic social organizations much more forcefully and directly.

The ability of these organizations to set the rules for people's daily behavior vests in them significant mobilizational abilities. They can skim surpluses and organize manpower. As long as states are limited in their domain of rule making, they are also limited in their ability to mobilize and organize the material and human resources necessary to fight wars effectively. Lamborn noted: "Much of what is traditionally meant by power does involve the government's capacity to mobilize resources."[4]

For a leader aiming to consolidate state power, attacking the prerogatives of local rule-making organizations always entails serious risks. These organizations not only mobilize resources, some portion of which eventually enters the state coffers and supports the armed forces, but they also maintain social stability. Attacks on the rule-making autonomy of the state can lead to diminished state revenues, social unrest, and outright rebellion. Nevertheless, the threat of war, especially of direct invasion may make it too risky for leaders not to try and strip domestic organizations of their prerogatives and thus to increase significantly the state's direct mobilizational capabilities.

The first half of the seventeenth century, as noted above, witnessed a significant consolidation of state power by a number of European monarchs. Probably nothing better exemplifies the relationship between the threats emanating from war in the state system—especially during the Thirty Years War—and the drive to consolidate power internally in individual states than the case of France. Its participation in the series of wars leading up to the Peace of Westphalia in 1648 (and even beyond to the Peace of the Pyrenees in 1659) was punctuated at the beginning and the end by major revolts against state authority. The first involved the subjugation of the Huguenots and magnates in 1629–1630, and the second was the Fronde (1648–1653).

The connections between domestic uprisings and the wars France fought to foil Hapsburg encirclement were many and complex, ranging from religious alliances to family splits. The international military threats that Louis XIII and Louis XIV faced were among the most important factors that indirectly precipitated domestic rebellion. The more the French monarchy could break the control of other domestic forces the more it could garner resources to wage international wars; and the more those wars demanded French resources, the more the monarchy aimed to consolidate power domestically in order to mobilize additional resources. The inevitable clashes of interests that occurred as state agencies attacked the prerogatives of the nobility in order to mobilize additional resources for war increased domestic tensions in France. Mousnier described the internal effects of the military campaigns associated with the Thirty Years War:

> These long and difficult wars demanded a major national effort and placed a heavy strain on French resources. The royal government was obliged to adapt to the war, to become a war government, resembling a dictatorship or monocracy rather than a kingship or monarchy. It became increasingly necessary to compel everyone, especially the royal family and royal officials, to obey immediately and completely. It became necessary to stop defeatist or enemy propaganda by any means and to foster patriotism and a military frame of mind. Above all, it was vitally important that the government find money for the troops; clothe and feed them; buy weapons, guns, and powder; arrange transportation; repair and build some fortresses and destroy others; and supply allies, such as the rebellious Dutch, Portuguese, Catalans, and Hungarians. The government greatly increased all kinds of taxes. It not only established new ones but even imposed some of them on towns or corporate bodies traditionally exempt from ordinary taxes. Thus it repeatedly violated provincial and local liberties and privileges in order to find money, and it even created a sort of revolutionary administration—staffed by tax farmers, traitants or partisans, supplemented by royal commissioners, intendants, and soldiers—which replaced the ordinary officials in the execution of royal power.[5]

French nobles claimed that the new demands of the state took it considerably beyond the constitutional authority it possessed. They argued that the new royal powers and functions violated the so-called unwritten fundamental laws of France. Some went so far as to lead attacks on tax collectors and sergeants-at-arms enforcing tax collection. Their assaults represented both personal dissatisfaction and fear of the king's attempt to reduce the autonomy and privileges of all sorts of estates in France, at the national, provincial, and municipal levels. The ministers of the king, first Richelieu and then Mazarin, realized—as did the nobles upon whose privileges they encroached—that the destruction of the old local prerogatives could increase royal revenue collection in a district by three or four times.

The voracious appetite of the French state within the country during the Thirty Years War created great risks for the king and his functionaries. They added to an already severe economic crisis, impoverishing part of the population, and fanned the flames of rebellion against them. In the Fronde, noblemen expressed their resentment against the state's domestic encroachments by leading peasants against the king. As a result, the state nearly collapsed. The risks involved in confronting the nobility were assumed by the state only when the dangers of not mobilizing additional resources became intolerable. The dire necessity to break the Hapsburgs' hegemony and their encirclement of France led Louis XIII and Louis XIV to push hard and quickly appropriate the privileges of the nobility. Once there was this motivation for state leaders to strip noblemen of their prerogatives, the state leaders reaped tremendous long-term benefits.

Confrontations led to the permanent debilitation of many rule-making organizations in France that had controlled parts of the French population since the Middle Ages. Cardinal Richelieu quickly saw the relationship between external war and internal consolidation of power by the state. He wrote: "War is sometimes an unavoidable evil and, in some circumstances, it is absolutely necessary and may even achieve some good. States need war at certain times to purge themselves of their evil humors. . . ."[6] My second hypothesis is thus that the more keenly a leader feels the threat of war and the need to mobilize material and human resources for it, the more likely he is to risk confronting domestic organizations that resist rule making by the state and to move boldly toward state consolidation of power.

Outside Support for State Consolidation of Power

Socially dislocating forces, including wars, can greatly weaken resistance to a visionary leader's attempts to use the state as the means of social transformation, and wars also can inspire leaders to confront resistance to state predominance by inducing them to mobilize resources currently controlled by resisters. The international environment can have yet another important influence on a leader's ultimate success. At certain world historical moments, international conditions may neutralize international powers opposed to the visionary leader's designs or may even support such a leader aiming to consolidate power domestically.

Such moments may be few and far between. For the most part, the modern state system has been highly competitive and the history of international relations has not been much more than the history of war. State rulers have rarely been eager to see other states increase their mobilizational capabilities significantly for fear that internally consolidated power elsewhere could be used against them in turn. Especially when there have been great asymmetries in power among states in the international system, hegemonic or leading states have not been inclined to encourage the internal transformation of other societies in ways that could lead to strong, competitive states.

Several bursts of state consolidation in Europe seem to have come when the hegemony of the leading state was declining. In the instance discussed above, Hapsburg domination in Europe reached its peak in the late sixteenth century. The series of wars that shook central and western Europe in the first half of the seventeenth century, accompanied as they were by a remarkable consolidation of state power, reflected the break in unity of the dynasty (different rulers in Spain and Austria) and its declining fortunes. Internal rebellions against Hapsburg rule characterized seventeenth-century Europe. Similarly, more than two centuries later, the unification and consolidation of the German and Italian states came in the wake of the diminishing gap, especially economically, between Britain and other European powers. By the 1870s, Britain's hegemony was in decline, leaving Europe open not only to the scramble for international predominance but also to an environment in which ambitious leaders could consolidate power in their states with less fear of the hegemon's negative responses.

In the twentieth century, the burst of successful state consolidation outside Europe in the two decades following World War II—in China, North Vietnam, North Korea, and several other states—occurred under somewhat different international conditions. Despite the preponderance of the United States' international power at the end of the war, the Soviet Union was able to establish and lead a second world-system. The Soviet-dominated system differed markedly from the U.S.-dominated one both in rules and norms of international interactions and in its blueprint for how societies should be organized domestically. The existence of two competitive world-systems had interesting, contradictory effects on the tendency of small states to consolidate power.

For most states, the competition between the world-systems, especially between the two superpowers, lessened the incentive for leaders to initiate major drives to strip fragmented social organizations within their societies of their prerogatives. Ironically, the nuclear balance of terror created an unusual stability for weak and vulnerable states, placing distinct limits on local conflicts, as seen in the termination of the 1973 Arab-Israeli War. In fact, the Cold War era was remarkably stable in its international structure, if not particularly peaceful. Not a single state disappeared due to invasion and only one, Pakistan, splintered into two states due to war. Even border changes, despite all extant claims, turned out to be minimal in this period. Thus the motivation, mentioned above, for state leaders to consolidate power internally because of the risks internationally of not increasing mobilizational capabilities was much less evident than in many previous eras. Rulers with only the most limited abilities to extract resources from their societies sat comfortably at the helms of states with low degrees of "stateness." In fact, authors went so far as to portray populations' "disengagement" from states in Africa.[7] State leaders could survive without taking upon themselves all the risks of directly challenging rule-making organizations simply because the threat of invasion was so low in the Cold War era.

In a few cases, however, the existence of rival world-systems had the opposite effect—promoting internal consolidation of power in state organizations. All faced invasion or had leaders who perceived invasion to be a real threat. Playing on the competition between the systems and each superpower's aim to recruit states, leaders drew international support for their domestic transformative goals. Most notable, of course, were those who adopted the rules of the Soviet system and accepted Soviet hegemony—North Korea, China, Vietnam, and Cuba. It is true that after achieving their domestic transformative goals, several of these later rejected Soviet hegemony, but, at the time of the onslaught against domestic fragmented organizations, the support of the Soviet Union was vital. It was not so much material support that made the difference; the Soviet Union's record was quite mixed in its openhandedness to revolutionary movements in distant lands. It was the counterweight the Soviets posed to potential United States economic or military actions against revolutionary movements and regimes—even in Vietnam—that was important in giving those states unusual opportunities for internal consolidation, even in the face of a leading state's opposition. The final hypothesis, then, is that the more the international system allows for a leader to avoid or cope with economic, political, or military actions by the world's leading powers directed against state consolidation of power, the more likely is that leader to risk undertaking such a process of consolidation.

Using the State as a Lever

In summary, historically, visionary leaders' abilities to use the state as a lever to realize their transformative goals has depended on more than their own talents or available resources. Certain rare world historical moments provided such leaders with an environment supportive of their aims to consolidate state power. Outside forces battered the domestic organizations that still made binding rules for parts of the population, diminishing internal resistance to state leaders' designs; external threats induced state leaders to challenge domestic resisters in order to raise the state's mobilizational capabilities, and changes in international configurations of power gave state leaders the chance to consolidate domestic power without all-out opposition from the world's leading states, possibly even with critical international support.

VISIONARY STATE LEADERS: THREE CASE STUDIES

Three important drives by visionary state leaders to transform their societies by consolidating rule-making power in the state organization illustrate the importance that world historical forces had on their efforts.

Cárdenas and the Institutionalization of Mexico's Revolution

Lázaro Cárdenas was president of Mexico from 1934 to 1940, two decades after Mexico's revolution. Nevertheless, many "revolutionary" aspects of modern Mexico date back to the Cárdenas reforms and institution building. In the wake of the revolution that began in 1910, many parts of the country suffered from near anarchy. Peasants throughout Mexico claimed lands held by powerful landowners, or *hacendados*; in turn, the *hacendados* organized private armies in order to maintain their hold. Agricultural production stagnated, per capita production declined, and railways suffered from decline and outright sabotage.[8] The state had only a limited ability to make binding rules or to offer able strategies of survival for the population. As Vernon wrote:

> During most of the first decade of the Revolutionary era, a national state hardly existed in Mexico. The institutions which made up the central government were a feeble version of a modern state. There was neither a genuine national currency nor a central bank, neither a true national army nor a civil service. Besides, during much of that period, the very jurisdiction of the national government was in question, there were only a few areas of Mexico in which the basic authority of the states was not being seriously challenged. The period from 1910 to 1940, therefore, was an era in which Mexico was developing the essential preconditions for the new role of the state.[9]

State leaders took important steps to build effective institutions prior to the mid-1930s, creating the beginnings of new revenue-collecting agencies, a national school system, a central bank, and other important institutions. Plutarco Elias Calles, in particular, weakened fragmented social organizations resisting the state from the mid-1920s until Cárdenas put an end to his influence in the 1930s. It was Cárdenas who led the important drive toward consolidation of state power in the late 1930s, preventing any newly mobilized groups in society from taking exclusive charge of the state organization. He went beyond neutralizing rival organizations, pushing hard for the state to become the effective rule maker in society and to effect the long-awaited social transformation.

Land reform was the centerpiece of the Cárdenas program. Despite the important participation of the peasants in the revolution and even in actions after the revolution, land holding in 1930 was still highly skewed, with farming land concentrated in the hands of a small minority.[10] Calles even declared the land reform program a failure. Seventy percent of the workforce was still in agriculture, and 70 percent of those in agriculture remained landless. Cárdenas went beyond mere technical changes to effect a more equitable distribution of land. He had a vision of various forms of communal social organization in which the *ejido*, lands held by villages rather than individuals, played a leading role.[11] The Cárdenas regime emphasized the collective *ejido*, one with a cooperative form of production.

By the end of the Cárdenas presidency, *ejidos* made up almost half of Mexico's cultivated land, compared to only 13 percent in 1930.[12] The population of the huge haciendas, which had dominated Mexican agriculture before the revolution, fell to barely a quarter of what it had been in 1910. The reforms broke the economic and political power of the *hacendados*, and Cárdenas then consolidated the peasantry into one of four sectors of the revamped revolutionary political party, the Party of the Mexican Revolution (PRM). The aim was a major social transformation of agrarian life through the alliance of the state and a mobilized peasantry. Indeed, "the agrarian reform destroyed the power of the large landowners and succeeded in its goal of eliminating or at least significantly reducing 'feudal' relations of production."[13]

Cárdenas faced a society in 1934 that had experienced massive social dislocation. Old strategies of survival had suffered badly as the result of at least two converging forces. First, the half-century leading up to the revolution had brought massive changes in Mexico's economy and society as its population was drawn into the world economy.[14] This process was capped by the severe jolt of the world Depression in the early 1930s as the bottom fell out of the commodity prices so important to Mexican producers. Second, the revolution and its aftershocks caused untold destruction. One million people, one out of every fifteen, died in the revolution. Fighting also destroyed much of the economic infrastructure. When Cárdenas approached the peasantry with concrete proposals for agrarian reform and political incorporation in a party controlled from above, he proposed not only the restitution of lands the peasants had fought for, but also concrete new strategies of survival for people whose old strategies no longer worked. His reform went beyond a nostalgic offer to return to the old communal system of land holding. He proposed new forms of production (collective and cooperative); vast sources of credit, principally the new Ejidal Credit Bank; and the political backing through the PRM to resist powerful figures bent on making and enforcing their own rules. In brief, the convergence of forces in the years leading up to the Cárdenas administration weakened existing social organizations, reducing obstacles and resistance to Cárdenas's goals for transformation of society in rural Mexico.

Other world historical conditions, however, may have worked against Cárdenas and his goal of social transformation through state predominance. The threat of U.S. invasion was certainly real during the revolution and even for some of the ensuing period. In 1913, the U.S.

ambassador had helped overthrow the Mexican president, and in the next few years U.S. troops actually carried out actions on Mexican soil. United States oil companies battled every change in Mexican petroleum policy and, as late as 1927, there were indications of possible military intervention in their favor. By 1934, however, conditions had changed dramatically. The world Depression had focused U.S. concerns on its own domestic issues. In addition, Roosevelt's "good neighbor" policy had led to a promise of nonintervention in the affairs of Latin American states.

Of course, on the face of it, the reduced threat of invasion by the United States strengthened Cárdenas's hand. His radical nationalization of the foreign oil companies, for example, did not draw nearly as negative a reaction from the U.S. government as did much milder moves against those companies by his predecessors. The reduced possibility of U.S. intervention, however, may have had the indirect effect also of encouraging outcomes that limited Cárdenas's chances of achieving his vision. Throughout his term, he incorporated diverse social groups into the party and the state. The absence of a serious outside military threat may have limited the degree to which he pushed to strip all these groups of their prerogatives and their independent rule-making capabilities.

In rural areas, local strongmen, *caciques*, adopted the rhetoric of the revolution while acting as mediators between peasants and the state. *Caciques* turned out the vote for the PRI (the Partido Revolucionario Institucional, the successor to the PRM), ensured high membership of the official peasant organization, and silenced dissenters.[15] They also limited the scope of state rule making and predominance. While state institutions and resources eventually reached even the most remote villages in Mexico, local *caciques* began to use the state agencies and state budgets to strengthen their own positions. They applied their own rules and used their own gangs to enforce them. The agrarian transformation stalled. Landlessness remained high—close to two million peasants were landless. Even landed peasants failed after 1940 to share proportionately in Mexico's growing prosperity. "Mobilization" came to mean peasant membership in institutions controlled on the top by state and party officials and at the bottom by *caciques* with their own agendas. Mobilization did not become an avenue for the expression of peasant interests: "Since the time of Lazaro Cárdenas in the 1930s, peasants in Mexico have not been in a position to make sustained independent demands on the political system for attention to their problems."[16]

Lack of a credible military threat by the United States may have made Cárdenas much more tolerant of independent-minded *caciques*—including the inevitable loss of revenues for the state—in order to "buy" rural social stability. In the aftermath of the revolution and local revolts in the 1920s, as well as continuing management-labor strife in the cities, such rural stability was eagerly sought by the regime, even at the price of state predominance.

The most Cárdenas was willing to do to limit the prerogatives of capital was to support laborers in actions against private employers and in a few cases (notably petroleum) to nationalize foreign capital. Dependence on foreign (mainly U.S.) capital—although attenuated somewhat by the effects of the world Depression and Cárdenas's policies encouraging local capital—still put severe constraints on him.[17] With the continuing hegemonic role of the United States in Latin America and the absence of another world power willing to support a major restructuring of Mexican society, Cárdenas's options were limited. Socialism could not be, under these circumstances, a realistic goal.

In sum, the Cárdenas regime, despite the many changes it instituted and despite the radical character of its vision, laid the basis in Mexico for the limitation of state predominance by private capital in the years after 1940. The Cárdenas vision was fulfilled only partially. World historical forces played contradictory roles. Working in Cárdenas's favor was the dislocation that preceded his years in office. Limiting his ability to see his vision through, however, were the absence of inducements to mobilize more fully, due to the lack of a credible war threat and the misfortune of ruling when international forces acted emphatically against the radical restructuring of society and consolidation of power in Mexico. The absence of a U.S. military threat did not mean that the United States could not use other forms of influence in Mexico. In fact, such influence further limited Cárdenas's chances of having his vision materialize. Cárdenas and other officials did play with various socialist and Marxist ideas, but the Soviet Union in the 1930s was not willing or able to give material or even moral support to a major challenge to private capital in other countries, especially one right on the U.S. doorstep.

Nasser and the Revolution from Above in Egypt

The 1952 overthrow of the monarchy in Egypt by the Free Officers was not accompanied by a major peasant uprising, as had been the overthrow of the old order in Mexico. The major agrarian reform that followed in Egypt, then, did not stem from prior peasant mobilization but was designed to lead to such mobilization. Gamal Abdul Nasser, the main force behind the overthrow of the monarchy and later the president of Egypt, had a vision of a major social transformation in Egypt, starting with the destruction of "feudal" elements in the thousands of villages along the Nile River. To reach his goals, Nasser had a clear idea of the institutional means he would need. His vision rested on the presumption of a strengthened, predominant state organization.[18] His hopes lay in the reorganization of the state, which could then supply viable strategies of survival to the Egyptian population. His plans for state predominance did not come in the wake of near anarchy and civil war, as in Cárdenas's Mexico, but in response to a weak governing organization unduly influenced by large landowners.

Rural reform seemed to be the perfect place to start a major social transformation. Landholdings were concentrated in the hands of a small minority—one-half of 1 percent of the landowners controlled more than a third of the cropland, while 93 percent of the landowners held title to only another third of the land. Half the rural population was landless. The new reform, the keystone to a larger social transformation that eventually was labeled "Arab socialism, " came only a month and a half after the coup d'etat in 1952.

In several senses, the law (and subsequent emendations) had great success. It eliminated the large landowning class as an economic and social force in rural Egypt and as a political force in Cairo. The small farmers, who made up 95 percent of all landowners, increased their holdings from one-third of the cropland to one-half. The law also included effective tenancy regulations, which lowered rents and afforded legal protection to tenants. Finally, the state penetrated Egypt's villages with institutions designed to offer peasants strategies of survival in place of those devised by large landowners. These agencies included agricultural cooperatives, local councils, and local committees of the national political party Nasser created.

In other ways, however, land reform led to only limited changes in Egypt's rural sector. The actual redistribution brought only modest gains to poor peasants there. Twenty years after enactment of the reform, the state had redistributed about 12.5 percent of the cropland. All in all, approximately 9 or 10 percent of the rural population gained land as a result of the reforms through 1970, the year of Nasser's death.[19] The average parcel of land distributed to beneficiaries amounted to less than 2.5 *feddans* (a *feddan* is slightly more than an acre). The average plot in Egypt is still barely larger than a single *feddan*, and two-thirds of the male agricultural labor force have no land at all or less than a single feddan.[20]

While state agencies penetrated every village and permanently changed the face of rural Egypt, all the new state institutions came to be dominated by people pressing rules for Egyptian village society different from those intended by Nasser. "To assume that the state is able to control the daily lives of peasant cultivators is to greatly overestimate the state's power of control over both its own officials and members of the rural sector. . . . The state remains quite incapable of determining the precise character and contest of local-level interaction."[21] Like the *caciques* in Mexico, middle and rich peasants in rural Egypt dominated the state's village-level agencies and the local committees of the national party. They turned the agricultural cooperatives and other new institutions into vehicles for their own enrichment and into means for pressing their own rules of the game on village social life.[22]

The Impact of External Powers   Egypt under Nasser enjoyed one advantage over Mexico in its struggle for social transformation, namely the configuration of the constellation of international powers at the time of its struggle. When Nasser embarked on his policy of social transformation through state policies, the timing was ideal in terms of diminished resistance from world powers and even in terms of positive external support for domestic restructuring and state consolidation. Great Britain's diminishing influence in the Middle East, especially in Egypt, left the region as a source of competition between the two great postwar powers, the United States and the USSR. Nasser used the superpower confrontation deftly in order to increase his maneuverability and to marshal badly needed support from outside Egypt.

Even before he assumed the presidency, Nasser led the delegation to the negotiations with the British that resulted in evacuation of British troops from Egypt. At the Bandung Conference in 1955, Nasser sought support for his charted course by building ties with leaders of other Afro-Asian states. When requests in 1955 to the West for arms purchases went unanswered, he invited the Soviet Union into the Middle East through an arms purchase agreement with Czechoslovakia. The United States reacted to Egypt's growing independence, including recognition of the People's Republic of China, by withdrawing support for one of Nasser's pet projeicts, the High Dam at Aswan. United States officials also induced Britain and the World Bank to withhold their contributions. Major events followed in rapid succession, including Soviet economic support for the project to replace the West's support; Egypt's nationalization of the Suez Canal; the attack by Britain, France, and Israel on Egypt in the Suez War; and the freezing of Egyptian assets in Britain, France, and the United States. Nasser emerged from the fray militarily battered but politically triumphant. He had established a degree of autonomy from the West through his policy of positive neutralism, which involved increased involvement with other Afro-Asian states and growing direct support from the USSR.

Other world historical forces, however, did not create encouraging conditions for the successful consolidation of power that Nasser sought. For one, he did not seem to take the threat of invasion seriously. In a sense, he was correct. The 1956 Suez War and the 1967 Arab-Israeli

War both involved foreign capture of Egyptian soil, but neither resulted in incursions into the populated parts of the country along the Nile. Neither Nasser's survival nor that of the state was immediately threatened. In both cases, he was genuinely surprised that fighting had carried over onto Egyptian territory. Even in 1967, with the buildup of tension prior to the Israeli strike, there is little indication that Nasser pressed to increase the state's mobilization capabilities rapidly. The short duration of the war also denied Egypt a period of crisis or "of grim determination to make all necessary reorganizations to ensure a successful conclusion to the war," as Marwick[23] said of Britain in World War I. The enormity of the Israeli threat in 1967 became obvious to Nasser only after the war. For the last three years of his rule, he sought to maintain social stability following the terrible defeat in 1967 that served "to discredit the Nasser regime and devalue its policies."[24]

In the years leading up to the Free Officers' takeover, Egypt had not suffered the social dislocation experienced by Mexico before the Cárdenas era. No convergence of forces had rapidly or deeply undermined the population's existing strategies of survival. The result was that Nasser found entrenched opposition to every attempt to strip other social organizations of their power. His response was to choose not to fight these entrenched centers of power when the stability of his regime was in question. On the contrary, he fell back on the social stability these other rule-making social organizations could provide.

In 1967–1968, in the wake of the military defeat, Nasser faced a disgruntled military and riots in cities, factories, and universities in Egypt. In the countryside, Nasser now had an important choice to make. Rich and middle peasants had long been key figures in the existing strategies of survival of the poor peasants, both as agents for larger landowners and in their own right as village chiefs. Nasser's own political party was in the midst of a major campaign, begun before the 1967 war, to uproot the power of these rich and middle peasants. Nasser had to choose between the social transformation the party was attempting to bring about and the immediate social stability the rich and middle peasants could provide. With his harsh criticism of the party, followed by the arrest of the top party leader, he in effect announced his willingness to accommodate the fragmented rule making of the rich and middle peasants in order to ensure social stability in the countryside.

In brief, Nasser, like Cárdenas, drew contradictory impulses from the world historical forces he encountered. Although the constellation of forces among the great powers gave him an unusual opportunity to forge radical domestic reform without the unchecked opposition of the world's leading state and even with sources of outside support, he faced other important obstacles to realizing his vision. The brevity of his wars in 1956 and 1967, the distance of his Yemen military adventure from Egypt itself, and the assistance of the Soviet Union in his war of attrition against Israel in 1969–1970 led Nasser not to undertake that "period of grim determination," risking domestic stability to reorganize society in the face of potential disaster from outside. In addition, Nasser ruled an Egypt in which old strategies of survival were well ensconced and resistance to a consolidating state was high. His attack against the great landowners did not come—as did that of Cárdenas—in the face of other social dislocations. For Nasser the risks of domestic resistance and instability were too high to see his vision through. He did not follow his attack on large landowners with battles against their agents in the countryside, the rich and middle peasants.

Ben-Gurion and the Creation of a New Society

The struggle of David Ben-Gurion for state predominance as the means to having his vision materialize did not begin in an independent state. Nor did it take place within an established society with time-tested strategies of survival. He developed his leadership, rather, in the context of British colonial rule (the League of Nations Mandate for Palestine) and of a society in the process of creation through immigration from the far corners of the world.

Zionism as an ideology and political movement dedicated to the ingathering of the Jews in Eretz Israel (Palestine) dates back to the last half of the nineteenth century. It was the events toward the end of World War I and in the several years following, however, that gave Ben-Gurion the opportunity to develop a plan of action for realizing his vision. At the end of the war, he wrote (with his colleague, I. Ben-Zvi):

> What was nothing more than hope and faith for 2000 years, has finally turned into reality. The proud dream of the victorious wanderer to return as an independent nation to its country is about to be realized. A people and its land—a downtrodden people and an abandoned land—are about to be reborn.[25]

The causes of this optimism came from Britain's conquest of Palestine and an important government resolution that preceded the military victory, the Balfour Declaration. This brief statement by the Secretary of State for Foreign Affairs endorsed the idea of a national home for the Jewish people in Palestine. The Balfour Declaration was subsequently incorporated into the terms of the Mandate for Palestine.

Ben-Gurion, as the emerging leader of the Jewish labor movement in Palestine in the early 1920s, was committed to a vision that included the most important issue to all Zionists—the transformation of world Jews into an autonomous single society through massive immigration to lands in Palestine that still had to be recovered. He also believed in the key roles that laborers and various forms of socialism, especially cooperatives and communalism, would play in the new society. In attempting to realize his vision he faced stiff challenges. First, immigration and land purchases were the source of the greatest controversy with the Arab inhabitants of Palestine and, eventually, with British rulers. The Jews, in essence, were trying to establish a frontier society without a frontier.[26] That is, Zionists wanted high Jewish immigration and land settlement in a country where practically all the land was already owned or claimed by others, one way or another.

A second challenge involved the leadership of the worldwide Zionist movement, especially the World Zionist Organization. Although there was broad agreement within the movement on some core issues, Ben-Gurion faced formidable leaders with significantly different visions of a future Jewish Palestinian society, including Louis Brandeis, Chaim Weizmann, and Vladimir Jabotinsky. Finally, Ben-Gurion faced the challenge of pursuing his vision within the context of British rule. In some ways, especially in the early years of the Mandate, Britain did not pose barriers to Ben-Gurion's plans. The Mandate, in fact, called for the creation of Jewish Agency to advise and cooperate with the administration of Palestine. The question was who in the Zionist movement would control such an agency.

While some of Ben-Gurion's rivals within the Zionist movement addressed these challenges through international consensus building or confrontation with the British by demands for immediate independence, Ben-Gurion built a power base within Palestine by addressing new immigrants' needs for strategies of survival. The labor organizations from the period before British rule had begun "to cater to the needs and interests of their members in many spheres. They produced separate journals and organized separate labour exchanges, soup kitchens, loan funds, cultural activities and agricultural collectives."[27] The party led by Ben-Gurion emerged after World War I as the one most adept at providing services. Although its ideology was not widely accepted in Jewish society in Palestine during the crucial decade following the war, it triumphed because of its brilliant use of resources garnered through the World Zionist Organization, as well as the resources and opportunities offered by the British.

Broadening his institutional base, Ben-Gurion joined other labor leaders and parties in creating a comprehensive structure for Jewish workers, the Histadrut. It was outstandingly successful in creating unmediated bonds of dependency between labor leaders and new Jewish immigrants.

> Nearly all phases of a man's life, and the life of his family, were embraced by the vast canopy of the of workers' organization. By the

eve of World War II, the Histadrut had become much more than a powerful institution in Jewish Palestine. For a majority of the Yishuv (Jewish society), the Histadrut was all but synonymous with Jewish Palestine itself.[28]

Ben-Gurion's base of power in Palestine led in the 1930s to his domination of the world Zionist movement, as he became chairman of the British-inspired Jewish Agency, the forerunner of the State of Israel. With no direct access to the society he wanted to lead and expand, a rival leader such as Weizmann found himself dependent on labor leaders—especially Ben-Gurion. The labor organization surpassed other organizations in its ability to mobilize the Palestinian Jewish population for common purposes. Weizmann and the entire World Zionist organization eventually accepted Ben-Gurion's argument that the interests of labor best expressed Jewish national interests. WZO leaders "soon realized they could not build a bureaucratic organization of their own to handle all of the necessary functions. . . ."[29] Thus, land purchases from Arabs—the highest priority of the Organization—could be controlled by the WZO only to a point.

Ben-Gurion's strategy paid off handsomely. By building an organization to meet the needs of new immigrants for strategies of survival, he was able to dominate the Zionist movement and to present himself to the British as the indisputable national leader of the Jews. His base of power met three severe tests at the time of independence and for several years after. First, the new state, assuming functions from both the British and the Jewish Agency, faced the war declared upon it by the surrounding Arab states. As prime minister, Ben-Gurion headed a tremendous mobilizational effort. Ruling a society that at the start of the war had numbered considerably less than a million people, he oversaw an increase in the Jewish armed forces from 30,000 to more than 90,000 soldiers five months after Independence. Second, he encountered in the course of the war two challenges within the Jewish forces to his authority as their commander. In both cases, he used the power he had so laboriously built in the pre-state years to enforce his will. Finally, the tremendous swell of Asian, African, and European Jewish immigrants after the War of Independence threatened the state's ability to provide viable strategies of survival for the population. Even as the number of Jews doubled between 1948 and 1951, the state prevented fragmented rules and strategies from developing along ethnic or other lines. Its control was direct, without the mediators between state and society, with their own rules, who so frustrated both Cárdenas and Nasser.

Consolidating State Power   Ben-Gurion benefited from favorable conditions for consolidating power in the state in all of the three world historical factors cited above. Massive migration is as potent as war and revolution in undermining existing strategies of survival in a society. From 1920, when the Histadrut was established, to 1951, the Jewish population in Palestine grew from about 80,000 to nearly 1.5 million. The social dislocation of the migrants presented a special opportunity to Ben-Gurion—not available to Nasser in his quest to realize his vision— to supply strategies of survival with minimal opposition from entrenched forces in the society.

War and the threat of war—with all the anguish they brought to Ben-Gurion—also provided him with special incentives to oppose any fragmentation of rules. Invasion came on the day of Independence. When Menachem Begin, then leader of an autonomous Jewish fighting force, even partially resisted full integration of units in a national army, Ben-Gurion thought he had no choice but to act decisively. During a ceasefire with the Arab armies, Ben-Gurion ordered a ship with arms for Begin's forces to be fired upon and sunk. Begin's cadres were arrested and his units disbanded. Similarly, the need to expand the armed forces rapidly and to improve their efficiency from the level of their semiclandestine activities under the British induced Ben-Gurion to develop mobilizational techniques that left no room for intermediaries imposing their own rules upon society.

Probably nothing played more to Ben-Gurion's advantage than the constellation of world forces. Unlike during the heyday of the colonial scramble in the latter half of the nineteenth century, the period after World War I—what came to be called the "sunset of empire"—did not see the acquisition of territory by Britain with a view to permanent rule. The very definition of the Mandate set out its temporary nature. Britain saw in a Jewish national home the possibility of establishing a bulwark to protect British interests—the land and sea routes to the East, especially against Bolshevik expansion—without Britain's ruling indefinitely in Palestine. As a result, British officials permitted a remarkable degree of autonomy, especially in a colonial situation, for the Jewish Agency and Histadrut. Similarly, in 1948, the U.S.-Soviet competition and the disintegration of Britain's role in the Middle East generally, and in Palestine in particular, provided Ben-Gurion with a special set of highly favorable circumstances for state creation and consolidation of power, just as they did several years later for Nasser. These conditions were most obvious in the November 1947 resolution in the United Nations, supported by both the United States and the Soviet Union, to create two states, including a Jewish one, in the territory covered by the Mandate for Palestine. In the aftermath of that important vote, a combination of complex motivations around the emerging Cold War—including Soviet support for any weakening of imperialism or colonialism and U.S. fears of Soviet expansion in that area as expressed in the Truman Doctrine—gave Ben-Gurion the opportunity to consolidate power without the active opposition of the most powerful actors in the region or world.

CONCLUSION

Cárdenas, Nasser, and Ben-Gurion all managed to change their societies, and the institutional landscapes of Mexico, Egypt, and Israel still bear the clear imprint of their efforts. Each saw the state as the tool that could effect a social transformation and realize his visions. They all expanded the agencies of the state tremendously in order to bring the population new strategies of survival and to challenge the fragmented and diverse ways of doing things that marked their societies. They wanted a uniform set of rules as the basis for a new society.

Their success in going beyond penetration of their societies with new agencies and realizing their visions, however, varied considerably. Uniformity of rules did not necessarily follow the state's agencies into the far corners of society. Much of the variation in these leaders' success must be explained by internal factors, specific to each case, which are beyond the scope of this chapter. Ben-Gurion, for example, benefited by the prior commitment of the great majority of Jews in Palestine to the most important symbols he espoused, the core elements of Zionism. His use of symbols from the Jewish religion struck a common responsive chord among the self-selected immigrants to Palestine in the 1920s and even among refugees in the 1930s. Nasser, on the other hand, suffered from his own and other Egyptians' ambivalence about social or group boundaries. The tags of Egyptian, Arab, and Islamic identities made it difficult to propose a convincing basis for solidarity in Egypt against "enemies of the state."

This chapter presents the argument that beyond such specific internal factors there have been additional necessary (but certainly not sufficient) conditions for these visionary leaders' successes in bringing about their sought-after social transformation. These conditions are related to world historical circumstances largely beyond the leaders' control. The differences that leaders found in the degree of social dislocation due to external factors, the intensity of the threat of invasion, and the efficacy of possible sanctions by leading powers go a long way toward explaining the variation in leaders' success in realizing their visions.

For both Cárdenas and Nasser, these world historical conditions had contradictory impulses. In each case, unfavorable conditions for state consolidation of power—the constellation of world forces in the case of Cárdenas, the absence of social dislocation in the case of Nasser, and the perception that invasion was not imminent in both—resulted in state accommodation to a class of mediators. The *caciques* in Mexico and the rich and middle peasants in Egypt ensured social stability at the cost of uniformity in social rules and of the social transformation each leader envisioned. Ben-Gurion benefited from favorable conditions for state consolidation of power in all three areas—social dislocation, the threat of war, and the constellation of world forces. Although his vision, too, was compromised, especially his hopes for a truly socialist society, he built a state without the need for mediators and effected the social transformation of millions of immigrant Jews.

My three hypotheses concerning the impact of social dislocation, the threat of war, and the sanctions of leading powers combine elements from the structure of international and domestic society and of individual perception. World historical factors can reshape the international and domestic environment and the structural level sufficiently to change the political leaders' risk calculations and their individual perceptions. An explanation based on these combined levels of what has been called risk analysis can be a useful tool in assessing the parameters within which bold, visionary leadership may emerge. The quality of any vision and its implementation, however, must be explained by factors beyond those singled out here.

PART III

Society Making

CHAPTER 5

Civil Society in Israel

In Part III the state still looms large, but the primary focus shifts to the construction and impact of society. In Israel, where society has stood in the shadow of the state, highlighting the effect of society on the state deflects theorist and country specialists alike from their propensity to center their analyses on the workings of the state. An analysis of democracy is an excellent starting point for a society-centered perspective.

Hopes for the blossoming of democracy in the Middle East cannot rest simply on changes within the state organization itself. Just as important as reforms in the procedures of the state and in the means to select key political leaders is a transformation within the broader society.[1] The growth of civil society is the mortar and bricks of any possible democratic project in the Middle East.[2] This chapter looks at Israel to explore the burgeoning of civil society and how that has affected state-society relations. Has the remarkable growth of civil society in Israel since the mid-1960s strengthened the democratic state? And, if it has not (as I will argue), why not?

What is "civil society" and how does it differ from "society"? In a narrow sense, civil society is the autonomous and inclusive public life beyond the close control of the state. Even as it includes groups with wildly different interests and goals, it has at its core a common agreement among its members over the constitution of the collective moral order, about the construction of society as a whole. One could think of it as a kind of uncontrolled common discourse. Of course, this does not signify people simply walking in lockstep. But it does mean some sharing of norms and values about how to resolve conflicts and clashing interests, how to organize power and authority, how people should behave toward one another in the public sphere, what property rights should entail, and what the boundaries of the society should encompass. The boundaries question involves not only the physical political boundaries of the state (a question of no mean importance in the Middle East) but also the equally crucial issue of who should be considered a rightful member of the society and thereby receive its benefits and rights. For example, transient visitors within the physical boundaries—or, in most societies, guest workers—are not considered to be such members.

Civil society assumes, too, some concurrence about the rightful existence of institutions other than the state organization that themselves promote, and operate within, the rules of this moral order. Local PTAs, charity groups, churches, businesses, and social clubs, for example, may be considered by the members of civil society as appropriately operating in the context of society's moral order. Even if an element of exclusiveness resides in these organizations (the Episcopal Church is only for Episcopalians, the PTA is not for childless couples), these institutions help create and reinforce both the inclusive norms and the boundaries of the larger moral order within which they operate. In short, there is both a passive and an active dimension to civil society: passive, in the acceptance of a certain order, and active, in its volitional element, which creates, maintains, and reproduces the moral order through institutions and individual behavior. The term *society* is broader than civil society because it can include, too, individuals and groups who reject that order (do not accept the passive dimension) and those who may accept it but do not participate in institutions or engage in public behavior to strengthen the order (there is no volition among them). Broader society, to be sure, may also contain a volitional element—organizations prescribing certain behavior, but not directed toward the acceptance and strengthening of civil society's outline of how society should be constructed; society, as opposed to civil society, may lack the inclusive dimensions normatively and institutionally binding its parts in a common framework.

Societies in the Middle East for the most part have, to date, still not hammered out strong, inclusive civil societies; both the passive and active dimensions of civil society have been extremely weak. The understanding of the moral order and of the construction of society is still highly fragmented, and institutions to press specific interests and points of view within the context of that moral order are still largely feeble. But can we assume that the growth of civil society, as it has occurred in Israel, will necessarily lead to the strengthening of democracy in the Middle East? I will propose here that the relationship between the emergence of civil society and a democratic state may be more complex in the Middle East than general writings on civil society would lead us to believe.

Theories have most often portrayed civil society as bolstering the state, enhancing its legitimacy and its ability to coordinate the diverse tendencies in society. The case of Israel, in contrast, indicates a variant pattern of state-civil society relations. Here, civil society grew alongside broad societal recognition of the legitimacy of the Israeli state, as most of the earlier theories would have expected, but civil society in this instance had a long-term corrosive effect on the state's ability to channel the diverse currents in society. To explain this anomalous effect of civil society, I will argue that we need to reject the undifferentiated portraits of civil society common to most of the literature. By breaking down civil society's active or volitional side institutionally, we can see how the particular patterns of growth of different parts of civil society can have a determining effect on state-society relations.

In the classical views presented by both Hegel and Gramsci, civil society emerged as an abutment to the state; it strengthened the predominance and hold of the governing organization by affirming it as the appropriate body to make and enforce society's rules.[3] In Hegel's version, it is the common agreement in society about the state as an ideal good that forms the backbone of civil society. Gramsci, in contrast, sees the cultural elements that will make up civil society as molded through the power of the state to accept a hegemonic dominance of a particular set of ideas supporting the state. In both theories, civil society supports the state's rule through a normative consensus in civil society. Such an understanding of the role of civil society does not contradict current (mostly Weberian) interpretations of the state. Even if the state's ultimate position rests on the possible use of violence in order to have its way, its day-to-day successes (and thus its long-term prospects) depend on voluntary compliance with its dictates even when the likelihood of violent retribution by arms of the state seems very small. Civil society from such a perspective helps ensure those successes by reinforcing the notions that the state is the proper organization to make most rules, that other organizations can make some rules and these will complement those of the state, and that the state's ability to maintain and defend a framework of rules, directly or indirectly, works to further the interests of those in civil society. In short, widely accepted theories in the social sciences see the state and civil society as mutually reinforcing through their common support of an ideology expressing the legitimacy of state rule.

In the last decade or so of communist rule in eastern Europe, a somewhat different understanding of civil society came into fashion, which is worth noting here, as well. It, too, does not fit the Israeli case very neatly.[4] In East Europe, civil society came to be understood as the antagonist of the state, quite unlike most of the associations that grew up in Israeli society. East European civil society expressed an alternative understanding about the norms and procedures for public life. As in the earlier interpretations of civil society, the emphasis in the communist states was on the role civil society plays in presenting a coherent image of what is befitting in the public sphere. But now the autonomy of civil society pits its notions against the unacceptable actions (and ideology) of the state and party. Rather than bolstering the idea of the state's rightful dominance, civil society hastens its downfall by chipping away at any widely held conception that the state's overpowering role is proper. Civil society, in these instances, offers a parallel moral order to that presented by the state, as well as alternative sets of practices.

The argument in this chapter rests on the premise that we need not think of civil society and the state only in terms of two sprawling institutional complexes, bearing on their shoulders some gargantuan notions—whether complementary or contradictory—of what is the proper way to order public life, much as Atlas bore the entire world on his shoulders. The relationship of state and civil society may not be best revealed by focusing on encompassing, coherent ideologies, whether reinforcing or conflicting, that support or bring into question the ultimate right of the state to rule. Focusing studies of civil society exclusively on questions of legitimacy, consensus, and hegemony (the passive dimension) may draw attention away from important cases in which the state's right to rule is not widely questioned but where the growth of civil society's institutions (the active or volitional dimension), nonetheless, dramatically affects the overall distribution of power. States may be enthusiastically cheered as the proper governing organizations, quite unlike the East European cases, while still finding that their ability to control society, to formulate policies, and to implement those policies may erode steadily, all in the context of a burgeoning civil society.

The organizations in civil society, at the same time, may find their autonomy and leverage increasing, but in an environment in which the overall framework that could reconcile and resolve their disparate interests, cultural perspectives, and views (i.e., the state) is atrophying. In these circumstances, the growth of civil society may be self-limiting, since civil society depends on a commonly accepted set of rules—a single discourse—for the interaction of different civil associations. The argument here, then, is that the state's ability to rule effectively may erode as civil society expands, even where the organizations in civil society overtly legitimate the state, and this erosion, in turn, may make civil society become increasingly uncivil. The widening realm of autonomous action among the groups in civil society may rob the state of key levers in controlling the population and deprive civil associations of the common language they need to coexist. The key to understanding the effects of civil society upon the state, as we shall see, is to identify the varying growth of different components of civil society; those components have very different effects on the nexus of state-civil society relations.

In the British-ruled Mandate for Palestine, the unceasing clash of Jews and Arabs, coupled with a colonial system that encouraged institutional bifurcation, prevented the sprouting of a countrywide civil society encompassing both peoples. And, even within the social boundaries of each communal group, the imperatives of the struggle, the need to mobilize people and resources as extensively as possible, and the challenge of organizing within a colonial framework, focused attention on each side's central political organizations. This period was crucial for both sides in the development of relations between politics and society. For Jews and Arabs alike, key groups scrambled to build central political organizations to confront the British and each other even before the societies themselves jelled in the context of the new, British-imposed boundaries. There was little room for the nurturing of autonomous civil organizations in either the Jewish or Arab communities, as political organizations demanded dominant control over the ordering of social life.

After the establishment of the Israeli state, the pattern of limited autonomy for civil organizations among its population (now including an Arab minority in addition to the Jews) continued, partly because of the persisting central role of the state in war mobilization and because of the previous pattern of state-society relations that had been established. Even as Israel was inundated with diverse newcomers, the emphasis was on state-directed "immigrant absorption" rather than on the promotion of a civil society that could bridge the vast cultural differences, especially those between Jews of European origin and those of North African and Asian origins. The state sought, too, to control and isolate what its leaders saw as the potentially subversive Arab minority, rather than fostering civil ties between it and the Jewish population. It is still difficult to read how far society has come in developing participatory civic life outside the control of the Israeli state organization. As late as 1988, Gadi Wolfsfeld could describe his book *The Politics of Provocation* as the first study of political participation in Israel, indicating that the notion of initiative from society in the public realm was still quite limited.[5]

The legacy of the relations between politics and society during the period of the Mandate and the Yishuv (the Jewish community in pre-1948 Israel) had a deep impact on everyday life after independence. The key institutions in the pre-state period were the fledgling organizations that would eventually make up the larger organizational complex of the state as well as the political parties, which were closely linked through personnel, function, and patronage to those other organizations. In Israel's first twenty years or so, public life was appropriated almost entirely by professional politicians staffing the state and what Gramsci called political society, the political parties. The preponderance of initiative did move toward the state from the political parties, which still remained key (but diminishing) links among elements in the larger society, but the pattern of leaving ordinary citizens on the outside looking in did not change substantially. A variety of works found the Israeli public standing on the sidelines with little sense that it could help shape the future of the society.[6] Not surprisingly, Israel had the largest public sector of any democracy in the world and devoted record proportions of its GNP to public services.[7] Israelis were inveterate political junkies, to be sure, stuffing themselves with information about public life in the form of news broadcasts, newspapers, and (loud) political discussions, but their initiatives in trying to shape the political and social landscape were paltry. As Wolfsfeld noted, "The high level of psychological involvement in politics can be traced to the obtrusiveness of political decisions into everyday life. Decisions about prices, salaries, reserve duty, and war are all made by a highly centralized government. Keeping abreast of politics in Israel is simply a necessity of life."[8]

If an event had a public dimension to it, the state or political parties saw it as their prerogative, indeed their duty, to lead the society in response. From health issues to charity drives, it was the government's and parties' initiatives that set the agenda and defined the extent and mode of public participation. In one book, the author began by saying, "A typical response of an Israeli to a proposed study of interest group development in Israel is, 'But how can you study interest groups? There aren't any.'"[9] Even the sphere of market relations was dominated by the large state enterprises and the heavy regulation of commercial activities by the state.

But, indeed, over time there came to be a multitude of autonomous social groups, and the market slowly came to develop a set of relations outside the direct control or oversight of the state. Various culture groups began to develop public practices (some with political overtones, some without) that became important motifs of the society. Moroccan Jews, for example, developed a set of pilgrimages and public celebrations that drew participation beyond their own culture group. As Drezon-Tepler and others have demonstrated, a public life beyond the controlling organizations of the state and the political parties began to reach a critical mass about two decades after independence. Following the 1973 war, civic organizations and activities seemed to mushroom. Many activities came to be centered in new formal associations; others took place through much less tightly organized groups or were not organized at all, but simply indicated similar civic behavior by people not formally linked to one another. The private sector produced an increasing share of national wealth, and government's hand in industrial and commercial relations seemed to lighten a bit (particularly with growing pressure from Israel's main international creditors). Various culture groups, ranging from religious factions to ethnic communities, organized to assert specific definitions of what the practices and beliefs of society as a whole should be.

All these represent heightened activity in society carving out autonomous realms of civic action, as well as increased contestation over what the content of state-society relations should rightly be. In a chapter of this size, it is impossible to look at all these components of society. Here, we will examine six different categories of those carving out an autonomous civic life, which differ in their relationship to the dominant political organization and in the degree to which they aggregate public actions (see Table 5.1). Their differing strengths stem from the particular legacy of earlier relations between politics and society and, as we shall see, have had a particular effect upon the contemporary state. I term these six types (1) fellow-travelers, (2) patriots, (3) do-gooders, (4) complainers, (5) protesters, and (6) interest brokers, as seen in the following table.

Fellow-travelers are seemingly the least interesting from the perspective of those concerned about the creation of autonomous associations that form the backbone of civil society. Many of these groups are nominally independent of the government but were originally organized (or at least inspired or influenced greatly) by political parties and government agencies. Most prominent here is the Histadrut, which is laced into party politics and government funding at every turn. A mainstay of its social power lies in its sprawling health maintenance organization, which is heavily subsidized by government revenues. But dozens of others exist as well, from some of the immigrant associations funded by the Ministry of Immigration and Welfare to an organization such as the Association on Behalf of the Soldiers (funded by the Ministry of Defense), which among other tasks has collected gum and pencils for soldiers at the front. Government or party funding is probably not an unflawed indicator of which organizations are fellow-travelers, since so many groups receive subsidies of one sort or another, even those that have established a modicum of independence. But for some, funding has limited the organization to promoting established public or party poli-

TABLE 5.1
Forms of Civic Life

	Adversarial to State	Supportive to State or Nonpolitical
Aggregative	Protesters Interest Brokers	Do-Gooders Fellow-Travelers
Nonaggregative	Complainers	Patriots

cies or to public education campaigns. One example is an environmental group, the Council for a Beautiful Israel, which was founded by a Knesset member in 1968. "Manned by professionals: architects, educators, lawyers, and other public figures . . . it was content to launch educational campaigns in schools, factories, gas stations, and the other institutions that were presumably conducive to raising environmental consciousness."[10] Nonetheless, even the limited autonomy of fellow-travelers creates an important volitional dimension in society outside the direct control of the state—that autonomous space has, on occasion, opened the way for yet more autonomy. The Histadrut is a case in point. It has increasingly gone head to head with government officials on key industrial and labor issues—both with the Likud in power and, more surprisingly, with the Labor party in control.

In contrast to the fellow-travelers, the other five categories have, indeed, worked to carve out a broad swathe of public space not dominated by the professional politicians of the state or the parties. Their efforts in forging a true civil society have been more telling. Patriots, the second category, have not been organized into associations at all but nonetheless have participated in a civic life quite supportive of the state. They have come together for memorial services for soldiers killed in Israel's wars or in loose friendship groups to help define the civic religion and other common civic practices outside the direct control of the state. During the 1982 Lebanon War, thousands of them assembled for progovernment rallies. They turn out to vote (Israel has one of the highest turnout rates for any democratic country where voting is not compulsory) and religiously tune into the national news broadcast nightly on state television. These sorts of activities, and the core of beliefs that sustain them, cannot be overestimated. They helped forge a common public space, with deeply shared values, for Jews coming from seventy different countries, with different languages, cultures, and religious practices.

While the effects of their actions have been complementary to those of the state, patriots have also placed severe limits on the expansion of civil society. For one thing, patriots, by definition, do not build formal organized groups, which have the most sustaining effects on the growth of an autonomous civil society. And what is even more important, a good share of the civic practices they have constructed have excluded the Arab population (almost one-fifth of Israel's citizens are Arab). Once the Palestinians in the occupied territories were added to the population as well, the practices of patriots became increasingly exclusive (or what Kimmerling has referred to as primordial rather than civil).[11]

Do-gooders, the third category, have operated on both sides of the civil society-state divide. At times, they have intersected with issues of public policy, acting much the same as standard interest or lobbying groups. But a prime motivation for organizing, as well, is to change values and practices in society, and not always to seek direct intervention of the state. Organizations such as the Society for Prevention of Smoking, the Heart Society, and the Cancer Society have aimed their messages at the Israeli public as well as at the institutions of the state. Yishai has made the point that, while they often appear to have a nonpolitical air about them, such do-gooder associations can become the tail that wags the dog.[12] The Heart Society, for example, has made a number of important decisions about appropriation of its resources that have established the parameters for the state's own health policy.

These sorts of groups, too, should not be underestimated in the creation of civil society in many liberal democracies. They have established a public domain parallel and often complementary to the state's realm, weaving diverse elements of society together in a broad variety of civic practices. Several very strong organizations of this sort have emerged in Israel, but many others have been among the weakest associations. Too often, the line between do-gooders and fellow-travelers has been blurred by the government and party officials. Do-gooders have slipped into being fronts for, or have been co-opted by, the state or the political parties. Whereas in liberal democracies, such as the United States, do-gooders have gained an important toehold in creating an autonomous social realm, in Israel all but a select few have found themselves standing on a very slippery slope.

Complainers, the fourth category, are not unique to Israel. In Western societies first, and then in others, there has been a burgeoning of ombudsmen, consumer complaint columns in the newspapers, radio call-in shows, whistle-blowing organizations, and more.[13] "Their appearance," writes Brenda Danet, "is a response to the call for greater accountability of public institutions, and for at least partial redress of the tremendous imbalance of power between individual citizens and these huge institutions."[14] Some of these organizations, such as the ombudsman, are centered in the state itself, acting as an internal check on the practices of government agencies. Others are autonomous of the state. In either case, they promote independent and safe means for voicing grievances, often (but not always) directed against the state itself, as well as being autonomous channels for influencing the behavior of the state.

In Israel, the government established the office of the ombudsman in 1971, one of the earliest moves in this direction outside Scandinavia. Additional municipal, army, and policy ombudsmen followed. Israelis also developed consumer organizations, a television show to air private complaints, and much more. These sorts of organizations expanded the domain of civil society, if not by binding people together socially (complaints are frequently individualistic in nature), then by limiting the domain of the state. For civil society to flourish, it needs arenas of social life relatively free from the overpowering control and influence of the state. Complainers acting through formal channels legitimize limiting the boundaries of state action and thereby open public space to other civic discourses and practices. They create independent channels of political and social communication.

But complaining in Israel, as in the case of the patriots, is marked by a tension in terms of the expansion of civil society. Despite the growth of complaint-handling organizations, many grievances go through channels that exclude portions of the public. These mechanisms are based on all sorts of particularism—familism, friendship groups, old army ties, and much more.[15] These bases of associations only exacerbate the tension between the two competing forms of social identity in the collectivity based on civil and more particularistic sentiments.[16] Kinship and friendship ties serve not only to stratify Jews in terms of in-groups and out-groups, they accentuate the tremendously difficult time Arab citizens in Israel have had in entering the corridors of Israeli civic life. With the addition of the occupied territories, the tendency to limit access of certain groups (Palestinians, above all) to the activities that would normally be thought of as properly in the realm of civil society has restricted the expansion of civil society all the more. In short, the differing abilities to have one's complaint heard and acted upon based on kinship and friendship group membership have retarded the knitting together of civil society. The independent channels of political and social communication have divided society rather than integrating it. The result is different playing rules for different groups, a situation antithetical to the flourishing of civil society. While complainers have enhanced the chances for civil society to flourish by helping to institutionalize the limits of state practices, at the same time they have often voiced their grievances within exclusive, rather than broadly civic, channels of communication.

The fifth category, protesters, burst onto the Israeli scene in the 1970s. The first instance was a set of protests against poverty and government social-welfare policy staged by youths from poor neighborhoods calling themselves the Black Panthers. Their sometimes violent demonstrations took the government aback, causing leading officials both to try and co-opt some of the Panthers' leaders and to delegitimize them. Few Israelis will forget Prime Minister Golda Meir's dismissal of the protesters as "bad boys." Another protest, this time in the form of a vigil, and much more sedate than those of the Black Panthers, rose directly out of the 1973 war. Even while the war continued to rage, a young scientist, Motti Ashkenazi, stood silently with his placard in front of the Knesset building day after day. His demonstration was aimed at the political leadership, especially Defense Minister Moshe Dayan and Prime Minister Meir, whom Ashkenazi identified as the culprits responsible for the deaths of his fellow army reservists in Egypt's surprise attack at the Suez Canal. Ashkenazi's protests were electrifying. Hundreds of other soldiers joined him in his vigil, which finally did serve as catalysts to force the resignation of the two political leaders.

Like complainers, protesters seek responsiveness and accountability by checking the state's practices. But, unlike much complaining, protesting is a form of collective action. Ashkenazi succeeded when others joined his cause, even if not in a formal organizational setting. Protesting goes beyond complaining by channeling dissatisfaction and forging ties among those objecting. It mobilizes political participation in a public realm outside the customary state channels, including those of the established political parties.

Throughout the 1970s, political protest gained ground as an accepted (if not always acceptable) form of citizen-initiated social action. In 1976, for example, Arab citizens organized a highly visible protest called Land Day, which later came to be commemorated annually. Important new groups, fighting against the ever-present seduction of joining the fray of party politics, emerged during the decade. Gush Emunim and Peace Now, the two most prominent ones, had a major impact in debates about the future of Israeli society and politics. But they certainly were not the only protesting groups. Throughout the 1970s, new protest groups formed and the number of demonstrations kept rising. The increase in the number of protests continued into the 1980s, especially during the 1982 war in Lebanon, after which the number seemed to level off. One count of protests found the number running over 150 per year in the first half of the 1980s.[17] And their impact, both among those in groups such as Gush Emunim and Peace Now and those protesting other issues entirely, was not insubstantial. As Wolfsfeld wrote, "Citizens who would have been shut out of the political process a few years ago are getting a real chance to be heard."[18]

But, like complainers and patriots, protesters have had a problematical effect on the development of civil society. Protesters awakened the citizenry to the need to take the initiative on public questions, often through organizations that go on to have a lasting effect on state-society relations. Too often, however, protests, like the actions of patriots, do little to create long-lasting ties in civil society, as a kind of permanent space outside the realm of the state. Moreover, when they are violent (which is relatively uncommon in Israel, although violence is more prevalent than in the past), they can undercut the building of a common framework of rules, so necessary for civil society. In fact, protests in Israel seemed increasingly to polarize the society about its overall social identity.

Perhaps the oldest form of autonomous associational life in Israel is found in our last category, the interest brokers. The prototype of an interest group in Israel is the Manufacturers Association, whose origins predate the state.[19] From 1921 through the post-Independence years, the association aimed to represent employers and to promote the interests of industrialists. "Its relatively high annual budget, . . . a well-staffed organization, and the expertise of its administrative workers," wrote Yishai, "have contributed to the association's efficiency. A wide membership and a cohesive organizational structure also constitute major assets."[20]

But for all the success of the Manufacturers Association, it was not typical of interest brokers in Israel. Through most of its life it was genuinely autonomous, remaining fairly free of party or government control (although it did have especially close relations with the General Zionists party at some points). The resources that it represented also set it apart in enabling it to have a substantial effect on government policy. Israeli interest groups, on the whole, have not found the same kind of nurturing environment as have such groups in, say, the United States. Like do-gooders, interest brokers have found themselves either co-opted by the state or smothered by it. Many of Israel's professional associations, for example, have been emasculated by their incorporation into the Histadrut, with its close ties to party and state. Where such co-optation has not been possible, the state has, at times, moved to nip in the bud the independence of interest groups. As Yishai put it, "The state is manipulative, its authority extending octopus-like over interest groups."[21] In 1980, the passing of the Associations Law enabled the state to delve into the records and affairs of interest groups as a form (or, at least, a threat) of intimidation. Yishai comments,

> By enacting this law, the state attempted to grasp the rope at each end, i.e., to ensure the freedom of association and to control the group arena. The absence of a similar law in many other democracies, however, highlights the prominence of the state in the Israeli context. The state was authorized by its early founders to overcome the divisions that beset the Jewish people in the Diaspora. . . . The state was thus ordained to rise above all sectional differences.[22]

Israeli civil society, then, has been shaky in precisely those areas where a number of Western liberal democracies' civil societies have been strongest. Do-gooders and interest brokers in Israel have remained weak, stymied in their efforts to create a space for durable autonomous associations and institutionalized social relations beyond the realm of the state. Because these sorts of associations have been co-opted or smothered by the state, the arenas of public life have been dominated by the state along with informal groups based on particularistic personal ties. The enfeeblement of that part of civil society made up of aggregating, inclusive, and highly institutionalized associations has been a legacy of the all-encompassing role of the state and the key parties before and immediately after independence, as well as of the enduring Arab-Israeli conflict. In the struggles to define the character of social relations in the broad public realm, interest brokers and do-gooders have not been as evident as in other democracies. The playing field has been dominated by the state. Uri Ben-Eliezer described the preeminence of the state in terms of the legacy from the period of the Yishuv:

> In contrast to the development of American society, people in Israel, particularly during the pre-state period, were organized in various social frameworks that did not necessarily give expression to the free will of their members. What indeed is the meaning of freedom of choice when receiving the documents necessary to even enter Palestine required a particular political affiliation; when the allocation of jobs through the labor exchange was governed by membership in a political party; and when receipt of medical services was conditional on membership in the trade union?[23]

State-society relations, however, have not remained static since the period of the Yishuv. From that time on, patriots have played a key role in supporting the creation of what Liebman and Don-Yehiya have described as Israel's civil religion, as well as in creating modes of appropriate daily behavior in the public realm.[24] Civil society did burgeon in the 1970s and 1980s. But the forms that civil society took in Israel at that time, complainers and protesters, have given Israel's state-society relations a special cast. Complaining often tends to be individualistic and nonaggregative. When people's complaints are addressed or the immediate issue passes, the complainers withdraw from the public realm. While protesting tends to be more aggressive, it too tends to bring people into civic arenas, where key questions of public behavior are being struggled over, for relatively short bursts of activity. Even groups such as Peace Now, which have been on the scene for more than two decades, have seen their visibility and prominence wax and wane depending on whether the time was conducive to launch protests (as it was during the war in Lebanon). The kinds of civic groups with staying power in such arenas, do-gooders and interest brokers, have been relatively weak in Israel.

Complainers and protesters, to be sure, have helped forge elements of public life outside the control of the state, and they have had an impact on the struggles about the shape of society. But both of these groups have set the civil society on an adversarial course with the state, while accepting the state as the proper address to direct complaints. Rather than creating arenas—public spaces—where the state is largely absent or at least negligible in the struggles over the establishment of the norms and patterns of daily behavior, these forms of civil society have had a dual effect. First, they have further accentuated the centrality of the state in many realms of life through their entreaties and protests aimed at government officials. It is not the appropriateness of the state's role in handling all these issues that they have questioned but how well the state has performed its role. The effect of complaining and protesting has been to put a tremendous burden on the state to make things right, while at the same time challenging the state in the way it has handled issues up until now. State accountability has moved to the center of the state-society nexus, while it has overburdened the state with more responsibility to make things right than it can deliver on. In Israel, the outcome was to erode the legitimacy of the state during the 1970s and early 1980s. Levels of discontent with government rose from the 10 to 20 percent range in the late 1960s to as high as 70 to 80 percent for the decade after the 1973 War.[25]

The prominence of protesters and complainers, as against do-gooders and interest brokers, has had a second effect on state-society relations: underscoring the exclusive particularism within the population. Complainers have used connections and pull to voice their grievances, and even protesters, some scholars have suggested, have relied "on primary relations and networks of families, friends and friends of friends as a basis for mobilization."[26] We have already commented on how this sort of fragmentation makes the creation of an inclusive civic life all the more difficult to institutionalize. It has had another effect, as well. Through their emphasis on back channels, complainers have further accentuated the heavy demands on the state to service multiple, particularistic fragments of the society. Certainly, this phenomenon is common to all democracies, but because these demands come in the absence of highly institutionalized civic associations that agree on the rules of the game, the upshot has been grave difficulty in state leaders' sorting out priorities and taking initiative in highest priority areas. In a self-reinforcing process, with the state frozen in this regard, the public all the more has resorted to back channels to gain state responsiveness, lending further divisiveness to social relations.

The growth of civil society is not simply a black and white question of whether it exists or not; the strength or weakness of different pillars of civil society, stemming from the environment in which it developed, is bound to have a profound effect on the nature of the state and its relationship to its citizens. Civil society cannot simply be analyzed as an undifferentiated institutional complex. In Israel, as we have seen, the prominence of nonaggregative elements of civil society (complainers and patriots) as well as ones with an adversarial relationship to the state (protesters and complainers) has overburdened the state. The paralysis of the state, in turn, has undermined its role as the framework for establishing universality among civil associations. With little direction from the state, public associations and behavior have inched increasingly toward particularism and exclusivism. Pull and connections have continued to dominate over broad and inclusive civic sorts of public participation. And the definition of society has rested on narrowly religious and ethnic criteria over more broadly civic ones. The next two chapters tease out how contingent factors—demography, the establishment of boundaries and, not least, war—affected the prominence of these ethnic and religious differences among Jews and between Jews and Arabs.

CHAPTER 6

Society Formation
and the Case of Israel

To my surprise, critics aimed many of their choicest criticisms of my book *Strong Societies and Weak States* at the use of Israel as one of the case studies.[1] Several complained that Israel was not a Third World state at all and that it skewed the entire analysis. That charge might indeed be true if we had an agreed-upon definition of Third World (Israel did fit into *my* definition) or if the term *Third World* held any analytic power at all (it does not). In any case, since the writing of the book and of the criticism, the demise of the Second World, the Soviet Union and its East European empire, made the very term *Third World* anachronistic.

For others, the problem with the case was a bit more serious. Israel is not representative, the argument went, because its society has been newly constructed; its origins are as a settler society. The process of state formation must be entirely different where state agencies (or their fore-runners) do not have to deal with a society that has been in place since time immemorial. Louis Hartz, in a now nearly forgotten body of work, offered his so-called fragment theory of state formation for precisely those few cases where societies have been largely transplanted and are, therefore, essentially new constructions.[2]

To his credit, Hartz did not simply assume that a new society started with a clean slate; he looked at exactly which ideas the transplants brought with them from the old country and how that baggage took on unique hues in the new setting. Nonetheless, his work lent credence to the notion that the handful of societies, such as Israel, that have been dominated by recent immigrants are somehow a different breed and poor examples to use in trying to grasp more common cases of state-society relations. Subsequent works on settler societies have implicitly made the same argument. In this chapter, I maintain that this distinction between new settler societies and old societies in Africa and Asia is invalid. Israel can be quite instructive in understanding the dynamics of state-society relations elsewhere because it illuminates processes that exist, but may be cast in shadows, in other cases.

What makes a society "new" or "old" and what do we mean by

society formation? As we shall note below, the concept of society has two dimensions. First is the potpourri of groups and organizations that are the basis for association, everything from the family to huge businesses. Second is an element more difficult to visualize—an outermost structure, formed by an intensity of interactions within and among these groups that falls off significantly beyond its limits, and reinforced by people's taking it as a basis for personal identification.

Such outermost structures, which constitute the boundaries between societies, are porous and fuzzy. Sometimes they are the same as the political boundaries, but that is not always the case; they can be the subject of serious dispute. It is not surprising that these outermost structures are not immutable. In "old" societies the outermost structures have been stable for some time, as have the major ordering of relations among groups. Society formation, on the other hand, involves the creation of "new" societies, that is, a significant change in outermost structures or a major reordering of relations among groups.

In the first part of the chapter, I look more closely at the process of society formation; in particular, I question the assumption that this term applies largely to settler societies. My argument here is that many scholars erroneously assume the existence of "old societies" in Asia and Africa. I contend that societies there are recent constructions, that outermost structures have changed substantially in recent decades, and that cases such as Israel can shed light on how the process of society formation occurs in Asia, Africa, and elsewhere.

In the second part of the chapter, emphasis is placed on the particular struggle in many societies between conceptions grounded in ethnic association and those based in civic membership. Society formation from the former Yugoslavia to Northern Ireland to the Sudan has centered on these two contending tendencies, of what society should be. My central question is: what moves societies toward one or the other? Of course, no single article or book can answer that question. But a closer look (in the third part of the chapter) at Israeli society, one that has vacillated between ethnic and civic principles in the process of society formation, can shed light on a struggle many other societies have experienced.

One answer to our question of why societies tend toward ethnic or civic bases is that immediate political contingencies—specifically, the territorial issues involved with the creation or change of state boundaries—deeply influence the central conceptions underlying the construction of society. Political boundary issues open a Pandora's box of questions about what the outermost structure of society is and should be. In the case of Israeli society, changes in political boundaries after World War I, in 1948, and in 1967, as well as the open question of ultimate boundaries after 1967, exacerbated the struggle between the two contending conceptions of society, that based exclusively on the Jewish nation and one geared to include non-Jewish residents of the territory as well.

STATES AND SOCIETIES

As I mulled over the criticism of the use of Israel as a case in *Strong Societies and Weak States*, I began to think that the problem was part of the larger issue for comparative studies of moving beyond theories generated by the experiences of the first modern states, those in Europe. Even today, so much of what we take as "normal" in state-society relations and in processes of state formation has been derived from the European, especially northwestern European, experiences (or, more accurately, myths associated with those experiences). The word *state* itself, representing the organization exercising supreme civil power in an extended territory, came into use only in the sixteenth century in the context of the vast political changes overtaking western Europe at the time. Can we indiscriminately use such a term for cases that have very different contextual conditions? Can we derive meaningful comparative theories in such circumstances?

Even more problematical is the concept of society. Its usage also dates back to sixteenth-century Europe. Society consists of a melange of organizations exercising social control; social, economic, and cultural relations within and among these organizations are marked by conflict and accommodation. By one measure, society is delineated by these partially overlapping arenas of social relations (labor markets, voluntary associations, and the like) and social control. These formal and informal organizations establish rules for appropriate behavior in society and for the ways people interact with one another. All sorts of sanctions and rewards, ranging from the use of gossip to the conferring of honor on a person, deter some kinds of behavior and encourage others. A society's character is formed by the rules people follow; the "appropriate" behavior they exhibit; the kinds of rewards and sanctions they employ; and, not least, the sorts of conflicts that develop over all of the above.

But society is more than these social organizations and the control they have over how people behave; another dimension, as we have seen, is society as "the outermost social structure for a certain group of individuals who, whatever might be their attitude toward it, view themselves as its members and experience their identity as being determined by it."[3] We can add that people's cumulating, shared experiences, particularly in dealing with institutions (especially those of the state), are key in creating boundedness, or that outermost social structure. Association within the boundaries of the social structure are likely to be more intense, and social ties more numerous, than across the boundaries. It is important to keep in mind that the outermost structure is not hermetically sealed, by any means, and it is often the relations with outsiders that make that structure tentative and subject to change.

It is not coincidental that the notions of "state" and "society" as identifiable concepts developed hand in hand. The understanding of a society that could be differentiated from other societies came to be tied to the emergence of distinct political entities, European states, that had some organic connection to the peoples they governed. By the eighteenth and nineteenth centuries, the conception of societies and states as differentiable entities, while still mutually dependent, developed even further. The intertwining of the two grew as a myth receded in Europe; that myth held that "society was naturally organized around and under high centers—monarchs who were persons apart from other human beings and who ruled by some form of cosmological (divine) dispensation."[4] With the attacks on such notions, political leaders now began to justify their power on the basis of the state's relation to its society, which they portrayed as bounded with a definite outermost structure. Political legitimacy of states came to be associated with the will of the people; state authority, political theorists and leaders claimed, derived from the representation of a people with shared experiences and some common identity. The assertion was that states' authority derived from the common will of those people, thereby assuming their basic unity (or an "outermost structure" for them).

States, the thinking continued, did not come on the scene of world history to unite disparate peoples (as empires did) but were an expression of, and drew their authority from, preexisting societies. Seen in this way, a state has "natural" boundaries, ones deriving from the organic society with its own general will, that it represents and governs. State boundaries, in this view, are not simply the capricious outcome of war or other political contingencies. The tendency to analyze the rise of the state in contractual terms, I believe, derived from an assumption that an already-present society contained people with enough in common so that they (or an elect group that could claim to represent them) could make a binding political contract, either with each other or the ruler.

Israel, with its newly formed society, is certainly not comparable with the more common cases—both in Europe and possibly elsewhere—with their preexisting societies. The Israeli state could not derive its authority from Israeli society, since Israeli society barely existed when the state was created. Israeli society was not organic and could convey no general will. If new states in Africa and Asia, in contrast to Israel, have drawn their authority from longstanding societies and have been representations of those societies, as the European model would lead us to believe, then the Israeli case would lend little to the understanding of other Asian and African cases. (As we shall see below, I find this understanding of new states deriving their authority from "old" societies to be mistaken; the case of Israel can actually be quite instructive for analyzing a broader array of states and societies.)

In the European context, the term *nation*, connoting an even more cohesive sense of common identity, was often substituted for the word *society* and for the word *state*. In English, the concept of nation actually predates those of state and society; in most cases, it has implied a people with a shared ancestry (or, failing that, a linguistic or historical bonding that forged an identifiably distinct people). The notion of a common heritage, most often found in a blood or kinship bond, underlies the notion of nation. Using the term *nation* to merge state and society reinforced the notion that states were direct outgrowths of the collective will of a people strongly identified with one another.[5] More recently, many academics have used the term *nation* to denote one kind of society—one tightly bound, often through a myth of blood or common founding, having a common purpose (expressed through nationalism). In the European context, whether one used the more tightly bound concept of nation or other more heterogeneously constructed types of society, it was society that came to be seen as the legitimating source for new, powerful states. Those states putatively represented the will of the nation or of society.

Even when the state was exported outside Europe, colonial officials often spoke as if somehow they were hunting for the natural societies or nations in this place or that, which could sanction the establishment of particular state boundaries and, ultimately, legitimate the colonial state itself. Some of the British rulers' disappointment in Palestine during the Mandate period stemmed from the dawning reality of the absence of such a natural society there, shattering their earlier naivete. Note the self-revelatory and didactic tone of the Palestine Royal Commission (or Peel Commission) report in 1937: "It is time, surely, that Palestinian 'citizenship' . . . should be recognized as what it is, as nothing but a legal formula devoid of moral meaning." In our terms, a Jewish-Arab society existed insofar as Jews and Arabs associated with one another in a wide variety of organizations, from work groups to municipal councils. What was missing, thus creating two societies in Palestine rather than one, was a common outermost structure.

The Peel Commission was not the only source warning that it was fiction to think of unified, preexisting societies in colonial territories, which corresponded to the political boundaries that European rulers drew on their maps. Academics have spilled much ink in recent years in order to tell us that Asia and Africa, with some exceptions here or there, do not have states whose boundaries correspond to existing nations or even to the looser concept of outermost structures of existing societies.[6] Note, for example, Benedict Anderson's take on the question:

> Nationality, or, as one might prefer to put it in view of that word's multiple signification, nation-ness, as well as nationalism, are cultural artifacts of a particular kind. To understand them properly we need to consider carefully how they have come into historical being, in what ways their meanings have changed over time, and why, today, they command such profound emotional legitimacy?[7]

Anderson's point stands for the broader concept of society, as well. Just as we take nations to be "cultural artifacts" rather than preexisting entities whose essence has remained unscathed since time immemorial, so must societies, which lack the tight connotation given by blood ties, be understood as human creations. Colonial leaders and heads of the new states found multiethnic or multinational peoples and multiple societies, which had to be formed into a single outermost structure if a common identity was to exist. These were vastly different from the commonly rendered European prototypes of already existing societies with a defined collective will.

A closer look at those Western prototypes in light of what we have learned from Asia and Africa indicates that preexisting societies as we know them in the eighteenth and nineteenth centuries did not exist in Europe any more than in Palestine or other places outside the West in the twentieth century. Eugen Weber's fine account of nineteenth-century France, for example, depicts how the state molded, indeed created, the French society; the state was not the simple outgrowth of an already formed French society.[8] In fact, both the French state and society came to be formed and re-formed in their ongoing series of interactions, alliances, struggles, and accommodations.[9]

The continuing survival of the notions of preexisting societies stems from their key legitimating role for states—in Europe as much as in areas outside the West. The myth of a natural society gives moral weight to the state's claim of preeminent authority. State leaders sought such affirmation for them and their states in the "moral meaning" of society, referred to in the Peel Commission Report, or in the "naturalness" of society itself, even if there was no "naturalness" of a more tightly bound nation (with its myth of common ancestry) per se. There is barely a state in Asia or Africa today, no matter how new its vintage and how diverse its population, that has not had its founders and subsequent heads ground it and define it in terms of a preexisting society in its territorial and social space.

State officials have sought, through the supposed naturalness of society, a moral justification and consensus for their use of coercion in everything from collecting taxes to fighting wars. Indeed, part of the project of state leaders in justifying themselves and the state has been to make the notion of the preexistence of their societies a truism. It is not surprising, then, that state leaders have nurtured myths of preexisting societies in order to legitimate the state and their own rule. Such myths are problematical when they become incorporated into social scientists' understanding of why states and societies are structured as they are.

The first serious look at the meaning of society in the comparative study of Asia and Africa challenged the interpretation that societies predated states. Under the chairmanship of Edward Shils, the Committee for the Comparative Study of New Nations at the University of Chicago formed in 1959; other members included David Apter, Leonard Binder, and Clifford Geertz. The committee had a decisive impact on the development of general concepts and theories encompassing the contemporary social and political experiences of peoples outside the West. As Apter, its executive secretary, put it, "Rather than emphasizing area specialization, such as Asia, Africa, or the Middle East, we prefer to consider certain common experiences that the new nations have entertained, seeking to compare broadly similar historical stages that they share. . . . Our object is to avoid becoming imprisoned in area parochialism at the expense of more theoretically useful comparisons."[10]

In the committee's most important publication, *Old Societies and New States: The Quest for Modernity in Asia and Africa*, it sketched out some very important thoughts about "society." Society is fashioned when something creates a framework for its existence, what I referred to earlier as an outermost structure; when contingencies change, as in the invasion of colonial rulers, so does the outermost structure encompassing society. In the world since the sixteenth century, that "something" or contingency creating such boundedness has most frequently been the state. Despite the claim by some later theorists that the state had been shunted aside in these early theories and had to be "brought back in," this early attempt at comparative studies, in fact, had a very strong notion of the state, with evident agency and autonomy, even if the particular word, *state*, was not always used. Substitute the word *state* the first time that Apter uses the word *nation* in the following passage about the committee's assumptions (the context indicates he really meant "state"), and it sounds very much like contemporary state-centered theory. "The new nations are engaged in a form of social change that makes nation building and material development simultaneous political problems. As a result, all aspects of life have a heavily political element."[11]

These new states, coming out of the colonial experience, encountered "old societies." By no means were the committee members simplistic about the coherence of these societies. Setting up a state, Shils argued, "must be done in the context of a traditional society, or, more frequently, in the context of a plurality of traditional societies. . . . The new states of Asia and Africa have not yet reached the point where the people they rule have become nations, more or less coterminous with the state in the territorial boundaries, and possessing a sense of identity in which membership in the state that rules them is an important component."[12] Leave aside for a moment the strong teleological element here (the "states have not yet reached the point," implying they inevitably would); Shils hints at a very important point: the imposition of a new state has the effect of re-creating society by establishing the framework for a new outermost social structure. Old societies are reconstructed into new ones whose boundaries are more or less coterminous with those of the state. It is the reconstruction of society, what I have called society formation, that is the key to understanding the dynamics of Asia and Africa. The reconstitution of their outermost structures demands much closer scrutiny, especially the state-society relations related to society formation. A case such as Israel, where society formation was obvious to all, can be a window into processes of society formation elsewhere. Relegating Israel to the margins of comparative studies is a fundamentally flawed enterprise.

Shils may have put too simple a gloss on the question of society formation. His work implies a state so autonomous that it seems not to be affected noticeably by the confrontation with the old society. In fact, the interaction of states and societies is a recursive process, with numerous, scattered struggles and co-optations.[13] In the end, both societies and states are transformed by these struggles and accommodations. Nonetheless, his conclusion that societies are reconstructed is an important insight. In our case, it casts a very different light on the Israeli experience; Israel's societal reconstruction would be more the norm than the outlier. Its self-conscious process of creating an outermost structure, a "new" society, has been comparable to the reconstitution of other societies under the pressure of Western political and economic expansion as well of postcolonial states. Israel leads us beyond simplistic notions of society's naturalness to the search for the particular contingencies that have been the underpinnings of society formation.

Unfortunately, Shils's insight was lost in subsequent years when the idea of "old societies" was too often taken as given. Rather than looking at the conditions that re-created societies, scholars frequently have assumed societies to have an enduring existence that preceded and transcended the state; discussions of change often came within pluralist and structural functionalist perspectives that saw society as a stable framework within which various sorts of competition and adjustment took place.[14] In part, this tendency to see longstanding societies as legitimating state authority, may have come about from an uncritical stance toward the state by academics and journalists, especially in the context of the Cold War. After all, as we have seen, the state's legitimacy and its very identity qua state (rather than, say, as a loose empire) depended upon the understanding of a preexisting society (with its "moral meaning" and "naturalness") justifying and authorizing the state's rule. An intact society legitimizes the existence and power of the new state.

Whatever the reasons for the paucity of studies on society formation, a new look at the question gives a very different cast to the Israeli case. Here is a society whose construction took place in the clear light of day first in its initial stages during the Yishuv period and then with the large influxes of Jewish immigrants after the creation of the state, along with the existence of a substantial Arab minority. While each society's formation has its own unique qualities, processes in each open vistas and questions that can help in deciphering the patterns of change in others. While in many cases these elements are veiled and relatively inaccessible, precisely because of the strong myths propounded by colonial and indigenous state officials about the naturalness of established societies, in Israel the creation of society was prima facie a project, allowing scholars to peer directly into the inner workings of the process. That project can tell us much about a process that needs our careful attention: the reconstruction of societies in Asia and Africa under the prodding of an expanding world economy and of first colonial and then independent states.

ETHNIC AND CIVIC BASES OF SOCIETY

If we reject the naturalness of societies and ask about their modern reconstruction, we are drawn to one of the most critical struggles over the structure and nature of society across the globe. Three decades ago Geertz pinpointed this tension, noting that people have demonstrated two strong motives: the need for a recognized identity, of being someone in the world, and the need for the practicality of economic progress, political order, and social justice.[15] The first, the need for a primary identity, is expressed in national or ethnic construction; the second (the practical impulse), in state and society formation, or the civic realm.

Geertz's distinction points to the two facets of society that we have indicated, the associative (relations in and among groups, often with their overtones of social control and getting things done, or instrumentality) and the outermost structure (bonding among individuals, with the emphasis on identity). Both are key elements in all societies, but they are often in tension with one another, and various societies, at different times, stress one over the other. Geertz writes:

> To subordinate these specific and familiar identifications [national, ethnic, etc.] in favor of a generalized commitment to an overarching and somewhat alien civil order is to risk a loss of definition as an autonomous person, either through absorption into a culturally undifferentiated mass or, what is even worse, through domination by some other rival ethnic, racial, or linguistic community that is able to imbue that order with the temper of its own personality. But at the same time, all but the most unenlightened members of such societies are at least dimly aware—and their leaders are acutely aware—that the possibilities for social reform and material progress they so intensely desire and are so determined to achieve rest with increasing weight on their being enclosed in a reasonably large, independent, powerful, well-ordered polity.[16]

Geertz's term *polity* at the end of this quotation is somewhat ambiguous, but to my mind it includes both the organizational dimensions encompassed in the state and the associative aspects represented by the larger society. For Geertz, these two elements—state and (civil) society—are coterminous, at the least, and in some ways indistinguishable. This is a point we will take issue with below. But for the moment, we can agree with Geertz that a critical tension exists between what he termed the primordial and civil. In fact, Kimmerling has adopted those terms specifically for the Israeli case.[17]

Numerous past and ongoing struggles shape the character of every society. In the contemporary world, as much now after the Cold War as ever, society's coherence based on civic association and its coherence based on bonds of common identity have frequently been at loggerheads. These are not simply theoretical tensions; they determine who is considered an integral member of society and who is an outsider, as well as the various rights and privileges assigned to different individuals and groups. By adapting Geertz's and Kimmerling's useful distinction, we can identify two tendencies in many societies, an "ethnic" one in which the outermost structure and question of identity revolve around myths of common ancestry or founding and a "civic," which emphasizes instrumental sorts of association among society's members.[18] We can also examine the crucial place of the state in the tensions between these tendencies. Each provides an answer as to how people can associate and identify with one another even in large groupings where each person does not know the vast majority of others.

The ethnic tendency seeks to collapse the differences between "nation" and "society." Full membership in the society and full rights accrue to those who are part of the nation or dominant ethnic group. I will avoid Geertz's concept *primordial* because of its association with negative terms such as primitive, but "ethnic" implies myths of common ethnology, especially sharing common origins. A person's place in society, to borrow some language from Gellner, comes by "virtue of prior membership of some organic sub-part of it."[19] Rights, privileges, and power vary among members within each ethnic group, but these sorts of internal status differences tend to be distributed according to skill, merit, inheritance patterns, and the like. Differences between ethnic groups, in contrast, are reinforced by particular property rights and legal strictures enforced by the state. And, outside the laws and institutions of the state, association in society—in the economic sphere, cultural activities, and political interaction—is largely structured on the basis of birth into a particular group based on the myth of blood ties.

Those supporting the civic tendency argue for membership and full rights to all who take on the duties of citizenship, which is conferred restrictively based on certain criteria, such as birth in the territory or to parents who are citizens, length of residency, profession of loyalty, and civic knowledge. Here, membership stems not from ethnology but from one's status as a "freeman," able to take on prescribed duties. Association is based on private or voluntary arrangements among individuals and groups, often founded in shared, acquired interests.[20] Once one achieves the status of citizen, one's ethnic identity is not the basis for, or limit to, mobility because of particular property rights or other legal strictures. Whereas ethnic-leaning societies discriminate in their constitution against nondominant nationalities (such as Gypsies in Romania), civic societies discriminate against those it restricts from achieving citizenship (such as "illegal" aliens in the United States).

Actual societies are neither wholly ethnic, constructed on the basis of national or primary identity in which association and membership are grounded in myths about common blood, nor entirely civic, constituted so that moral meaning comes not from shared ancestry but from voluntary (sometimes contractual) associative ties among those in the territory, regardless of birth group. Rather, actual societies are amalgams of the two ideal types. Even many that are closer to the civic end of the spectrum, for example, have long maintained property rights excluding women from full rights and privileges. But using these two tendencies, which exist in all societies, enables us to sort out different paths of society construction and how rights become hierarchically assigned, both in legal terms by the state and informally through society's norms. The actual mixture of the two tendencies is dynamic and moving. We can ask what sorts of conditions lead to the dominance of one over the other and to the particular mix of the two.

Construction and reconstruction of societies in the Balkans, Africa, Asia, and elsewhere have frequently centered on these two contending tendencies of what the normative basis, or moral meaning, of society should be. The interesting question is what moves societies toward one pole or the other—what sorts of factors influence the outcomes of societal struggles? Those factors range from natural phenomena, such as devastating earthquakes, to interactions with other societies through commerce or war. State organizations play key roles in mediating these other factors and in pushing societies toward either ideal type.

In this regard, states have had dual, often contradictory, motives and ways of acting. From early modern times, state leaders have claimed for their organization a universal role in the claimed territory, discouraging inherited status differences among groups in favor of a society of "freemen" whose civic ties to one another are sanctioned by the state and also justify the state's existence. At the same time, state leaders have sought to create a legitimizing core, national or ethnic, whose members would consider the state theirs, often at the expense of hard-to-assimilate groups in the territory (enhancing integration of the core by highlighting differences with the "other").

Understanding the forces moving a society toward the ethnic or civic poles, then, entails looking at the critical role of the state, both as an actor and as a prize (to be secured and itself molded) for groups competing to define the society. The Israeli case is an excellent one in highlighting these struggles and in isolating some elements that move societies toward a dominant ethnic or civic character, as well as how the mixture of the two types manifests itself.

THE CONSTRUCTION OF ISRAELI SOCIETY

Israel's experience suggests several key hypotheses that might shed light on other cases, where societies are undergoing key changes. First, states, both colonial and postcolonial, play critical roles in the construction of societal boundaries coincidental to the designated political borders. Second, once formed, societies do not remain static entities. They continue to be changed by conscious state policy, by the unintended acts of states, by internal dynamics, and by transnational forces. The result is that societal boundaries may begin to diverge substantially from the state's political boundaries. Demographic shifts, in particular, play a critical role in changing societies so that societal and political boundaries may not coincide. And, third, change in, or uncertainty about, the state's boundaries tends to strengthen ethnic tendencies at the expense of civic forms of association. In short, the importance of territoriality and demographic shifts in the era of the modern state carry over to the construction and reconstruction of societies. Israel, where territory and discontinuous demographic changes have been prime issues and where state borders have been both in question and in flux, can shed important light on how such issues result in particular sorts of society formation. We can point to three critical junctures and their aftermath in the history of Palestine/Israel in order to draw out these hypotheses and the process of society formation generally—the British creation of Palestine, the 1948 war, and the 1967 war.

The Creation of Palestine

Perhaps the single most important event in the formation of what would become Israeli society was the British hewing of Palestine out of the larger Ottoman Empire. The shaping of society within the newly bounded territory had a number of different facets and countless ramifications, but we can indicate several particularly important ones here: the designation of the new boundaries, the establishment of Jewish communal institutions, and the failure to create an Arab-Jewish society.

The establishment of the political boundaries for Palestine was a set of acts that took some time and that met with varied social responses. Prior to the demarcation of those borders, the small Jewish population in the country lacked a central focus that could lend some structural coherence to the creation of a society. As Horowitz and Lissak wrote, "The cleavages between the 'Old Yishuv' and the 'New Yishuv,' between 'Ashkenazim' and 'Sephardim,' and between Ottoman subjects and foreign citizens who enjoyed the protection of foreign consuls (according to the Capitulation agreements) hampered the formation of institutions representing the entire Jewish community in Palestine."[21] Only with the beginning of British rule and the establishment of the colonial political boundaries did the local Jews begin to develop autonomous institutions—from the Histadrut to Knesset Israel. In short, the setting of political borders also gave a framework for the integration of disparate groups into a Jewish society. In society formation, the two key structural elements—creating an outermost structure and forging the numerous internal institutions or groups that mark the character of the society—are contingent upon one another. The array of new British and Zionist organizations in Palestine was critical in Jewish society formation, bridging some of the previous cleavages among Jews and thus preventing social fragmentation. Zionist organizations had been active even before Palestine was created; through their ideology and organization, they gave continuity to the Yishuv from Ottoman rule to the formation of the Mandatory state. British state organizations were entirely new, of course, and lent a whole new dimension to Jewish society (frequently underestimated in the literature on the origins of Israel).

The new coherence to Jewish society created by the demarcation of a country called Palestine by the British allowed Zionist leaders to challenge domination by Jewish institutions from outside Palestine. In particular, the World Zionist Organization, whose potential leverage lay in its distribution of funds, threatened the creation of an "outermost social structure" in Palestine itself. In fact, the opposite occurred: the labor movement's preoccupation with creating institutions inside Palestine so empowered it that, by the early 1930s, it dominated Diaspora Zionists and the WZO, at least in issues regarding Palestine. But it is essential to remember that a good part of the success of the Palestinian Jewish institutions was contingent on the political creation of Palestine as a state by the British; state boundaries created the societal boundaries and facilitated the Zionist organizations that could thrive in the new society.

British control, then, provided a framework for the establishment of a Jewish society whose outer social boundaries were those of the newly mandated territory. The critical elements that the colonial state provided, besides the boundaries themselves, were the rights of the Zionists to create countrywide institutions for all Jews and of Jews worldwide to immigrate to Palestine. This demographic shift created a critical mass of Jews needed for the new institutions to function. It allowed for Zionist ideology and organization that had existed even before British rule to flourish and dominate in the newly forming society.

Certainly, the creation of a relatively cohesive society does not automatically follow the demarcation of political boundaries. In fact, the result could have been the re-creation of multiple Jewish societies in Palestine, rather than one. The Religious Community Ordinance, issued by the Mandatory state in 1926, opened the door for the development of unity-producing Jewish communal institutions, the most notable of which was Knesset Israel, that went far beyond the religious basis for organization intended by the British. At the same time, the law left open the right of any group—in the particular case, the haredim (or non-Zionist Orthodox Jews)—to withdraw and establish its own recognized religious community. While that in fact did occur as Agudat Israel and others established the separate Edah Haredit, the danger of further withdrawals and fragmentation was averted. Indeed, the looming threat of disintegration prompted the labor Zionist core into determined efforts to make institutions as inclusive as possible (including such mechanisms as proportional representation in Zionist organizations, which gave even small groups a voice in setting agendas and coming to decisions).[22]

Besides Jewish society formation, the creation of Palestine as a political entity had a profound effect on the reconstruction of Arab society as well. Even more so than in the case of the Jews, it would be difficult to speak of a cohesive Palestinian Arab society before the Mandate. The Arabs lacked the pre–World War I ideology and organization that Zionists had achieved, making the breakpoint that came with the creation of Palestine as a political entity much sharper than it was for the Jews. The final determination of Palestine's borders after the Great War and the relationship of the Arab population to the swirling processes of society formation both hinged on the curious episode of Emir Faysal's Arab kingdom in Damascus. Faysal's role began with his father's agreement to organize an Arab revolt against the Ottomans during the war in exchange for British support for an independent Arab kingdom. Following the Great War, Faysal's army stood in Damascus, and he harbored hopes of establishing his dominion over what today constitutes Syria, Israel, Lebanon, and Jordan. But that moment of glory was to be short-lived. French troops swept in from Beirut, routing Faysal's forces and sending him into exile. For Palestine, that moment was critical. It induced the British to find a substitute kingdom for Faysal (Iraq), as well as a sinecure for Faysal's brother, Abdallah. That sinecure turned out to be yet another kingdom, Transjordan, which the British lopped off the intended Palestine Mandate, forcing the Zionists to think very differently about the reach and definition of the Jewish home and the contours of their budding society.

For the Arabs, Faysal's brief 1920 reign in Syria and his flight from Damascus had even more momentous results. Young Palestinian notables had attached themselves to him in the hope of dissolving the new Palestinian political boundaries (designated by the British to encompass a Jewish national home), and a Palestinian Arab congress had endorsed that line. In Palestine, the first major outbreak of Arab violence against Jews in 1920 was tied to the drive to expand Faysal's kingdom to include Palestine.[23] When that effort foundered, the Arabs of Palestine found their blueprint for society formation in shreds. With the Ottoman Empire gone and the idea of a greater Arab kingdom remote, leading Arabs had to take stock of the possibilities of what the boundaries of their society would be. As one leader put it, "Now, after the recent events in Damascus, we have to effect a complete change in our plans here. Southern Syria no longer exists. We must defend Palestine."[24]

In sum, the uncertainty of political boundaries in the years surrounding World War I led to inner turmoil among Arabs about what their outermost structure would be. That debate continued through the rest of the twentieth century, but the failure of Faysal and the British determination of the final boundaries of Palestine muffled it considerably. New social boundaries for the Arabs of Palestine, of course, did not emerge immediately. Yet, the institutional and ideological foundation of a Palestinian Arab society, which increasingly drew disparate Arabs into a new outermost structure, emerged as a result of acts by the British through their Palestine Mandate. Even more dramatically than in the case of the Jews, the political boundary making of the colonial power carved out the boundaries of a Palestinian Arab society. The new Mandatory state was a key factor, then, in setting the limits of the new Arab society. Within those limits, important new institutions arose—literary groups, the Muslim-Christian Associations, labor unions, and others—that worked to create that outermost shell of society. New myths emerged as well, suggesting a core of shared history, beliefs, and identity among those in the society. But the scope of the shell, the reach of the new Arab organizations, and the target of the myths were all deeply influenced by the country's new political boundaries.

For all the talk and myth making by both Arab and Jewish leaders about the long lineage of their societies, it was a rather simple, finite set of political acts that induced the formation of their societies. The territorial dimension is as crucial a component in defining societies' outermost structures as it is in defining the scope of states—a point sometimes lost or obscured in the sociological literature.[25] Societies and states draw their features and character from many contingencies, especially in their interaction with one another; but probably no set of contingencies surpasses the importance of those involved in boundary making.

What came out of British decisions was by no means everything that the British rulers intended or for which they hoped. Simply creating the territorial limits within which society formation would take place did not predetermine what sort of society, or societies, would form in the newly defined space of Palestine. From the early 1920s until the late 1930s, they tabled any number of schemes intended to find the key to an elusive Jewish-Arab Palestinian society. Indeed, the two decades after the establishment of the Mandate were filled with futile British tinkering to find just the right mechanisms so as to make a Jewish-Arab civil society in Palestine work. To be sure, the very creation of British political institutions in Palestine increased direct and indirect ties between Jews and Arabs immeasurably, and those ties continued to grow until the Arab Revolt in 1936.

But British rule also had the unintended effect of helping to prevent any semblance of a civic binational society in Palestine. As Horowitz and Lissak stated, "It was the very establishment of a governmental center, with key positions filled by British officials, which facilitated the political separation of Arabs and Jews. It relieved the need for Arab and Jewish political elites to cultivate direct relationships, since it was possible to conduct most of the political bargaining through the British authorities in Jerusalem and London."[26] The state, and its many offices, also became a series of prizes for which Jews and Arabs competed, inducing internal and competitive organizing by the two groups.

The new territorial reality, then, did not forge an inclusive society within the new political borders of Palestine but two societies, each bounded within the same territory and each seeking an exclusive, national or ethnic basis for association. Both societies would struggle for the rest of the century with the practical and theoretical question of the relationship of nonnationals (the "other") in the bounded territory to a society grounded in nationality. What was each side intending to do with people who would be inside the political boundaries but outside the social boundaries?

The 1948 War

The 1948 war and its aftermath precipitated two sorts of changes, territorial and demographic, both of which would have profound effects on society formation. In the aftermath of the fighting, Palestine ended up partitioned among three states—Israel, Jordan (controlling what it dubbed the West Bank), and Egypt (ruling the Gaza Strip). Jewish and Arab societies were now faced with their third set of political boundaries in Palestine in only the first half of the twentieth century, not to speak of others that had been proposed but never realized, such as the demarcations of the Peel Commission Report in 1937 and of the UN partition plan in 1947.

While all these changing sets of actual and proposed borders had only minimal effect on the distribution of Jews in the territory, they did raise important questions for leaders about the ultimate territorial scope of a Jewish state and its coterminous society. For example, the minority Revisionists, even in the 1950s, continued to focus on eventually creating a state that spanned the two banks of the Jordan River, and they assumed that Jewish society would eventually stretch to those territories. They did not accept the British act of severing Jordan from the intended Palestine Mandate as a legitimate act. Not only did Zionist leaders need to think about the scope of society but also the nature of membership in it, particularly the relationship of non-Jews to the society they were building. No matter what the exact boundaries proposed in the various plans, it was clear that any Jewish state would have a substantial Arab minority. The questions dealt with the forms of inclusion and exclusion of Arabs in the territory the Zionists would rule.

From the time of the Zionist debate over whether to accept the recommendations of the Peel Commission in 1937, the dominant factions within Zionism argued that political sovereignty over even a piece of Palestine was preferable to the construction of a stateless society while waiting for control over all Palestine.[27] Or, to put the matter differently, the mainstream leadership held that the territorial scope of the Jewish state could be dictated by political contingencies; Jewish state and society would be formed and bounded within the limits set by the British (or, later, the UN). Of course, the Jewish leaders did not believe these political contingencies to be solely a product of chance; Zionists had affected the British and UN decisions about the proposed territory of the Jewish state through their settlement policies for immigrant Jews and other means (indeed, by creating outlying settlements, Zionists sought to stretch the conception of what could be allocated to the Jews). Nonetheless, the labor Zionists, even before 1948, accepted the need for a state, even a half-a-loaf state, as the means to realize their visions of a new Jewish society.

Dissident Zionists held out for a state defined by "original," noncontingent conditions (e.g., the original biblical, or at least British, promise) and the "potential" society that could fill that space. Both dissident and mainstream Zionists understood the significance of the boundaries of a new state in society formation, and the mainstream labor leaders, at least, appreciated the converse—how society formation could influence the selection of the new borders for the state. Shmuel Sandler framed the debate within Zionism as follows:

> Is the main goal of the Jewish national movement the establishment of a Jewish state in which the Jewish people as a majority and enjoying sovereignty will control its destiny, public life and institutions? Or is the return of the Jewish people to the land of its ancestors and regaining control over all the Land of Israel the main purpose of Zionism?[28]

Whatever the differences between the groups in their ideologies on the territorial issue, the actual creation of the new state and its boundaries through the UN vote, the withdrawal of the British, and the 1948 war overwhelmed all Zionist leaders. The enormity of having a sovereign Jewish-run state quashed, for two decades, active contention among Jews about the boundaries of the Jewish state (even if some of the opposition continued to make a formal point about different ultimate borders for Israel). After 1948, the new political borders gained almost universal Jewish acceptance, indeed even their own sacredness. As state agencies took the initiative in organizing everything from charity drives to cultural programs, Jews and even many Arabs began to see the boundaries of their society—Israeli society—as coterminous with the happenstance borders of the 1949 armistice lines. The new sovereign state had a major hand in the content of society formation; it not only established a formal legal framework, it imposed a series of practices on the population, from language use to land use, that chiseled out a common outermost structure.

The dissidents' understanding of society formation as a process dependent upon the realization of the "true" boundaries of the Jews did not die altogether. It remained alive enough to re-emerge after the 1967 war as a powerful alternative to the mainstream view—more on that in a moment. But for the period between 1948 and 1967, a surprising stability suffused Israeli society, even in the face of waves of new immigrants. The growing sense of the sacredness of the new state boundaries encased the new society in seemingly stable outer limits and allowed for the creation (mostly through state initiative) of a reinforcing set of societal institutions and myths to develop within those boundaries. Social and political struggles were over the control and content of those institutions and beliefs, not over their ultimate legitimacy and scope.

The 1948 war had profound demographic effects, as is well known. Arabs went from two-thirds of the total population of Palestine to less than 10 percent of the population in Israel (about one-fifth the proportion envisioned for Arabs in the Jewish state by the UN partition plan). Jewish numbers quickly tripled with the influx of Holocaust survivors and, especially, Jews from other Middle Eastern and North African countries. The continuing state of war somewhat muffled the debate on Jewish-Arab relations in Israel; Arabs were placed under emergency military rule until a year before the 1967 war. Nonetheless, the mainstream position that society was to be formed under the guiding hand of the state at least theoretically left open the construction of a Jewish-Arab society with a common outermost structure. What the precise content of such a society would be was not entirely clear; Jews would form a nation within the society and Arabs would be included as individuals, possibly with some recognition of religious or communal status (but not national status).

Using Michael Sandel's conceptions of citizenship, Yoav Peled attempted to sort out the relationship of Jews and Arabs to the state (in formal-legal terms) and to society (in terms of status and access to a civic, moral dimension). He argued that Jews have had a republican citizenship in which they have played an active, committed role in constituting society and state—a moral community. Arabs, in contrast, have had a liberal citizenship, which involves "a residual, truncated status . . . , citizenship as a bundle of rights. Bearers of this citizenship as status do not share in attending to the common good but are secure in their possession of what we consider essential human and civil rights."[29] Jews and Arabs could both participate in the civic community, but the assignment of social privileges gave Jews the upper hand; they received national rights beyond the human and civil rights accorded to Arabs, and they had a greater opportunity to participate in society and state formation. The contradictions between the two tendencies in society, the ethnic and the civic, were glaring and, as Geertz had predicted, caused no small measure of consternation.

Even while the question of how to form a society including a large Jewish majority and a growing Arab minority remained somewhat theoretical, it did have important practical implications. Policies on Arab education, political participation, and military service all turned on the broader conception of the sort of society Zionist leaders sought to construct. The fact that between 1948 and 1967 the border question seemed to be settled (even though the boundaries were officially only armistice lines and neighboring states did not accept their permanence) gave great impetus to the notion that a society with a dominant tendency toward civic association was a reasonable goal. It was in these circumstances of relative stability that the outermost structure of society was created and the (somewhat tortured) nature of civic society developed. The continuing regional Arab-Israeli conflict and the domestic use of military administration of Arabs both often served to shunt aside the larger question of the place of Arabs in a Jewish state and Jewish-dominated society. Still, as Peled's work implies, important patterns were explicitly and implicitly developed that defined the civic roles Arabs and Jews would play. The most important of these was, in 1950, the "granting of Israeli citizenship to the country's Arab residents [which] constituted a renunciation of the ethnonational principle. . . ."[30] State institutions, too, reflected a civic tendency, with principles making them universal rather than in the service of the Jews only. In practical terms that meant the establishment of the rule of law, with its implied universality for all groups; the development of strong legal institutions, most notably the Supreme Court (later to be used liberally by Arab citizens and residents of the territories conquered in the 1967 War); and the emergence of other key agencies designed to protect the citizenry, including the offices of the Attorney General, the State Comptroller, and the Ombudsman. The labor-dominated state, then, was instrumental in promoting the civic tendency in society formation. It did this, ironically, even as it repressed and tightly controlled Israel's Arab citizens.

While Jews as Jews automatically had national rights that were denied to the Arab minority, their position in relation to the society was in some ways even more problematical than that of the Arabs. Since labor Zionist leaders saw Israeli society as constructed, they felt that they needed to imbue members with the "proper" attributes to sustain the new society. There was no question that on a national or ethnic basis, all Jews would be accepted by the new state as citizens, but on a societal basis those Jews who arrived would have to be reshaped so that the society could be "properly" constructed. This distinction between the ethnic Jew and the societal Jew underlay Israeli policies of immigrant absorption.

It was, then, the mainstream Zionists' conception of society that dominated after 1948 and that guided society formation, especially regarding the local Arabs and the newly arrived Jews from Arabic-speaking countries. As I have hinted (but do not have space to elaborate here), this conception was rife with contradictions, which were evident in the policies of the state.

The 1948 war and its illusion that the current political boundaries were stable gave impetus to forces in society pushing for a civic character. Demographic changes—the influx of Jewish immigrants and the remnant of a relatively small and unthreatening Arab minority (at least compared to what had been projected in the UN partition plan)—induced political leaders to confront head-on the question of how to construct society. They invented new social identities for non-Jews (as Israeli Arabs) and for immigrant Jews (as fully absorbed, citizen-warrior Zionists). The perception of territorial stability led to increased debate about the removal of military administration from Arab areas and the eventual civic role of the Arabs in the state. That debate, at least implicitly, was about the basis for association in the society and the allocation of rights and privileges where a growing percentage of the population was not from the dominant ethnic group. Only a year elapsed between the end of that internal military administration and the next war, but even so one could discern an important civic component in society's mix, reflected in the rule of law, the emerging role of the courts, and institutions such as those associated with the Attorney General's office.

The 1967 War

In the third period, the 1967 war and its aftermath, the civic conception faltered, and the long-dormant contending position gained new strength. It saw society as an outgrowth of the "true" (noncontingent) territorial legacy of the Jews. Perhaps what was most important was that the newly revived conception did not have a place for Arabs in the society. Even in terms of the state, Arabs would be subjects with specific (limited) rights, but society itself was the Jewish nation, and no common identity beyond the national one existed. In this view, the centrality of the territorial promise to the Jews (whether by God or by the British) together with the myth of common Jewish ancestry combined to dictate the limits of society. Society was not a civic construction of mortals but derived from the rights (especially, territorial rights) of the preexisting nation, the Jews. Thus, civic rights and national rights were one and the same, and only the Jews had such rights.

Not only did this conception have clear implications for Arabs, it also meant that the newly arrived Jews would be seen differently from the way they had been viewed up until 1967. Since societal membership depended exclusively on national membership, immigrant Jews in this conception would be much more likely to be accepted as is (without the necessity of transforming or "absorbing" them). This understanding partially accounted for the fairly rapid movement of immigrant Jews from Middle Eastern and North African countries to opposition political parties. What eventually became the Likud party (and its several offshoots) won the hearts and votes of these immigrants. While the Likud's Zionist ideology certainly contained an element that expected personal transformation of Jews as free people in their own land, it was more willing than Labor to accept immigrants from Asia and North Africa fully, because of who they were (part of the Jewish nation) rather than on, in part, who they were to become (the new citizen-warrior Zionists).

What accounted for the revival of the ethnic tendency in the formation of society? Once again, it was the territorial and demographic changes that underpinned the new situation. The capture of the West Bank and the Gaza Strip established new boundaries for Israeli political rule, which reopened the possibility of a society encompassed in its originally promised borders. Especially as small numbers of Jews created new settlements in the occupied territories in the early 1970s, they rekindled the question of the proper permanent boundaries of society. And new institutional dynamics followed this debate, including the establishment of nonparty social movements (Gush Emunim was the most prominent). Religious, cultural, and social fault lines among Jews changed dramatically after 1967. Political and social struggles changed from ones over control of legitimate institutions whose scope was widely accepted to those marked by broad disagreement on the limits of society and over which boundaries were truly sacred.

At the same time, the military administration of the occupied territories pushed the issue of Arab citizens' place in society to the back burner once again. Also, uncertainty over whether Arabs in the territories would be permanent subjects of the state complicated any attempt to deal with the role of Israel's Arab citizens. In short, with the state's own borders in flux, the question of society's boundaries and character had something of a life of its own. The boundaries of state and society no longer coincided.

Not least among the factors undermining the dominance of the civic tendency was the demise of its strongest proponent, the labor Zionist leadership that controlled the state. Besides the often cited internal reasons for Labor's fall from power in 1977 (including internal corruption and growing numbers of scandals), another key one exists: Labor had not come to terms with the enormity of change that the 1967 war had brought to Israeli society. Not least of these changes was the desanctification of society's outermost structure that had existed before the war. The newly assertive role of haredim and Jews from Arabic-speaking countries after 1967 made Labor's conception of society one among several vying for dominance. The symbols and affective attachments that it had cultivated came under severe attack. The future character of Israel's society was now up for grabs.

CONCLUSION

The same sort of uncertainty about political boundaries that so deeply affected society formation in Palestine and Israel have rocked a number of other regions in the wake of the end of the Cold War. The demise of the Soviet Union undermined the sense in the Balkans and in parts of Africa that political boundaries were permanent and inviolable. Analogous sorts of questions had arisen in the Balkans when Ottoman and Austro-Hungarian rule had disintegrated in the early decades of the century. When state boundaries come into question, as in Yugoslavia, people's sense of security through state protection diminishes, compelling them to turn to their societal ties with others as an alternative form of protection. In situations where changing boundaries or state disintegration leave people feeling that the most elemental personal and property rights are at risk, they seek some refuge in the institutions and associations of society other than the state itself. But for what sort of society do they search? Even where civic institutions have taken on a sense of sacredness, their contractual foundation—contracts that, in any case, need to be backed up by a state—may seem to provide only the flimsiest sort of protection at precisely the moment when people feel most vulnerable. It is then that the ties of blood may seem much more compelling.

Establishing a civic basis of association in society is a delicate enterprise. It entails some risk taking by groups and individuals, who must depend for their security on the forging of a public space and fair rules to govern interactions in that space, all with people that they mostly do not know personally. Uncertainty over who will be in the society and who not, over the scope of state boundaries, undermines the stability necessary to undertake that fragile exercise. A civic basis for association depends, in the end, on firm outermost limits for society, ones coincidental with the boundaries of the state, which is the ultimate guarantor of that critical public space.[31] When the state fails, or its own boundaries become a matter of dispute, the foundations of the civic tendencies in society quickly erode.

Institutions of everyday life depend upon the population's clear sense of their reach—who is inside an institution and who is outside, which sorts of interactions they govern and which are external to their realm, what is private space and what is public space. Institutions' efficacy is defined within a particular physical and social space. When state boundaries are in flux, the reach of institutions—their space—is questioned, undermining their efficacy. It is at that point that we see severe conflicts over what the new institutions will be. This is the struggle over society formation.

Israel's struggle to reconstruct its society, then, is by no means a unique one. From Poland to Cambodia, from Angola to Peru, similar questions are in the air about the conception of society, about what ties people in particular territories together. In Israel, the changing dimensions of the territory and the newness of so many of the people in that territory put into boldface the struggle that Geertz pointed to more than thirty years ago. Immediate political contingencies, not least of which is the perceived permanence of political boundaries, help determine whether society formation will tend toward association based on "the gross actualities of blood, race, language, locality, religion, or tradition" or will be grounded in "practical necessity, common interest, or incurred obligation. . . ."[32]

PART IV

Social Crisis

CHAPTER 7

Changing Boundaries and Social Crisis: Israel and the 1967 War

FROM DOOM TO BOOM

The sudden end of the June 1967 war brought not only unrestrained rejoicing in Israel but, just as palpably, a collective sigh of relief. What Israelis had called the "waiting period," between Egypt's blockade of the Straits of Tiran on May 22 and the beginning of the war on June 5, had been a time of unbearable tension in the country. Israelis saw the closing of the straits as a tripwire for war and waited those fourteen days with a sense of impending doom.[1] This was a moment, as Itzhak Galnoor recounted, of "public confusion, lack of confidence in the political leadership and some threats of military insubordination."[2]

The dark warnings of Arab leaders about what would happen to Israel if their forces were to triumph had been all too explicit. Only a week before the outbreak of fighting, Egypt's president, Gamal Abdul Nasser, had threatened that "this will be a total war. Our basic aim is the destruction of Israel." And the head of the Palestine Liberation Organization, Ahmed Shukairy, had added to the sense of looming tragedy, "Those native-born Israelis who survive can remain in Palestine. But I estimate that none of them will survive."[3]

I recall receiving a letter from Israel in May of that year describing a sense of resignation and foreboding on the part of the writer and her fellow kibbutz members. She wrote of people going about their daily chores with their heads hanging; a sense of fatalism gripped Israel's Jews. But the sudden and complete military victory in June stood Israelis' emotions on their head. The war itself was a fleeting, almost surreal, interlude. Bill Stevenson, a veteran British war correspondent, recounted how "the clocks stopped in Israel on Monday, June 5, 1967, and they started again a week later."[4]

The drastic mood swing began in the last couple of days of the war. On June 9, the fifth day, one Israeli woman wrote of "the two weeks of dreadful tension when all of us faced what we thought might, quite literally, be extermination, and the death of the young State, and our own total abandonment by the world. And then, the four breathless, incredible days and heights of victory."[5] Indeed, that sense of being collectively plucked from the precipice at the last possible moment—a feeling of miraculous, redemptive deliverance shared by religious and secular Jews alike—inaugurated a period in which Israelis seemed all but oblivious to the postwar currents sweeping them up. Like a death-row convict celebrating wildly after having been granted a pardon minutes before execution, Israelis followed the Six-Day War with a six-year spree that veiled many of the domestic difficulties caused or exacerbated by the war.

These six years, which ended with the October 1973 war, or what Israelis call the Yom Kippur War, both followed and preceded sharp economic downturns in the country. But that interwar period wiped out thoughts of recession and unemployment. Per capita income grew at among the highest rates in the world, at 8.5 percent a year, and personal consumption reflected the spreelike atmosphere, ballooning ominously at a rate of about 12 percent annually. Collectively, Israelis were recklessly living beyond their means.

Profound social and political difficulties simmered beneath the surface of this economic explosion, involving an increasingly beleaguered state organization and its relations with the Israeli population. Indeed, the central dynamics of state-society relations came under severe strain in the generation following the 1967 war.[6] I will underscore three of the central problems: First, at a time of continuing tension in the Middle East—so high that it prompted a nuclear standoff between the superpowers in 1973—the Israeli state found itself with diminishing capabilities to govern its own society effectively. Second, deep and abiding divisions about what the character of Israeli society should be rent both political and social life. And, finally, the society's model of social integration came to be seen as a failure, resulting in more intense and open social conflict.

Why did such fundamental problems afflict the state, society, and state-society relations in the wake of Israel's greatest military triumph? In this chapter, I will argue that the boundary changes that the war effected unglued important social and political relationships. Three core ideas related to boundary changes will be developed:

1. *Upsetting understandings of institutional reach.* The stability that social and political institutions bring to everyday life depends upon the population's understanding of their reach. Boundary changes bring into question the reach of those institutions and, in so doing, lead to crises in society's central dynamics.

2. *Challenging the principle of universalist exclusion.* Reconstituted boundaries of the territory governed by the state open to question the established principles about the character of the state and its

relationship to its population. In Israel, the civic principles of the pre-1967 period had the paradoxical effect of using the principle of universal citizenship as a method of exclusion, especially for Jews of Middle East background. The boundary changes opened the way for a contending ethnonational set of principles, which these Jews found much more inclusive.

3. *Undoing labor segmentation and social fragmentation.* Territorial boundary changes can have a deep impact on social boundaries. In Israel, the new borders changed the character of the labor market, opening the door to new types of social and physical mobility and undoing the old social boundaries that had been marked by social fragmentation and segmentation. For society, the change in social boundaries led to heightened tensions; for the state, the change resulted in new, increased demands on it without a corresponding growth in capacity to deal with those demands.

From a comparative perspective, the timing of this volume, the beginning of a new century, is opportune for revisiting the issue of the effect of the 1967 war through its transformation of boundaries. After World War II, the Cold War had imposed an extraordinary stability on states' boundaries. Significant border changes came only with the dismantling of the colonial empires, and, even there, many new states' boundaries remained the same as when the territory had been ruled by Europeans. One would be hard-pressed to name more than a handful of cases in which state boundaries changed or states disappeared entirely during the more than forty years of the Cold War.

But its end brought a host of boundary changes in a short period, including the disintegration of the Soviet Union itself, Yugoslavia, Czechoslovakia, and Ethiopia. As one of the few cases of state boundary changes in the decades leading up to the 1990s, Israel and the 1967 war offer some important insights into the process of how border changes affect labor markets, state-society relations, and ethnic relations.

In the following section, I will look first at the social dynamics that undergirded Israel's state and society in the two decades leading up to the Six-Day War. I will then analyze how the crisis transformed those dynamics. Finally, I will tie the crises in state, society, and state-society relations to the 1967 war's transformation of state boundaries.

STATE AND SOCIETY BEFORE THE WAR

Three key features had marked pre-1967 Israeli society: the important and growing role of the state in people's daily lives; increasing consensus among Israel's Jews about the extent and character of the state; and a focus on societal integration, at least among the more than 90 percent of the citizenry who were Jews. But, in the wake of the war that had so united this population, each of these cornerstones began to show worrisome fissures. Before analyzing how border changes that resulted from the war affected these three elements, I will survey the three.

Israel's first prime minister, who dominated political life for nearly half a century, worked single-mindedly from the moment of the state's founding in 1948 to make the state the dominant and central institution in people's lives. Through an orientation that he called *mamlahtiyut* (which can be translated loosely as *statism*), David Ben-Gurion was determined to bring about a revolution in Jewish society.[7] His first target was the abiding wariness of nationalism that had marked Jewish writings and thought since the Enlightenment.[8] And, what was even more important, he battled the very institutions that he and others had built in the generation before Independence. His own political party, Mapai, and the powerful labor federation that he had headed, the Histadrut, along with numerous other organizations had played key roles in creating a viable Jewish presence in Palestine during the thirty years of British rule. While Ben-Gurion certainly saw an important role for them in the period of statehood, he feared their divisive, even sectarian, tendencies. His aim was to shift the ability to allocate key resources in the society from the political parties, the Histadrut, and the once-powerful Jewish Agency to the bureaucracy of the new state and thereby build a political center that would gain the loyalty and obedience of the population.

In its first two decades, the success of the new state in centralizing the allocation of key resources and in overcoming the long-standing distrust of nationalism among Jews was truly impressive. It quickly became the central focus of people's lives, engendering not only endless complaining about its oversized and often unresponsive bureaucracy but also fierce loyalty that had a religious-like fervor.[9] Tension continued to fester between the institutions that had predated the state and Ben-Gurion, and by no means did their leaders lose every battle with him. Health insurance, for example, remained outside the state's direct control. But the swelling state bureaucracy assumed responsibility for education, welfare, labor exchanges, and more. Centralization brought increased state capabilities—from the battlefield to the control of the economy to the regulation of everyday social relations. An import-substitution economic strategy also heightened the activity of the state in the economy. All in all, the state organization grew to alarming proportions and insinuated itself into the daily lives of everyone living within the crazy-quilt boundaries Israel ended up with after the 1948 war.

Beyond the growing role of the state organization, a second feature of pre-1967 Israeli life was a developing consensus about the nature of that state. Prior to 1948, the Zionist political institutions were understood by Jews and non-Jews alike to have two highly sectarian qualities to them. First, those organizations represented and advocated for the Jews, against the claims of Palestine's Arabs and, sometimes, against those of the colonial British rulers. Second, sectarianism also marked the relations among the Jewish political institutions. There was a unified framework incorporating the Jewish groups, but inclusion in it was voluntary. At various moments, key groups simply dropped out. And, of those that remained inside, representing most of the Jews, each had significant autonomy to pursue its own ends.[10] S. N. Eisenstadt, Israel's leading sociologist, labeled the weak framework consociational, one in which the framework served largely as a mediating forum among groups rather than one that set the tone for all political debate.

Once an independent state existed, important changes occurred in people's thinking about political institutions. The old mediating framework's "place was taken by an ideology of national social ethos articulated within a constitutional democratic-pluralistic State, based on universalistic premises, universalistic citizenship and the access of all citizens to the major frameworks of the State."[11] This quotation from Eisenstadt points to a fundamental element in the character of the state, as well as an underlying tension. The change was critical, altering the political framework from a sectarian one claiming to speak for a people or nation—the Jews of Palestine, but not others in the country—to one asserting the right to represent all peoples within its boundaries. Both Jews and Arabs fell under the new state's "universalistic premises [and] universalistic citizenship." Eisenstadt's reference to "the access of all citizens to the major frameworks of the State" meant that the new political entity, at least in theory, provided equal rights to non-Jews and equal entrée to the administrative services of the state. Its "universalistic principles," in the words of Erik Cohen, "would govern relations between all citizens."[12]

To put the matter a bit differently, the state (unlike the prestate political institutions) was constituted so as to interact with a civil society—a population united by its civic ties in which all held the key role of citizen—not simply the Jews in society.[13] The declaration of independence, the Basic Laws that were to be the backbone of an as-yet-unwritten constitution, the judiciary, and many other key state institutions were created on the basis of an imagined society made up of equal citizens. While the construction of the state was geared to such a civil society, no such society bound through civic ties yet existed. Further complicating the picture was the fact that political leaders also defined the state as Jewish (what Eisenstadt obliquely referred to as a national social ethos), which put some of civil society—the Arabs—at a disadvantage. I will come back to this tension because it is so central to the internal dynamics of Israel, especially after the 1967 war. It is worth noting here that Arabs faced a kind of Alice in Wonderland existence: a set of laws and institutions designed to give them, like everybody else, equality and day-to-day practices that discriminated against them at every turn.

Before the war, however, this inconsistency tended to be somewhat muted. A combination of the terrible dislocation of Palestine's Arab community during the 1947–1948 war and the effects of the state's military rule of the Arab population until 1966 dampened Arab demand for equal access to the state's services and agencies.[14] The promotion of a fragmented labor market in which the state prohibited Arab movement beyond their own localities reinforced the low profile of Arab citizens. In short, state policies and the trauma of 1948 veiled the dissonance that Arabs faced every day.

In what can only be understood as a supreme paradox, these conditions, which created the invisible Arab as a clearly less privileged citizen, allowed state leaders to proceed in building the civic orientation of the state, one whose institutions were geared to be universal rather than in the service of a particular group. In practical terms that meant the establishment of the rule of law, with its implied universality for all groups; the development of strong legal institutions, most notably the Supreme Court; and the emergence of other key agencies designed to protect the citizenry, including the offices of the attorney general, state comptroller, and ombudsman. The character of the state, even with the encouragement of a markedly Jewish ethos or civil religion and even with the repression and strong control of the Arab population, was being forged in the years before the 1967 war with strong universal components, premised on the development of a society forged by civic ties. Indeed, evidence mounted that even many of the country's Arab citizens related positively to the civic dimensions put forth by the state.[15] No more important sign for the development of a universalistic state was evident than the granting in 1950 "of Israeli citizenship to the country's Arab residents [which] constituted a renunciation of the ethnonational principle."[16]

Consensus developed not only about the character of the state but on the extent of its reach. From 1937, when the British tabled a plan to partition Palestine between the Arabs and the Jews, Zionists had engaged in a loud debate about whether or not to compromise by taking only a portion of the promised Palestine in exchange for political independence in that truncated territory.[17] Once independence was achieved, however, this debate quickly faded. Shlomo Avineri, the renowned political philosopher and onetime director-general of Israel's foreign ministry, noted a new implicit understanding about what the character of the state should be:

> One issue which was central to the political debate within the Jewish Yishuv (community) in the late 1930s and the 1940s—the debate about partition—was over. The armistice lines of 1949 were considered by practically all Israelis as the realistic definite borders of Israel. If, prior to 5 June 1967, the Arab countries had been ready to sign a peace agreement with Israel on the basis of the existing frontiers, there would have been an overwhelming Israeli consensus in favour of accepting this, perceiving this Arab readiness as a major concession and a tremendous achievement for Israel. With very few exceptions on the lunatic fringe of Israeli politics, there was no irredentist call in Israel during the period of 1949–1967, advocating an Israeli initiative to recapture Judea and Samaria, or even the Old City of Jerusalem. This post-1948 consensus was visible across the spectrum of Israeli politics.[18]

Avineri's point is a very important one. The haphazard and irrational borders with which Israel was left after 1948 took on a kind of sanctity of their own. They imparted a stability to state and society. The state molded its reach to them and people simply assumed that those arbitrary lines would permanently define the extent of Israeli society. Borders, then, affect both institutional development (by defining the limits of an institution's reach) and public culture (by providing the frame for a sense of we-ness, or common identity—what it meant to be an Israeli).

Finally, besides the growing role of the state and the developing consensus on its nature and territorial reach, a third mark of the pre-1967 period was an emphasis on social integration among Jews. The huge influx of Jews immediately after the 1948 war posed serious challenges for both state and society. Not only did the country's Jewish population triple in the three years after Israel's founding, but the majority of the new Jews were from the Middle East, culturally distinct from the dominant groups that had migrated earlier from eastern Europe. The state's response was an attempt to assimilate the new Jews into the dominant eastern European culture through an ideology of *mizug galuyot,* or what we might call the melting pot.

While this model had worked relatively well in absorbing early waves of immigrants during the prestate period, it ran into serious bumps in the 1950s. The proportion of immigrants was now extremely high, and the Middle Eastern Jews came much less prepared or willing to take on many of the values and symbols of the dominant groups.[19] Critics have emphasized the shunting of Middle Eastern Jews into low-paying, low-status jobs—often in remote parts of the country with very little infrastructure. The immigrants quickly became the blue-collar class in a labor market that gave them limited opportunities for physical or social mobility. Here, the boundaries did not simply divide "us" from "them"; they provided the bases for the distribution of people in society, including their centrality or peripherality. New immigrants were relegated to the outer reaches of the frame. Just as the borders provided the space within which imagined civic equality would develop, the border also framed the scaffolding for real social and economic inequality that emerged.

In terms of income per person, by 1967 families originating from Africa and Asia (mostly the Middle East and Arab North Africa) had a bit less than 50 percent of the income of their counterparts of European origins.[20] Even after taking into account factors such as length of residence in the country, education, and age, an "ethnic gap" in income of 5–15 percent persisted.[21] Erik Cohen added a cultural dimension to the problem of economic inequality: "Oriental culture, in which at least some of the Oriental communities [African and Asian, mostly Middle Eastern] had been deeply steeped, has made no perceptible imprint on Israel's cultural life. Oriental civilization was generally considered 'backward' or 'Levantine,' and Oriental immigrants were asked to shed their way of life as quickly as possible."[22]

These criticisms and gaps notwithstanding, the period before the 1967 war "was marked by the relative success in the absorption of immigrants. . . . A society made up of numerous, highly varied cultures underwent a rapid and sometimes painful process of consolidation."[23] This point is not made in order to minimize the problems. Rather, the period before 1967 is remarkable for the emphasis on integration in public, academic, and government discourse, even as real, serious problems abounded. Indications existed of seething anger and deep resentment on the part of many immigrants—against Ashkenazim, old-timers, the Histadrut, and the Mapai (the Labor Party). But the cauldron, while bubbling, rarely boiled over. Practically all Jewish groups were absorbed into almost all state and civic institutions (as followers and receivers of services rather than leaders), including schools and the military. Immigrants and old-timers alike participated in and promoted the new civil religion—only Arab citizens were largely excluded from that.

Israeli institutions and civic culture held out the promise of upward mobility for new immigrants. Indeed, as one sociological study gathering data on mobility and opportunity put it, "Israel has developed into an extraordinarily meritocratic society. . . . It is a country that both beckons to potential immigrants and integrates them into the mainstream of social life."[24] After 1967, as we shall see, serious protests arose against this formulation. Critics claimed that the meritocracy demanded accepting the dominant European Jews' rules of the game, especially the primacy of education, while Middle Eastern Jews had inferior educational opportunities and less access to education. But before the war, the emphasis was much more on integration into the Israeli institutions and civic culture than on a critique of them.

WAR AND THE CRISIS IN SOCIAL DYNAMICS

The years following the Six-Day War brought unrestrained euphoria to Israel. But in a period of heady economic growth and consumption, and of a self-image as a regional powerhouse, Israeli state and society demonstrated clear signs of stress. The three processes that we have discussed—the state's increasing centrality, the emerging social agreement about its character and reach, and the emphasis on social integration of Jews into the new Israeli society and culture—all developed in the context of new, fixed boundaries. When the 1967 war suddenly changed those boundaries, these three processes changed dramatically. Military, economic, and political shocks that came a bit later—the 1973 war and the long period of economic stagnation in its wake, as well as the 1977 defeat of the Labor Party (formerly Mapai), which in one form or another had dominated politics for half a century—exposed and exacerbated social dynamics stemming from the 1967 war.

The State's Diminishing Centrality

The Israeli state, so domineering in the first two decades after Independence, suffered surprising blows after the 1967 war, both to its centrality in society and its capacity to govern. It is difficult to disentangle the issue of state centrality and capacity from Ben-Gurion's resignation in 1963 and from the once-dominant Labor Party's painful demise. The state's legitimacy rested in no small measure on continuing allocative roles still played by the party and Ben-Gurion's own towering stature in coping with threat and crisis.[25] Nonetheless, one must not underestimate the amount of state institution building that had gone on in the first twenty years of the state to facilitate policy making and the bridging of differences among key groups. After the war these institutions' capabilities eroded; "it became more difficult to overcome crisis and potential breakdowns with the old tools of accommodation and compromise."[26]

Several key signs of the changing status of the state were the mushrooming public protests and labor strikes directed against it, especially by newly independent groups "outside the rigid structure of Israeli politics; growing debt and faltering ability to finance public expenditures;

reduced dependence of the population on state capital; and difficulties in mediating among competing demands by groups in the population, leading to high inflation, among other economic and social plagues."[27]

Israelis have always been political animals; political decisions have been too important to their daily life for them to remain aloof.[28] Anyone who has sat on an Israeli bus as the hourly news is broadcast knows that. But in the prewar period high attentiveness was not matched by organized activity to influence government or by social initiative, especially by organized protest groups.[29] By the 1970s, this diffidence vanished. This process must have been spurred by the international political mobilization of 1968 and the following years. But it had a decidedly local flavor in a country with such a quiescent society and domineering state. Where once the relationship between state and society had been analogous to a marriage in which the husband had taken all the public roles and the wife had faded into the background, now it resembled one in which the wife was newly assertive, making all sorts of new demands for changes in the relationship.

Leading the way at the beginning of 1971 was a group of mostly young Jews of Moroccan origin who called themselves the Black Panthers, after the notorious black militant organization in the United States (again, the connection to international factors, especially the rise of a new identity politics, is evident). While the Black Panthers' demands were comparatively rather mild—they asked the government to clear slums, provide housing, and stop discrimination—their effect was electrifying. "Although the number who actually joined the Black Panthers was not very large," wrote Cohen, "the spontaneous movement quickly gained popularity and triggered off the expression of widely-felt resentment and dissatisfaction among Oriental Jews."[30] Other protest groups formed later, especially following the 1973 war. Social movements, including Gush Emunim and Peace Now, began to see organized demonstrations as a legitimate tool, and both organized a series of massive protests over the next two decades.

As time went on, much protest centered on the boundary question, the future of the occupied territories. The war had dramatically changed Israel's borders, creating a sense of uncertainty about the appropriate reach of the state and its character. Violence against the state came from both sides. Jewish settlers from Gush Emunim (less than 10 percent of those surveyed) battled soldiers and police when they felt state leaders were contemplating giving up parts of the newly conquered lands, what came to be called territorial compromise.[31] On a far more massive scale, Palestinians in the West Bank and the Gaza Strip rallied, violently and nonviolently, against the state. Their protests culminated in the Intifada, an unarmed but violent continuous struggle, which began in 1987 and petered out by 1993. Palestinian citizens of Israel, too, joined the stream of demonstrations. Starting in 1976 with rallies that ended in a confrontation with the army and the shooting of several Arabs, Israel's Arab citizens have marked Land Day as a means of expressing their frustrations with the state. All in all, a state that had escaped having more than occasional outbursts of unorganized political protest in the pre-1967 period found itself increasingly preoccupied and wearied by all sorts of planned public protest after the war.

Labor unrest was a second avenue of protest. As in the case of the Black Panthers, much of the impetus for the wildcat strikes that blanketed the country after 1967 came from dissatisfaction among Jews of Middle Eastern origins. Strikes were not unheard of before 1967, to be sure. A wave of labor stoppages crippled many enterprises in the mid-1960s. Even then, the strikes were concentrated in the public, not private, sector.[32] That wave, however, had subsided in the prewar recession and a reinstitution by the state and the Histadrut of strict labor discipline. Within two years after the war, however, the strike craze was fully under way, again concentrated in the public sector. In 1970, strikes resulted in 390,000 lost workdays, three-quarters of them in the public sector.[33] In one startling statistic, the number of persons involved in labor stoppages and lockouts for every thousand workers, rose from twenty-three in the years 1948–1959 to 218 in 1975–1988.[34]

As the state became a target of surging unrest after 1967, its centrality to people's lives diminished, as did its capabilities. As one professor of business put it, "The constant rise in the standard of living and the receipt of personal reparations money from Germany materially reduced the dependence of citizens on the political apparatus or the government system."[35] Not only did the economic dependence of the population on the state decrease, the state showed signs that it could not control social demands put upon it. Even as productivity lagged, the state continued to promote increases in public and private consumption. The only way to do that was to find outside money to continue catering to growing consumption. It is not surprising, therefore, that one clear sign of the state's increased weakness was ballooning foreign and domestic debt.[36] The state could not take the steps necessary to make Israel live within its means.

The state's inability to balance available domestic resources against demands for growing consumption led to a host of serious problems. Investment dropped, balance of payments worsened, and the state's liquidity diminished.[37] But the two clearest signs of state weakness were debt and inflation. By the early 1980s, the state spent nearly one-third of the country's GNP on transfer payments and debt service, and, in 1985 the debt burden reached 127 percent of GNP.[38] Spiraling inflation was another sign of the state's inability to mediate demands even as it made substantial cuts in domestic financing of defense. The fifteen years after 1970 wreaked economic havoc on Israel, as first the Labor government and then the Likud government lost control of the economy. At the beginning of the 1970s, clear signs of accelerating inflation already existed; by 1979, rates reached a level of more than 100 percent per year and soared to nearly 500 percent in 1984.

Growing Disagreements about the State's Character and Reach

At the same time that the state's centrality and capabilities diminished, bitter debates broke out about what the character of the state should be. No single powerful figure, as Ben-Gurion had been in the prewar period, could dominate the controversy. What had seemed to be settled before the war—the civic, universal model of the state in the territory under its control—became a source of bitter dispute, both inside and outside the halls of government.

The territorial controversies are well known and need little comment here. Avineri captured the deeper importance of the new political battles:

> What appeared to have been closed in 1948–9 by the dual impact of the acceptance on the part of Israel of the UN partition resolution and the outcome of the War of Independence, became once more an open question. The national consensus that Israel had to be defended, and defended at all cost, from within its 1949 borders, was broken and for the first time since Independence the question of the Israeli boundaries was reopened. While there was virtually no dissenting voice regarding the unification of Jerusalem, the future disposition of the West Bank and Gaza became the focus for the most acrimonious and divisive debate in Israel since its inception. For the debate is not only about policies, it is about the boundaries of the polity itself.[39]

Deep social and political conflicts about the nature of the state followed closely on those over Israel's eventual permanent international boundaries. At issue was whether the state held, for the Jews, a kind of stewardship over the historical Land of Israel or instead served as the representation of the population—largely but not exclusively Jewish—in a given territory, even if that territory was somewhat arbitrarily defined by twentieth-century circumstances. The tension between its ethnonational foundation as the *Jewish* state and its universal, civic nature—first and foremost found in its rule of law—now burst to the top of the public agenda.[40] The Jewishness of the Israeli state and society has remained a central topic of public and academic discourse to this day.[41] Certainly, the rise of the Likud after 1967 and its control of government for nearly fifteen years starting in 1977 were not unrelated to deeper questions about the character of the state.

In the renewed ethnonational conception, the state was downgraded from the centrality of *mamlahtiyut* to the role of guardian of Jewish society. That society was defined independently of the state, as a product of the *true* territorial legacy of the Jews. Jewish nationhood was defined through its relation to the ancient homeland, and the state was simply an expression of the nation. As Alan Dowty summarized this view, the Jews, like any other people have "a distinct character that is inextricably linked to [their] statehood. The essence of nationhood was particularism, not a vague set of liberal principles that few states observed in practice anyway (especially when their survival was at stake)."[42]

The Arabs would have only a limited role in such a state, much more as subjects than equal citizens. In the ethnonational image, then, society was not a civic construction in which the state played a pivotal role in forging the society by developing universal institutions, as had been widely accepted before 1967. Society's very existence, the dissenters contended, stemmed from Jewish national rights, largely territorial rights.[43] Arabs did not share in those rights; and this implied that they were not full members of society and that the state was not theirs in the same way that it was the Jews'. While I will concentrate below on group relations among Jews, it is worth noting that the problematic status of Arabs after the war led to "a reality of growing hostility, estrangement, and hatred" that governed relations of Jews with Arab citizens.[44]

Faltering Images of Social Integration

In addition to the eroding position of the state and the divisive debates about its ultimate reach and character, a third social dynamic coming out of the boundary changes of the 1967 war was the faltering of Israel's model of social integration among Jews, which led to deteriorating group relations. The slide down the slope of ethnic enmity took many observers by surprise. If anything, the 1967 war's initial impact was to strengthen social integration, especially feelings of solidarity among Israel's Jewish population. One anthropologist captured its effect: "The virtually traumatic experience of the Six-Day War in 1967 . . . was highly concentrated in time, packed with action, and dramatic in its outcome. The hypertension of this drama, whose result was seen by many as a miracle, streamed down to all levels of the nation. All strata of the highly variegated and motley society experienced themselves united by the bonds of common peril and salvation, an experience that overrode all the other particular exigencies of various social strata and individuals."[45]

It became a truism in Israel that the participation of Jews of Middle Eastern origin in the deliverance of the country from its moment of peril in 1967 cemented their place in society. The heroism of many of their children in the war itself established the credentials of the Middle Eastern immigrants as central members of the society. Additionally, by the mid-1970s, evidence appeared indicating that the ethnic wage gap was beginning to shrink.[46] Indeed, the widening income differential between Jews of European and Middle Eastern backgrounds in the prewar period stabilized in the late 1960s and then shrank to its lowest point since 1951—at precisely the time that the Black Panthers burst on the social scene.[47] While noting that domination by Jews of European background remained at the highest levels of society, one observer pointed out that "the economic expansion after the Six-Day War brought with it increased entrance of Orientals into white-collar occupations. They became bank tellers, secretaries, sales people, and moved into service jobs such as television and radio repair, became bus and taxi drivers, food-stand and boutique owners; they also entered the ranks of the expanded regular army, especially in N.C.O. positions."[48]

But the solidarity born in the experience of the war and the narrowing economic differential afterward did not prevent a serious deterioration in ethnic relations among the Jews. Perhaps, as Virginia Dominguez has argued, the problem of ethnicity comes only after a collectivity such as Israeli society develops a sense of collective self.[49] Whether the 1967 war had such an effect or not, both the sensitivity and open dissatisfaction of Jews of Middle East background increased rapidly within a few years of the war. Smooha, for example, found that leaders of Jews with Middle Eastern origins were much more likely than leaders of, say, Romanian Jews to cite invidious comparisons and other forms of discrimination.[50]

Public and academic discourse came to be focused on issues of discrimination, prejudice, unequal access, and segregation. Jews of Middle Eastern background became more conscious of, and outspoken about, their inferior status. No event had more impact in crystallizing dissatisfaction than the actions of the Black Panthers. Their demonstrations were followed by a host of new studies confirming the ethnic gap and active discrimination. Ethnic parties sprouted up, and ethnic anger was taken out on the ruling Labor Party, as Jews of Middle East origin flocked to the opposition Likud.

If the dominant discourse before 1967 had been one of social integration, in the aftermath of the war the talk was of "immigration without integration."[51] Anger welled up; one Yemeni intellectual challenged some of the sacred cows of Israeli society by stating that the children of Middle East Jews had died in the war "in order that the Abromoviches and similar people . . . might be appointed as civil servants."[52] The Black Panthers displayed the same sort of animus: "Their whole attitude," wrote Cohen, "was permeated by the conviction that the Orientals had been oppressed and cheated by the Ashkenazi-dominated establishment or even used for its ulterior purposes."[53]

It is important to add that the sense of dissatisfaction did not lead many of the non-European Jews down the path of separatism. Even the few ethnic parties did not trumpet a separatist ideology. From the violent protests of the Black Panthers to the treatises of academics and writers, the call most often was for inclusion and equality, not a breaking off from the dominant groups.[54] The prosperity of the immediate postwar period made the prospect of integration continue to seem attainable. At the same time, it heightened the frustration of second-class status, resulting in an increasingly vitriolic reaction against the methods and outcomes of the existing model for integration.

The three postwar crises that I have singled out—the diminishing centrality of the state, deep divisions in society about the nature of the state and its final borders, and growing ethnic tensions—intersected with one another. Israel faced growing social polarization, intractable divisions between Jews and a growing Arab minority, as well as ethnic venom expressed by one segment of Jewish society against another; and, on the future status of the occupied territories and the character of the state as universal or ethnonational, Israelis also faced off against each other. And, throughout the fray, no referee was in sight. The diminished Israeli state seemed paralyzed by the social divisions and unable to make hard choices. Its declining capacity to guide the society left Israel by the early 1980s with an economy spiraling out of control and an inability to come to terms with the question of where the society was headed. The war that had been heralded as redemptive, as the antithesis of the Holocaust, seemed within several years of its conclusion to have had satanic effects on Israeli state and society. What was it about the 1967 war that so unsettled state-society relations?

SHIFTING BOUNDARIES

Fixed boundaries lend stability to political and social life. People's behavior becomes predictable, social values become ensconced, and the established social roles of institutions—from the family to businesses to the state—become the defining elements for the character of interactions in a society.[55] Institutions of everyday life depend upon the population's clear sense of their reach—*who* is inside an institution and *who* is outside, *which* sorts of interactions they govern and *which* are external to their realm, *what* is private space and *what* is public space. These whos, whichs, and whats may institutionalize exploitative and brutal relations, or egalitarian and caring ones; ones based on individual autonomy, or those promoting group sensibilities first. Whatever the specific character of the institutions, their structure of benefits and sanctions carve out stable social roles and modes of interaction.

Institutions depend upon the permanence of boundaries. Shifting boundaries lend all sorts of uncertainty to the underpinnings of institutions. Boundary flux changes the calculus of incentives; it undoes the understanding of the institution's reach and, with it, the whos, whichs, and whats that provide the parameters for behavior in the society. Ideas and practices embedded in institutions have meaning and influence in a certain space, both social space (say, that of a family) and physical space (as in the jurisdiction of a municipal agency). Sudden shifts in the boundaries of that space can subvert the rules and practices that characterize a single institution. Changes affecting multiple or central institutions in a society can lead to crisis in society's central dynamics, both by opening routine rules and practices to question and by lending uncertainty to the relevance and efficacy of society's central institutions, such as the church or state. The effect of boundary changes is particularly salient when the new borders are hotly contested.

Ian Lustick is one of only a handful of political scientists who analyze the relationship of boundary changes to broader questions of state-society relations. His brilliant book *Unsettled States, Disputed Lands* analyzes how and when boundary changes may occur outside the context of war.[56] He asks which circumstances move a polity from a point where lopping off some of the territory that the state controls (Ireland for Great Britain, Algeria for France, and the West Bank and Gaza Strip for Israel) is unthinkable to a point where such an act is an actively debated policy choice.

Raising the question of border changes, as Lustick does, is important in a broader theoretical sense, as well. When the concept of the state reentered academic discourse in the 1980s, all too frequently it was treated as a given; as an independent variable it seemed inviolable and unchanging.[57] Rosenau remarked that scholarly discourse seems to assume that "the state is to politics what the hidden hand is (à la Adam Smith) to economics."[58] Along with several other scholars, Lustick shifted the focus of comparative politics, asking how the state may change from a seemingly impenetrable rock to something that is shaped and transformed by the currents in society or in the larger international system.[59] His insight that states are not permanent fixtures but may contract or expand in size (or disappear altogether) furthered the entire enterprise of state studies.[60]

It is the possibility of border changes that concerns Lustick. In technical terms, the shifts in boundaries are his dependent variable, and he looks to changes in state-society relations for his answers (the independent variable). The question I am exploring stands Lustick's formulation on its head. What is the effect of boundary changes and continuing contestation over those changes, which now comprise the independent variable, on state and society, which here comprise the dependent variable?

It would be incorrect to say that by themselves the boundary changes stemming from the 1967 war caused the crises in Israel's social dynamics. We can follow Galnoor, however, in stating that the war created a "broken path."[61] By undoing Israel's boundaries, the Six-Day War chipped away at the hold of key institutions and unraveled the understanding of the character of state and society, opening a new period of intense debate about the future. Conquering and then holding territories that had been ruled by Jordan, Syria, and Egypt undermined existing institutional patterns in Israel and precipitated crises in Israel's central social dynamics. Reopening the question of Israel's borders in 1967, after a twenty-year hiatus in which the state's territory seemed to achieve some permanent status in the minds of many in the international community and among Israelis themselves, led to divisive debates in the country about the fundamental nature of society. These debates spilled over into the political realm and had profound effects on state-society relations and relations among groups in the society.

Boundary Changes Open New Questions
about the Construction of Society

In addition to the territory marked by the 1949 armistice lines, at the 1967 war's end Israel ruled the Golan Heights, the Sinai Desert, the West Bank, and the Gaza Strip. The latter two, with their dense Palestinian populations and their relation to Jews' construction of a "territorial legacy," had a particularly profound effect on social dynamics in Israel. At the simplest level, the occupied territories presented Israelis with choices on issues that the vast majority had previously assumed were closed. In the immediate aftermath of the war, Israeli leaders seemed not to have assimilated these choices, giving indications that they assumed the territories would be returned in exchange for peace and recognition by Israel's enemies. But quickly the issue of choice pushed itself onto the public agenda, leading to debates about what had previously been undebatable—incorporating new territories permanently into the state.

But the change in political boundaries had several other key effects that went beyond the question of the territorial reach of the state. First,

the conception of an expanded Israeli state was accompanied by a rationale for its enlargement; that is, the new reach demanded a set of principles different from those that had supported the zigzag boundaries
that had existed from 1949 to 1967. What emerged was a debate that
went far beyond the question of where to draw the lines for Israel's permanent borders. The controversy was an intense, still ongoing division
between those supporting the old principles (with their heavy emphasis
on universalism and citizenship) and the new rationale based on the ethnonational rights of Jews over the state's other citizens.

The bitter dispute over the meaning of the state not only divided
those in Israel along ideological grounds but also deeply affected group
relations. Most obviously, the debate affected Israel's Arab citizens and
their relationship to the dominant Jews. But it also injected itself into
group relations among Jews. The ethnonational principle offered the
hope of quicker and more complete integration to frustrated Jews of
Middle East origin. The established model of a universalistic state
implied, as I noted earlier, a civilly constructed society. Such a society
placed demands on citizens to conform to modes of interaction through
civil behavior. Exactly what civil behavior entailed, however, turned out
to be defined by the dominant European-Jewish groups. Much of the
discrimination against those from North Africa and Asia, as Jews from
a Middle East background knew all too well, was based on the claim or
assumption that they did not possess civil attributes. Their acceptance
into full membership in society, then, was attenuated and subject to
unspoken tests, which in the eyes of those controlling major institutions
they repeatedly failed. "They were thought," noted Arnold Lewis, "to
exhibit instability, emotionalism, laziness, boastfulness, inclination to
violence, uncontrolled temper, superstitiousness, childishness, and lack
of cleanliness."[62]

An ethnonational definition of society would subject Jews of
Middle East background to no such tests. Ethnonationalism would
mean automatic acceptance for such Jews, as is.[63] In part, their grad-
ual switch to the Likud reflected a desire to hook into that party's
model of society. Israel's universal institutions, by their very exclusion of those who did not fit the criteria of "civil," had created their
own in-group qualities. Run, as they were, almost exclusively by Jews
of European roots, they created what Danet called an institutional
culture marked by *mishpahtiyut,* or familism.[64] "It is almost a com-
monplace," wrote Cohen, "that all the major institutional spheres of
Israeli society—the government and the Knesset (Parliament), the
political parties, the Histadrut (The General Federation of Labour),
the major economic enterprises and corporations, the universities,
state schools, and the cultural activities—are dominated, on the

national and often also on the local level, by people of Ashkenazi [European] origin and by expressly Western values."[65]

The effect, oddly, was that institutions based on universalism used universalism as a method of exclusion, creating their own ethnic in-group.[66] The change in Israel's boundaries opened the question of what sort of society would be most consonant with rule over an extended territory and well over a million Palestinians in the newly conquered territory. Those Jews who had been excluded from the central institutions before the war took advantage of the reopened question about the nature of society to push for a redefined ethnic in-group. The new group would be ethnonational, not civic in character, leading to their automatic inclusion, as well. Outliers would then be the Palestinians, both citizens and those in the occupied territories.

Boundary changes thus account for a new contending model of what society should be. This model opened the door to inclusion in central institutions for Jews of Middle Eastern background and, at the same time, to new negativism toward, and exclusion of, Arab citizens (and certainly noncitizens in the territories).[67] It is not surprising that Danet found almost no drop in the institutional culture of familism, between the war and 1980, in what were constructed as universal institutions.[68] What may have changed is that after 1967 a multifaced battle developed over the lines of who was in, and who was outside, the family.

Boundaries Change the Labor Market

The effects of the wartime change in boundaries did not end with struggles over where the final borders should be drawn or with ideological divisions about the sort of society that went along with different boundary configurations. Another key impact of the war's final demarcation lines was on the country's labor market. The war created a new reservoir of low-wage workers in the conquered territories who had access to work opportunities in Israel across formerly impenetrable lines. This new worker pool affected the entire labor market, most markedly those who had occupied the lowest rungs of the labor ladder before the war. The high-level mobilization of the Israeli economy before, during, and after the war lifted the country out of recession. Palestinians from the territories filled much of the new labor demand by taking low-paying jobs. The mobilization and the existence of the new Palestinian labor pool from the West Bank and Gaza Strip enabled Israeli Arab citizens and Jews from Middle Eastern countries to take advantage of all sorts of positions at the next level up—they became subcontractors, foremen, supervisors, and the like.[69]

Their occupational mobility often demanded new physical mobility as well. The result was that the Israeli economy, and its labor market in particular, shed much of the fragmentation and segmentation that government policies, wittingly or unwittingly, had engendered during the first two decades of statehood.[70] Those barriers to physical and social mobility, the internal boundaries, had been most obvious in the case of the Arab population of the country but had existed for new Jewish immigrants from other parts of the Middle East too, as we shall see below. Because Israel seemed so militarily secure now, and because demand was so high for all sorts of labor, state leaders may have seen the breakdown of the old segmentation and the social relations that went along with it as largely cost-free. In fact, the costs turned out to be staggering: reorganization of society, with its new Gazan and West Bank underclass, prompted the erosion of the state's privileged position, leading to important and profound changes in state-society relations.

In the years of high immigration right after the creation of the state, governmental policies had attracted new immigrants, especially those of Middle Eastern origin, to so-called development towns. Subsidized housing and low-interest loans were the biggest inducements drawing immigrants to these isolated new communities, "outside the main stream of Israeli society geographically as well as socially."[71] More than any other settlements in Israel, these towns were ethnically constituted, with as many as two-thirds of residents from a Middle Eastern background.[72]

The state also gave incentives to certain kinds of industries to locate in the development towns, especially ones using labor-intensive technologies and low-skill labor.[73] In effect, an ethnic division of labor developed in Israel that was geographically based. Isolation meant that new immigrants from Middle Eastern countries were concentrated in jobs and locations that impeded their physical and social mobility. Concentrated at the lower end of the occupational ladder and shunted to the geographical margins of the country, Jews with Middle Eastern roots formed a labor force within a labor force. Spatially, Israel was divided by what Oren Yiftachel has called "internal frontiers."[74]

Segmentation and fragmentation, then, were the hallmarks of the pre-1967 economy. The deep recession immediately before the war fell hardest on precisely those in the isolated, low-skill industries.[75] "To sum up," wrote Swirski, "residential segregation, the predominance of intragroup marriages, the segregated and unequal school system, and the ideological apparatus that portrays the Orientals as culturally deprived or backward—all work to reproduce the ethnic division of labour that emerged in Israel during the fifties and sixties."[76]

Arab labor in Israel was even more disadvantaged. Even before the creation of Israel, many Arabs (especially those living in the coastal portions of Palestine that became Israel) had begun to commute from their villages to low-skill jobs in the cities. With the imposition of military administration of the Arabs after Israeli independence, that pattern continued. Now, however, severe restrictions were placed on how far and under what conditions Arab workers could commute to outside jobs, making them available for the lowest-skill labor but only in their local regions. They, too, formed a niche within a fragmented and segmented labor force.

Even before the 1967 war, signs emerged that the social boundaries associated with the segmented labor market, with its clear ethnic division of labor, were beginning to fray. The end of military administration ended the forced confinement of Arab labor. Since the geographic isolation of Jews from Middle Eastern origins was maintained through incentives, rather than force, it is not surprising that many began to move from the development towns. One study in the early 1960s found that interurban movement from these communities was four times the national average.[77]

But it was the boom after the war, coupled with the reconfiguration of the labor market through the addition of Palestinians from the conquered territories, that opened wide the gates to new physical and social mobility, undoing the old social fragmentation and segmentation.[78] Economic boom created a high demand for labor at all levels of the Israeli economy; in fact, unemployment rates until the late 1980s averaged just 3.6 percent. Amir described the result: "The 1967 war changed the composition of the labor force in Israel; there now existed accessible reserve labor which was cheap, unskilled, and nonorganized [Palestinians from the occupied territories]."[79] For both Arab citizens of Israel and Jews from Middle Eastern background, the demands higher up on the occupational scale, coupled with the availability of low-skill labor to replace them at the low end, resulted in new social and physical mobility.[80] The changing of the internal social boundaries and the external physical boundaries became coupled processes.

The mobilization of new social groups increased demands upon the state—many of them, as we saw, expressed in terms of ethnic and labor protest.[81] Indeed, the end of the old residential isolation and labor market segmentation broke down the state's ability to dampen demands put upon it. As new political and social demands strained the capacities of the state's relatively young institutions, it became less and less able to regulate intergroup relations and to put brakes on Israeli consumption. And, with the reemergence of the ethnonational model of society expressed by the Likud, many Jews with Middle Eastern origins found a ready way to express their dissatisfaction.

It might also be noted, in conclusion, that some of the elements leading to the crisis in Israel's social dynamics also put limits on that crisis. The unrestrained economy, with its soaring levels of personal consumption and low unemployment, allowed for high mobility and thus very focused bread-and-butter demands by Jews from Middle Eastern backgrounds. Their aims were not separation but inclusion and participation. They did not build exclusive institutions but integrated into established ones, such as the Likud itself. At least for some of the problems we have discussed, that meant an avenue for the creation of new institutional stability in the future.

CONCLUSION

When the 1967 war broke out, the Israeli state was only twenty years old. Its institutions had not hardened over many decades or centuries. Still, in a short period, those institutions had created remarkable stability in the relations between the state and those it governed. State organizations from the Knesset on down had become naturalized, that is, many in society, especially among the Jewish population, accepted the reach of those institutions and the rightness of their establishing codes for social behavior. To be sure, there was no shortage of grumbling about particular rules, but little questioning arose about the appropriateness of those organizations to make the rules.

Immediately after the harrowing days of May and early June 1967, very few Jewish citizens saw the outcome of the war as anything but an unmixed blessing. What they and Israeli political officials could not foresee was how unsettling to state institutions and the relations between the state and society the change in boundaries brought about by the war would be. If the prewar boundaries had taken on a kind of sanctity in those two decades, all sorts of doubts came to the surface about what the new proper boundaries and reach of political institutions should be. In a setting where the state had been elevated to a very special status comparatively, the postwar border changes, mixed with a number of other domestic and international factors, weakened the state and transformed its relation to society.

As I write these words, early in the new century, in the midst of intense negotiations with the Palestinians and Syrians, the questions of Israel's permanent boundaries, including who constitutes the nation, the nature of citizenship, and the proper role of state institutions are as contested now as they were thirty years ago. If a glimmer of hope can be seen on the horizon that some of the most wrenching disputes will recede, it is that today's debates are much more focused now on the signed agreements with the Palestinians and what they require of Israel.

The absence of a viable alternative to the Oslo Process, as well as a growing sense of inevitability about the return of the Golan Heights to Syria, has channeled many of the divisions into questions of how to implement the agreements and how far concessions should go. Those are not inconsequential questions. But, if they can be resolved and final agreements between Israel and the Palestine Authority, and between Israel and Syria, can be ratified, the effect could be similar to Israel's withdrawal from the Sinai Desert and its settlements there, such as Yamit, in the late 1970s. In that case, emotions ran very high at the moment; then, as now, musings about the possibility of civil war could be heard in the street. But the permanent settlement with Egypt came to be nearly unquestioned within a few short years after the withdrawal occurred. If the Israeli people and state are fortunate, the same will occur in the context of a final peace with the Palestinians and the Syrians.

CHAPTER 8

The Odd Man Out: Arabs in Israel

with
Baruch Kimmerling

In the excitement of Israel's birth, in the agony of its wars with neighbors, and in the painful march toward a final status agreement with the Palestinians, Israel's own Palestinian citizens often have stood on the sidelines, on the outside looking in. But, for Israel, this population has represented much more than a neglected minority. The place of this group in Israel lies at the crossroads of those issues that have beset Israel in its society formation, the issues raised in chapters 5, 6, and 7. Questions of who is part of civil society, of the ethnic or civic direction of society, and of the glue that holds society together all swirl around the place of Arabs in Israel.

As among Israel's Jews, Israel's Arabs' identity (even the question of what to call them) has had a complex relationship to the state. In chapters 6 and 7, the emphasis was on the battle over what it means to be an Israeli, and who is included in that designation. While the civic understanding of citizenship was meant technically to include Arab citizens, continuing practices of discrimination left the question of Arab identity in limbo. This chapter explores the odd relationship of the Israeli state to the Arabs, looking at the attempt to create a new identity of the Israeli-Arab. But, as with state policies toward Jews from Middle East countries, those attempts had unintended consequences. Instead of the Israeli Arab, there emerged the Israeli Palestinian, an identity laced with contradiction.

During the nearly half-century since al-Nakba, the disaster the Arabs of Palestine experienced in Israel's war of independence, the struggle to refashion a Palestinian nation has necessarily had a double focus: Arabs in the West Bank and Gaza maintained the distinct character of camp society and the largest intact population in towns such as Nablus. The newly formed satellite communities outside Palestine signified cosmopolitanism, mobility, and, in time, agitation against the existing international order. Between 1948 and the 1967 war, those who did not leave the Jewish state occupied a position as uncertain and ambiguous within Israel as in the eyes of other Arabs. Mostly fellaheen (peasants) during the British Mandate, Israeli Arabs heard distant echoes of the political vocabulary being forged in exile, which was recreating Palestinism. Transformed by their passports into the pariahs of the Arab world, they were also cut off from the huge waves of outward migration to more distant Arab countries—the West Bank alone had nearly 300,000 such emigrants before the 1967 war and another quarter of a million through 1975.[1] The war finally inaugurated a process of reintegration. Even then, while many began to think of themselves as Palestinians and to support the ideals of Palestinian nationalism, their experience as Israeli citizens psychologically and socially separated them from that of dispersal and longing.

In any event, from its inception, the state of Israel had developed two distinct personalities. For Jews, it was one of the few vibrant, participatory democracies in Asia, Africa, and Latin America. For Arabs, it represented a system of control and was the distributor of key resources—a state for which its Arab citizens had limited emotional attachment. As citizens of a country formed for them, Israeli Jews had, beyond simple feelings of civic responsibility, those of proprietorship toward the political institutions—the army, the flag, and the national anthem. Correspondingly, a predominant concern of government officials and academics was absorbing waves of Jewish immigrants into a new society and culture.

The state leadership certainly did not intend such absorption to involve the Arabs, especially as they came to compete with Jewish immigrants for land, water, welfare, and jobs. Their formal rights were initially counterbalanced by the harsh realities of military government, isolating them from the rest of the population, fostering dependence, preventing the creation of significant local institutions, and transforming them into a voting bloc that supported the ruling political party. Later, they would find their civic participation offset by continued national alienation. What sociologists have called the civil religion of Israeli national life—Independence Day, the Sabbath, school and work holidays on Jewish festivals, and so on—held little meaning for them.[2]

FROM MAJORITY TO MINORITY

Just after the 1949 armistice, the approximately 150,000 Israeli Arabs comprised slightly more than 10 percent of all Palestinians and about the same percentage of the Israeli population. Three-quarters of them lived in villages in the western Galilee and the Little Triangle—a part of the country adjacent to the coastal plain annexed to Israel in the armistice agreement with Jordan. These villages had not experienced mass exodus, nor the same sort of social decimation as Haifa, Jaffa, and other cities.

This apparent stability was deceiving: The 1948 war had left an Israeli Arab society as disoriented, in many ways, as those in the refugee camps ringing Israel. Although not officially exiles, between one-sixth and one-half of all the Palestinians in Israel were internal refugees.[3] Some would manage to return to their original villages, as would others who had fled the country.[4]

Nonetheless, Israeli authorities continued to expel concentrations of Arabs after the fighting subsided.[5] Citing their rights as citizens of the state, such uprooted Christian Maronites from Birim and Iqrit used the Israeli courts in an unsuccessful struggle to return that lasted several generations.[6] And many of the few thousand young men who were not exiles were war prisoners, leaving the Arabs without a significant part of their productive potential.[7]

Other Israeli Arabs faced a double bind, facilitating the confiscation of their land: The military barred them from their original homes, but since they were classified officially as "present absentees," the state could claim their "abandoned" land through the Absentee Property Act of 1950. One estimate is that as much as 40 percent of Arabs' land (half a million acres) was confiscated through the act.[8] After resettling Arabs (and compensating them for about a quarter of its worth), Israeli officials would use the land for people who were themselves uprooted, simultaneously thinning out a population that—reflecting a bitter legacy—they believed was threatening to the state:[9] a fifth column. In fact, broadcasts from neighboring Arab states continuously suggested just such a role to the Arabs in Israel. In this context, the land transfer was viewed as a means of disabling a major tool for undermining Israel's right to exist—the Arabs' claim to possession of the land.

Even where they held onto their plots, the Arabs found it difficult to stay in farming. The state severely limited their water and electricity quotas, particularly when compared to the more productive neighboring Jewish communal and cooperative farms (kibbutzim and moshavim).[10] And the Arabs found themselves excluded from the country's powerful marketing, credit, and purchasing cooperatives.[11] Arab-owned citrus groves all but disappeared; in the 1950s, the fellaheen fell back on subsistence production, with supplemental marketing of olive oil.

It is thus not surprising that many Israeli Arabs abandoned agriculture altogether. In this respect, at least, they resembled the Palestinians scattered in most other countries—in Zureik's terms, they underwent a process of depeasantification.[12] The land became the domain of those with the machinery to exploit it. By the 1960s and 1970s, Arab agriculture in Israel would undergo significant mechanization and cash cropping, Israeli research organizations speaking of a shift from fellah to farmer.[13] In earlier decades, however, it would have been more apt to speak of a shift from fellah to wage earner. The shrinking Arab land base and the preference given to Jewish commercial agriculture simply continued the process that was well established, already, in the Mandate period—the movement of fellaheen into nonagricultural, unskilled and semiskilled wage labor. Approximately three-quarters of urban Arab workers, one study has found, had no training at all.[14] As Israel moved from labor surpluses to labor shortages, many Palestinian Arabs ended up integrated into the national economy, working in Jewish industries and construction companies as the lowest group on the social ladder.[15]

The transformation was rapid and thorough. By 1963, the fraction of Arabs in farming was slightly more than one-third (compared to just over 10 percent of the Jews); a decade later, it was one-fifth. Arabs entered what is often called a split- or a dual-labor market:[16] Jews filled the skilled and higher-paying positions, while Arabs settled into those that were lower paying and often seasonal, demanding little technical skill. Even during the Mandate, Palestinian Arabs had found themselves at a disadvantage compared to the more skilled, technologically sophisticated Jews. The post-1948 power of the Jews in the society's central institutions only heightened the disparity.

Israel's rapid economic growth not only produced disorientation, but also a rising standard of living for Palestinian Arabs and a gain in their rights as citizens: They now had access to the Histadrut and the benefit of a law opening state employment offices to them. But hovering behind such gains were the costs of being a weak minority. Even when state employment offices accepted applications from Arabs, they tended to give preference to Jewish applicants for jobs in Jewish areas.[17] All Arabs experienced major and minor favoritism toward Jews. Barred (aside from Druze and Bedouin) from army service, they found benefits, jobs, even housing, open only to those who had served in the military. And sellers and real estate agents often greeted Arabs seeking housing in predominantly Jewish areas with outright discrimination.

It is also important to note the trauma involved in any sudden transformation from national majority to small, fairly powerless minority. While now in the latter category, "it does not necessarily follow that [the Israeli Arabs] have developed a minority self-concept."[18] Compounding the trauma was the absence of any effective national leadership to deal with their Jewish counterparts. Those who remained, noted the first Israeli adviser on Arab affairs, "were like a headless body . . . the social, commercial, and religious elite had gone";[19] even among the Christians, making up a disproportionately high 21 percent of the Israeli Palestinian population, there were few remaining representatives of the Mandate period's middle and upper classes.

Like the Palestinian refugees in nearby countries, the Arabs in Israel thus looked to local leaders, many of whom were clan heads, gaining new prominence as they played key mediating roles between their relatives and Israeli state and party officials. In fact, the clan heads filled an even more central niche than local leaders in the refugee camps, and interclan rivalries took on far greater intensity than those of the Mandate period.[20] In the camp society of Gaza, Jordan, and Lebanon, the old village chiefs gave way in the two decades after 1948 to a young, educated national leadership; in Israel, the Arabs found themselves cut off from it and barred from generating a broader leadership of their own. Even when increasing urbanization and education began to undermine the old local clan leaders, starting in the mid-1970s, the Arabs in Israel could not produce a countrywide leadership to represent them. A series of Israeli government policies, reflecting lingering Jewish fear that the Arabs would form a spearhead for Israel's avowed enemies, was aimed at forestalling its creation—and with it, a revitalized Palestinian identity.

No policy rankled more than the imposition and maintenance of military government for the Arabs. Drawing on Mandate regulations dating back to 1936 and 1945 (to thwart Arab and then Jewish rebels), the government established military administration in the fall of 1948, while the fighting raged. In 1950, the government organized the administration into a military government, maintained until 1966. It resembled emergency powers in other countries, restricting freedom of speech, freedom of movement, and so forth. It provided an easy way to shove the Arab minority aside—in order to focus on the pressing problems of creating a new state administration, assimilating hundreds of thousands of immigrants, stimulating economic growth, and building military capabilities to face the next round, which neighboring Arab states repeatedly promised would soon come. Perhaps for the Arabs the military government's most onerous aspect was its severe restriction on movement. Journalist and poet Fouzi El-Asmar recalls the situation in Lydda right after the 1948 war: "The Arabs were not allowed to leave their own ghetto [practically all Arab villages or clusters of villages were designated as closed areas][21] without a permit from the authorities [i.e., the military governor], and the most infuriating thing for us was that our area and the other areas in Lydda which were inhabited by Arabs were under military command, while the rest of the city in which Jews lived, was not. We were not allowed out without special licences until the early fifties, while the Jews, of course, were free to walk anywhere except in our neighbourhood."[22]

The effect of the restrictions on free movement was to fragment the population even further (by limiting contacts among Arabs) and to make it more difficult to find employment in the larger labor market. Several years before its demise in the 1960s, the hand of the military government became much lighter. In part, the liberalization was due to the fact that Arabs in Israel did not prove to be disloyal or subversive. In part, it was due to the tragic events in the Little Triangle village of Kafr Qasim, in 1956, spawned by the harsh restrictions on movement.

For Arabs, Kafr Qasim became a symbol; for Jews, it was the catalyst removing one of the many veils shrouding the Arab issue. The events unfolded at the beginning of the Suez war—the second Arab-Israeli war, following fast upon the first one and (in light of Nasser's pan-Arab appeal) intensifying Jewish fear about the disposition of the country's Arabs. On October 29, 1956, at the outset of the fighting, military authorities clamped a curfew on Arab villages, starting at 5 P.M. In Kafr Qasim, workers had been toiling in the fields; not having heard about the curfew, they drifted home after five. The village chief, having learned of the curfew at 4:30, had cautioned the local military unit's NCO that the returning laborers would have no way of knowing about it. Similar situations occurred in other villages, but in Kafr Qasim the military unit lined up the returning workers and shot them. Forty-seven were killed.

For the Arabs, Kafr Qasim took on a symbolic importance almost rivalling that of Dayr Yasin, the village where Jewish Irgun forces committed atrocities in the 1948 war. El-Asmar writes of

> a turning point in my political development. I spent so much time talking about the incident to my friends, who were also greatly affected to varying degrees. We asked ourselves: "What will happen next? When will our turn come? What had these poor workers done?" We dwelt on these and a thousand other questions. From these unanswerable questions, I arrived at the conclusion that in all truth this had happened simply because these people were Arabs, despite the fact that Arabs in Israel had kept the peace since the creation of the State.[23]

The response of the Israeli government offered little reassurance. At first, it tried to cover up the events. Once they became public, officials expressed outrage and brought the members of the military unit to trial, but Arabs openly questioned whether the punishments fit the severity of the crimes. Eight men received sentences ranging from eight to seventeen years in prison, but in the end none served more than three and a half years.

Along with Dayr Yasin, Hebron, Gush Etzion, and similar incidents that became symbolically important in the Arab-Israeli conflict, Kafr

Qasim encouraged Arabs and Jews to demonize each other. The absence of routine contacts, exacerbated by the military restrictions, made the process easy: The two peoples resided in segregated neighborhoods, attended different schools, almost never intermarried; they met only in the workplace—and then, usually, as boss and worker.

For the Arabs, still reeling from their defeat in 1948, Kafr Qasim dramatized the weakness of their position as a national minority. Israeli policy was not simply aimed at subduing the Arabs through sheer force, but controlling them in ways that denied their connection to a larger Palestinian society and its nationalism, thus thwarting unity among them. One political scientist has identified this policy as segmentation,[24] resembling the system of divide and rule made much use of by the imperial powers earlier in the century and still used by many states to handle their populations. As with Jordanian policy during the same period, the Israeli political leadership worked consciously to nullify the Arabs' Palestinian identity. But its approach differed from Jordan's in having no goal of integrating them into a larger state identity. As Israeli Arabs, they were designated as neither Israeli—in the ways that Jews could be Israeli—nor Palestinian.[25]

Israeli citizenship would bind Jews and Arabs in a civic sense, enabling Arabs to secure a relatively fair share of resources and assure their civic rights, but they would forego any national identification, any means of membership in a close-knit collectivity.[26] The Law of Return, conferring rights of immigration and instantaneous citizenship on any Jew, reflected the status of Jews as automatic members of such a collectivity, as did the continuing functioning of nonstate organizations such as the Jewish Agency, bestowing benefits on Jews only.[27] (Only the Law of Return and military service officially differentiated Jews from Arabs.)

The experiences of a group called *al-Ard* (The Land) reflected how the authorities moved against those aiming to speak for broad sectors of the Arab population. The al-Ard group of nationalist intellectuals, who published a magazine starting in 1959,[28] attempted to create an Arab party list in 1964 to run in the upcoming Israeli national elections. Lustick describes the events that followed:

> The Military Administration moved hard and fast. Permission for the Arab Socialist List to appear on the ballot was refused, el-Ard's leaders were separated and banished to remote Jewish towns, many members were put under administrative detention, and the organization itself was finally declared illegal. Subsequently several of its leaders were offered a choice of imprisonment or exile from the country.[29]

Al-Ard raised fears among Israeli officials that the Arabs were about to reopen the old, finally dormant political struggles of the Mandate period. The Arab party, troublingly Nasserite and pan-Arab in its stance, did not recognize the right of a Jewish state to exist, certainly not within the enlarged boundaries of the 1949 armistice.[30] It also saw the Arabs of Israel as an integral part of the dispersed Palestinian people. Israel's High Court finally banned the group, finding that its core ideology contradicted the very existence of the state.

Working to fragment the Arab population into numerous different minorities, such as Druze, Circassians, Bedouin, and the like, Israeli officials turned to the clan as their institutional link.[31] In the 1950s and 1960s, clan leaders served as the village conduits for government investments in education, social services, and infrastructure. This status—depending on the continuing largesse of the Israeli government, the Histadrut, and the major political parties (especially the Labor Party, or, as it was formerly known, Mapai)—thus gave them a newfound discretionary power. Their co-optation was demonstrated in 1963, when a move to abolish the military government failed by a single Knesset vote: Two of the negative ballots came from Arabs.

Not surprisingly, the older clan leaders began to lose their followers' confidence even as they continued to deliver important benefits. At the same time, Israeli officials put obstacles in the way of any other organizations taking over. They confiscated, froze, or took control of the Muslim religious endowments, the *waqfs*, which had played such an important political and economic role in earlier periods. And quite effectively, they drew activist students away from community leadership roles with well-paying positions in the Histadrut or state agencies. Between 1948 and the 1967 war, such policies were generally successful. But they also had an unintended effect, producing new social groups—including small numbers of elites—who sometimes subtly, sometimes openly, forged the elements of an Arab identity running counter to the official vision.

No policies had more impact in this regard than those involving education. Education for Arabs in Israel has sustained a built-in tension since the state's inception. On the one hand, the state has controlled all of it, Arab and Jewish alike, in a highly centralized manner, with the curriculum completely controlled by the Ministry of Education in Jerusalem. On the other hand, the Arab and Jewish educational systems have led almost totally separate lives at least up to the university level. With a few exceptions in several cities (Jaffa, Haifa, Nazareth), Jewish children have attended school with other Jewish children, Arab children with other Arab children—and Arab teachers. This has allowed, amidst Jerusalem-imposed uniformity, the emergence of an educational milieu with a distinctly Arab personality.

Both the Arabs and Jewish officials have seen the education of Arab children as a key resource for achieving important goals: for the Arabs, political and socioeconomic progress;[32] for the Jews, both overall Arab modernization and the creation of the "new Israeli-Arabs," with their various subdivisions of identity, their religious and ethnic fragments. Soon after the guns fell silent in 1948, the Knesset passed a compulsory education law, which overwhelmed Arab schools with droves of new students. Ministry of Education personnel promptly drafted Arab teachers, many poorly qualified, to staff the classrooms. Makeshift schoolhouses and two-a-day shifts became the norm in most villages.[33] Textbooks were almost nonexistent.[34] Setting a pattern for other government offices, the Ministry of Education established an Arab Department, led and in large part staffed by Jewish civil servants. Much as in the Bureau for Indian Affairs in the United States, a certain paternalism became its standard operating procedure.

In many respects the results of the crash program were impressive, dwarfing British educational efforts in earlier decades. The great majority of Arab children became not only literate but conversant in Hebrew as well as Arabic. By 1955, the Israelis had doubled Arab enrollment percentages from prestate levels. And even that figure is somewhat misleading, since it incorporates nomadic Bedouins, of whom only a negligible number attended state schools, and girls, still enrolled at less than one-third the rate of boys. But in one important respect the Israeli enterprise did evoke the Mandate period: As the Arabs gained in the classroom, they nonetheless continued to fall farther behind the Jews. For example, while the compulsory education law led to truly universal education among Jews at the elementary level, in 1973 only four-fifths of Arab children attended school regularly.[35] In fact, their pre-1967 elementary school enrollment was closer to the levels of West Bank Palestinians than to those of Israeli Jews; in high schools and universities, the disparity was even greater.

The educational system, in an odd way, fed upon itself. For educated Arabs, many Israeli offices employing white collar workers, both in government and in the private sector, were off limits—Arabs were simply not hired. Furthermore, at the time Israeli investment policies discouraged the creation of autonomous economic sectors in Arab areas, severely limiting career possibilities for educated young Arabs. The result was that education and law became virtually the only careers open to the growing number of graduates. Soon, many of the best students returned to the schools as teachers, raising the level of education substantially. In 1962, for example, the Arab failure rate in the state high school matriculation exams was 90 percent; three years later it had dropped to 70 percent.

Even if the Israelis could point with some pride to such achievements, their goal of reshaping Arab consciousness into a new Israeli-Arab identity had more mixed results; the development of Arab education within a dominant Jewish culture was bound to cause confusion. Note the ideals articulated in the 1953 educational laws: "To base education on the values of Jewish culture and the achievements of science, on love of the homeland and loyalty to the state and the Jewish people, on practice in agricultural work and handicraft, on pioneer training and on striving for a society built on freedom, equality, tolerance, mutual assistance, and love of mankind."[36] The actual curriculum adapted these statements for Arab schools and Arab students, but the Jewish cultural thrust continued to be very strong: Arab students around the country studied more hours of Jewish history than they did of Arab history.[37]

In some important ways, formal education was thus a disorienting experience for Israeli Arab children, represented a bilingual and bicultural experience, with both cultures being somewhat out of place. Anomalous in schools where all the students were Arab,[38] Jewish culture still established the norms for achievement—the matriculation exams, entrance into all the country's universities, facility in Hebrew. The limited professional career opportunities that did exist depended on mastering a curriculum including Hebrew literature, Jewish history, Zionism, and the like. The relationship to Arab culture was equally anomalous, since Israel's Arab minority was cut off from the centers of Arab culture and learning in Cairo, Beirut, and elsewhere. Its isolation came not only from Israeli policies but also from being shunned by other Arabs in the coffeehouses of Europe, and by Arab governments. Inversely, in Israeli schools, the Arabic component of the curriculum included classical Arabic language and literature and Muslim history, without any reference to contemporary Arab or Palestinian developments. The implicit message to the students was that the Ottoman Empire represented the end of their history.[39]

Israeli officials had hoped that children's educational experiences in the state's highly centralized school system would create the new Israeli-Arab man and woman, an identity autonomous of those being forged in refugee camps and Palestinian satellite communities outside Israel. The values implicit in a modern education would break down the Arabs' old parochial perspectives, the appreciation of both Arab and Jewish history creating a minority that identified itself with classical Arab culture and, in a civic sense, with the Israeli state. The formation of new identities, however, is far more complicated and confusing than the officials imagined. The disorienting experience that Arab children faced within school, compounded by the contradictory pulls they faced in the larger society, resulted in the emergence of a rather different perspective.

It did not emerge immediately. In the 1950s and 1960s, the Arabs in Israel did not have the resources to recreate an autonomous cultural life, especially given the restrictions of the military government. Caught between the pull of local Arab culture and the efforts of Israeli educational officials, they remained largely quiescent, both on a political and cultural level. When asked by Israeli sociologists in the summer of 1966 to state their core identities, those in a sample gave the following rank order: Israeli, Israeli-Arab, Arab, and Palestinian.

A short time after, other factors led to a strikingly different order: Arab, Muslim/Christian, Israeli-Arab, and Israeli.[40] No doubt the intervening 1967 war had shaken up existing Arab understanding. But the war also made manifest the educational system's virtue of offering both Jewish and Arab students the tools to challenge the truths taught them. What may have mattered even more than such critical skills was the educational system's fostering of new groups in Arab society. Despite efforts to prevent Arab national integration, high schools and universities brought together students from far-flung villages and towns to explore their common experiences and construct their own view of the world.

In this manner, a fragile, narrow new Arab elite emerged out of the Israeli educational system. It would never manage to play a social and political role similar to that of the old notables before 1948 or of the exiled educated element in the Palestine Liberation Organization. Nonetheless, those who rose out of peasant society through school ranks in Israel provided the basis for an emerging, collective self-identity, as Israel's Arabs struggled to clarify their relationship with other Palestinians and other Israelis.

What sorts of people made up this elite? As Khalil Nakhleh suggests, foremost among them were "people of the pen."[41] A number of school teachers began to achieve recognition beyond their local communities by publishing poetry and short stories. In 1954, they established the League of Arabic Poets (including Jewish members writing in Arabic), which gave way in 1955 to the League of the Arab Pen. Through their verse, often recited in public forums, they expressed the pent-up grievances of the Arab minority as a whole.

It is important to note that in the Palestinian Arab context both inside and outside Israel, politics and art were almost never differentiated. The only nonpolitical poet with stature in the 1950s was Mishel Hadad. The most important Arab writer in Israel was Emile Habibi, a communist activist. (His best-known book is *The Opsimist*—a mixture of "optimist" and "pessimist"—an ironic description of the Jewish-Arab reality in Israel.) Likewise the most important literary periodical remains *al-Jadid*, also issued by the Communist Party. It was a vehicle for poets and political activists such as Samih al-Qassim, Mahmoud Darwish, Zaki Darwish, Salim Jubran, and Tawfiq Zayad.[42]

In the period leading up to the 1967 war, "few Israeli Arabs defined themselves publicly as Palestinian Arabs or just as Palestinians," writes Aziz Haidar, but in the work of some of these writers one could discern signs of a renewed Palestinian identity.[43] A handful eventually left Israel and joined the armed resistance. Others stayed in their teaching positions, using symbolism and allegory to "write protest poetry and to communicate with the readership under the watchful eyes of the Israeli censor."[44] They also railed against the clan leaders for working hand in glove with the Israeli authorities.

Until the mid-1960s, the Zionist political parties did not accept Arab members in their ranks; instead, they created affiliated lists, or so-called Arab slates, populated largely by clan heads or their designated representatives, the only exception being the left-wing Zionist Mapam party. Allied with the writers, a small number of political leaders now managed to gain a foothold outside the framework of the clan heads.[45] Most rose to prominence within Israel's Communist Party, but some joined Mapam. With the top leadership of both parties being Jewish,[46] the immunity of the parties themselves, along with the privileges of party activism—access to publications, participation in local seminars, travel to conventions in communist countries, interaction with Jewish intellectuals—enabled this small group to gain invaluable experience and contacts, as well as access to Eastern-bloc universities for their children.

The graduates of both Israeli universities and those in communist countries eventually joined the emerging elite, mostly as a small core of professionals, especially teachers, lawyers, physicians, and pharmacists. Although most of their education was financed by their clans, seemingly grounding them within village society, they became cultural oddities. Their Hebrew was often flawless, certainly superior to that of the Jewish man in the street; they read the same books and newspapers, attended the same plays, and hummed the same tunes as their Jewish middle-class counterparts. (In fact, after 1967, many Gazans and West Bankers commented on how "Jewish" these Arab men appeared.) Nevertheless, they played an important role for other Arabs, providing an important bridge to the dominant Jewish culture. Lawyers, in particular, became skilled at advancing Arab interests through the adept use of the courts and Israel's democratic institutions.[47]

Like the cultural and economic leaders who had emerged on the coast during the Mandate period, these intellectuals, professionals, and party activists could not create a comprehensive leadership by building political parties or other institutions. One writer notes that the "Arab elites, on the whole, are few in number relative to the size of the community. They are also a bitter and frustrated lot. . . . Finally, they are economically and politically marginal, rarely occupying positions that enable them to influence or contribute to the development of their society"[48]—a judgment that seems overly harsh. The elite did fill an important function in defining possibilities and directions for the Arabs of Israel. They did so at a time when old social institutions had been eviscerated and new ones were threatening the foundations of Palestinian Arab life.

AFTER 1967: ECONOMIC AND POLITICAL TRANSFORMATION

In the years leading up to the June war, the old patriarchal system based on the clan was in disrepair. Much of its strength had come from its pivotal role in the distribution of land and of government benefits tied to agriculture during Israel's first two decades. But with a declining number of Arabs in farming, and as work lives expanded beyond the village's physical and social boundaries, its special position in Arab society had begun to vanish. After 1967, its economic strength ebbed quickly and it moved farther toward the community's margins. The process accelerated when the Labor Party weakened and then, in 1977, fell into opposition; much of the vitality of the early brand of politics had rested on the ties of the clan heads to the party.

Even the marriage system that had sustained the clan fell into disarray. The prevalence of wage labor meant that the family's arrangement of marriages and the old standards determining bride price, or dowry, disappeared. In the post-1967 period, young women from outside the village, or at least outside the clan, no longer were the most desirable brides. According to tradition, marriages were within the patrilineal clan, with villagers prizing outside brides because they could enhance its political alliances. Now, such carefully arranged unions gave way to personal choice.

In that respect, the old system did not entirely vanish after the June war. In the town of Shafa Amr, Majid al-Haj found more traditional marriages still prevalent—even if young Arabs reported that their selections were made through their personal choices, rather than family arrangement.[49] Nonetheless, as one anthropologist puts it, "The marriage system has become ineffectual. . . . At best, the system is accommodated to individual strategies promoting personal or (nuclear) household viability or need. . . . The 'end purpose' of a marriage strategy is personal well-being. . . ."[50] Once questions of bride price and the basis of selection of mates changed, so did other aspects of family life. Increasing individualism, for example, made it much more likely for young couples to set up separate households, rather than moving in with their extended families.[51]

Corresponding to these social changes, new organizations were appearing with political potential—for example, those consisting of internal refugees from various destroyed villages. Yet even as the clan heads' local stature suffered, the new, more individualistic Arab community faced an Israeli political system still working through them. And government policies continued to stifle the possibility that the educated elite would emerge as a comprehensive leadership, prepared to help the Arabs in Israel confront the changes setting in after 1967.

Some of these changes had already been evident in preceding decades, now simply intensifying dramatically. Others were real breaks with earlier patterns, partly growing out of the resumed relations with other Palestinians in the West Bank and Gaza. Two trends, in particular, were central to a reshaping of Arabs' social life in Israel: the end of agricultural society, with the Arabs adopting a different role in the Israeli economy, and the development of a new politics.

The economic surge in the years following the June war affected both the standard of living of the Arabs and what anthropologist Henry Rosenfeld has termed their "latitude and scope in the economy."[52] Many became self-employed, owning small workshops and—in several instances—large-scale industries. They went, Rosenfeld notes,

> from unskilled laborers and service workers, often at the most menial of tasks over the past decades, to an increasing hold in construction . . . ; from a readiness to undertake jobs in manual labor that many Jews were leaving, to the gaining of skills, experience and know-how in the labor market, and the ability to provide these, and workers, as sub-contractors for Jewish contractors in building, defense projects, road construction, public works, and in a huge variety of enterprises many of them, directly or indirectly, state development projects.[53]

Just as Jews from Arab countries escaped low-status, unskilled manual labor in the 1950s and 1960s by moving past the Israeli Arabs, who filled such positions, now these jobs were handed on to commuters from the West Bank and the Gaza Strip. Even those remaining in wage labor forfeited temporary work on construction sites and in the fields to their West Bank brothers.

By the 1980s, an Arab industrial sector was also forming, employing as much as 30 percent of the Arab industrial labor force and about 6 percent of the Arab work force.[54] Unlike an earlier period when authorities frowned upon investment in Arab villages and towns, small manufacturing enterprises were now opening there, often with clear Jewish approval—if not material support. Arabs started smaller businesses (e.g., garages) servicing mostly local Arab clients. A 1985 field survey of such businesses, and of industries and development projects, points to their strength.[55] Correspondingly, agriculture itself was becoming less a peasant society's linchpin than another in a series of businesses; the attractiveness of wage labor outside the village eliminated underemployment and forced farmers to raise wages and their own productivity.[56]

The autonomy of the Arab economy should not be overstated, industrialization in the Arab sector still being quite limited. Palestinian-owned businesses tended to be small, devoted to trade and commerce, subcontracting, crafts, and transportation.[57] Many of the enterprises continued to be wholly or partially dependent on Jewish industries, contractors, and employers. An Arab clothing industry, for example, emerged to supply a larger, Jewish-owned textile industry and its design houses.[58] Industries owned by Arabs tended to be in traditional sectors, such as textiles and food processing, while Jews owned the more sophisticated manufacturing concerns. State policies continued to encumber Arab economic activities much more than Jewish ones (although Jewish businessmen might have wondered how that was possible). State intervention assisted politically favored groups, which included Jews but not Arabs.[59] Nonetheless, lacking state investments or the advantages accruing to an area designated as an industrial zone, but finding informal, innovative ways to bypass state policies (the so-called black economy),[60] the Israeli Arab achievement by the 1980s was remarkable.

The economic vitality and the mobility in Israel after the June war helped make it possible. One researcher has pointed to approximately three hundred Arab families becoming big investors, with another two thousand moving up to the middle ranks.[61] Along with the intellectuals and professionals, whose numbers had risen to more than four thousand, these entrepreneurs comprised the most influential force in Israel's Arab society.

Such prosperity had a marked impact on less privileged Palestinians—most notably, on village women. Increasing numbers entered the labor force, corresponding to the growing demand for workers. In the town of Shafa Amr, 11 percent of the working age women did so by the 1980s.[62] But if there existed a dual labor market for Arabs and Jews, internally one emerged for Arab men and women: Because Arab economic growth was not accompanied by significant urbanization—the inhospitality of the larger society meant that Arabs continued to live in their villages—and cultural mores kept women much closer to home, they found themselves limited to the opportunities in their immediate localities. Nearly three-quarters of industrial workers in Arab industries were women, filling the lowest-status and lowest-paid positions. Now they were part of a rhythm in society reflecting wage labor rather than agriculture, but still cut off from the mobility and autonomy that could change their status. The new marriage system and labor opportunities may have translated into a slight relaxation of the difficult conditions wives traditionally had endured, chipping away at the husband's dominance; at the community level, however, women's positions did not noticeably improve.[63]

In general, the transformation of the Israeli Arab economy did not come without important problems. Arabs still had to deal with a wider society that frequently suspected their motives and discriminated against them; they had to participate in a political system continuing to prefer working through clan heads and failing to address some of their most pressing needs. Perhaps no problem better illustrates this reality than that of house construction. The Arab population in Israel rose from the 150,000 remnant after the 1948 war to more than three-quarters of a million by the end of the 1980s. At times the rate of natural increase soared to more than 4 percent per year, an almost unheard-of figure among demographers. For the decade of 1972–1982, the figure was 3.7 percent, translating into a rate that would double the population in less than twenty years. The pressure on housing grew correspondingly; nearly two out of five Arab households included seven or more people, and more than one-fifth held more than four people to a room. (The rates for Jews were 5 and 1 percent, respectively.)

Two other factors made the housing situation even more difficult: the lack of rapid urbanization to take pressure off the villages, and the fact that the new prosperity brought both the desire and ability to build more and larger homes (a source of great prestige in the society). But such construction was no simple matter since Israeli law demanded that it conform to a local municipality's master development plan, and Arab villages simply did not have the resources to undertake such projects. Construction on current agricultural lands, almost the only plots available in Arab villages, also demanded special permission from the Ministry of Agriculture. Village representatives frequently lacked the clout to gain the necessary waivers. And Israeli officials systematically denied Arab communities the resources—from building permits to official recognition as a city—to develop comprehensive town plans.

The result was an explosion of illegal construction in village after village, probably comprising 30 percent of all housing. Some of it came to be accepted de facto by Israeli authorities. The rest became the source of bitter controversy, leading to the bulldozing of new houses. At a protest against a housing demolition, reflecting a change from the political quiescence of previous decades, security forces killed one Arab and twelve others were injured.[64] A separate episode, the House Day general strike of 1988, also demonstrated that Arabs were increasingly seeing their grievances in national terms.

The housing crisis points to the development of a new politics among the Arabs in Israel. Within a decade after the 1967 war, a wave of political activism rolled over the community, rekindling some of the Jews' worst fears. The Arabs continued to find an effective independent political movement beyond their grasp, but their orientation within Israeli politics altered dramatically. The event making this clear came on March 30, 1976, in a violence-marred general strike. The National Committee for the Defense of Arab Lands—the first political organization claiming to represent the entire Israeli Palestinian population—called the strike and dubbed it Land Day. As in the past, the immediate issue was proposed expropriation of Arab-owned land by the state, announced by the government in February 1976. In the Galilee, where the expropriations were slated to occur, villagers clashed with army units, leading to six Arab deaths plus many injuries and arrests. For many Arabs, the events echoed those in Kafr Qasim, twenty years earlier. But the Arab community now demonstrated a sense of assurance and political awareness totally absent in 1956.

In some ways, the strike represented the coming of age of Rakah, the Communist Party, which had created the National Committee. Born in petty factional disputes leading to a communist split in 1965, the party emerged in the mid-1970s as the voice of Arab grievances. More than one-third of Arab votes in national elections were going to Rakah, and in the 1977 elections, when it was in coalition with a largely Jewish party (the Democratic Front for Peace and Equality), half the Arabs voted for its list. Before Land Day, it had succeeded in breaking the Labor Party's near stranglehold on elective offices in Arab municipalities by gaining the office of mayor of Nazareth, the sole Arab city at that time. Now the new mayor, Tawfiq Zayad, led the general strike, albeit with qualified success in terms of mass involvement. Rakah did come with baggage limiting its appeal: Many Arabs rejected its atheism, and some younger nationalists reacted against its calls for Jewish-Arab worker solidarity. Nonetheless, the party was the closest the Arabs came to a broad-based organization expressing many of their nationalist aspirations.

Other groups besides Rakah, also began to express nationalist sentiments. Arab university students and graduates formed the Arab Academic Union in Israel in 1971, which affirmed that the country's Arabs were part of the Palestinian people and Arab nation.[65] A movement called *Ibna al-Balad* (Sons of the Village) picked up momentum in the late 1970s, partly because it presented itself as an alternative to Rakah. Starting in 1974, Arab mayors came together in the Committee of the Heads of Arab Local Councils. Later this organization evolved into the Supreme Follow-Up Committee, which in effect became the recognized representative of the Palestinian community in Israel. It included leading political figures and cultural leaders along with the heads of the municipalities.

Precisely the sorts of Arab community integration that Israeli policy had long sought to prevent were now occurring. The Supreme Follow-up Committee, in particular, managed to emerge as a forum for overcoming the debilitating factionalism that had plagued the Arabs. Attempts by the authorities to stress the solidarity of Arab subdivisions foundered on an emerging sense of community, cutting across the old lines.[66]

Land Day, declared a national Israeli Palestinian festival in 1992 and acknowledged by annual demonstrations and a general strike, led to newfound respect for its participants among Palestinians in the West Bank and the Gaza Strip. The immediate reaction of Israeli authorities was one of alarm. In September 1976 a highly controversial document, called the Koenig Report, was leaked to the press. In it, Israel Koenig, who had been a highly placed official in the Interior Ministry, stated that the Arab majority in the western Galilee posed a threat to the state's security, and argued for settling Jews in the area, suppressing Arab political activity, and encouraging Arab emigration. But in the following years, the same disinterest that had existed earlier crept back into Israeli policy, punctuated periodically by a gesture of good will, an enticement to follow one party or another, or a clamping down on Arab political activity. With time, Israeli officials grew increasingly distracted by events on the West Bank and Gaza, especially after the outbreak of the Intifada in December 1987. Two weeks later, a general strike by Israel's Arabs in solidarity with the revolt raised concerns that it might spread to Israel proper. But those concerns also seemed lost to distraction once the strike was over.

Israel's Arabs were becoming more responsive to outside Palestinian political currents, the two most important being Palestinian nationalism, as expressed by the PLO, and a revived Islamic consciousness. For its part, the PLO leadership treated the Arabs of Israel with a studied indifference—as if, along with the Israeli government, they looked through them rather than at them—for the first two decades after it reorganized in 1968. The PLO would address them as a community only in the 1988 Israeli elections, when it suggested which choices would best serve the Palestinian national cause. While many Arabs in Israel lined up with those wings of the PLO supporting the creation of a Palestinian state alongside Israel, their feelings about the PLO as the spokesman for all Palestinians remained more obscure. Partly, the obscurity derived from Israeli restrictions on any form of contact with the organization. But it also certainly stemmed from authentic, continuing ambivalence at their own position—the one fragment of the Palestinian community not facing dispersal, and not really fitting into a national culture being reconstructed in exile, *ghurba.*

Like other Arabs, those in Israel were not left untouched by the Iranian Revolution of 1978. By the mid-1980s, Islam was clearly ascendant in the Muslim population, vying for a central role in the definition of the community. This became most obvious in the municipal elections of 1988, when Islamic political forces won majorities on a number of councils, including that in Umm al-Fahm, a former village that had grown so large it was accorded the legal status of a city, after a protracted political battle of its residents with Israeli officials. The Islamic movement was now the most important political rival to Rakah.

The roots of Islamic activism in Israel lay in a group of students who were involved in the Islamic revival on campuses in Nablus and Hebron during the 1970s. A charismatic figure, Abdallah Nimr Darwish, led an underground group, Usrat al-Jihad (the Family of Holy War), discovered by Israeli officials in 1981. Darwish and others were jailed for secreting arms. Upon their release, they turned to ground-level community welfare projects as a means of political organizing, much as other Islamic groups in Gaza and the West Bank were doing. Their influence spread, as they created community centers around mosques and self-help circles to combat drugs, prostitution, and alcohol. Groups of youngsters undertook sanitation and cleanup campaigns in local villages. In some ways, their mundane activities made the activities of Rakah—fighting for national equality and civil rights—seem somehow misplaced, because the communists now appeared removed from the everyday problems of the people.[67]

The shift of Islamic political leaders from clandestine activities to the provision of routine services was reflected in their orientation to Israel and the Jews. At first, their magazine *al-Sirat* (banned since 1990) was very militant, preaching for *jihad* and complete Islamization of the country. In time, their radical political slogans gave way to advocacy of "two states for two nations," their entry into the fray of Israeli elections seeming to moderate their stance at the very moment that Islamic groups on the West Bank and in the Gaza Strip were demonstrating increased militancy. Once again, Israel's Arabs seemed out of step with the activities of other Palestinians.

The Arab public in Israel at the turn of the 1990s was neither the subdued, traumatized group it had been four decades earlier nor the revolutionary force that many Jews had feared it would become. Its self-definition as a distinct and cohesive group, crystallizing with Land Day in 1976, stemmed from the political events of 1967, from the vast social and economic changes that they underwent afterward, and from the experience of living in Israel for more than forty years. Their identities were increasingly Palestinian (in surveys over two-thirds felt so) but in ways quite distinct from other segments of the people.[68]

The dissolution of the sealed frontiers to the West Bank and Gaza in June 1967 had ended two decades of isolation from other Arabs, offering access to both the basis for a re-created Palestinian identity advocated by Israel's Arab writers for several years—the symbols and longings in the refugee camps—and the resistance that would soon coalesce in the PLO.

At the same time, it highlighted major differences with other Palestinians. In a survey comparing their position in 1968 to that of their counterparts under Jordanian rule, Israel's Arabs found themselves with better economic and cultural conditions, higher morale, and more political freedom. Their only real envy was for the intensity of both religious observance and patriotism in the West Bank. Few of them seemed ready to trade their positions in the Jewish state for the lot of their brothers.[69] Other surveys showed a willingness to have Jews as friends, a reluctance, by a vast majority, to leave Israel, even if a Palestinian state were to come into being, and a dwindling number (less than 10 percent by 1980) denying Israel's right to exist as a state.[70] In general, they developed a sense of themselves as participating in a legitimate political entity.[71] And a substantially greater number reported feeling more at home in Israel than in Arab countries. Here is Smooha's summary of his survey:

> Israeli Arabs are a Palestinian national minority, destined to live permanently in the Jewish state. They avail themselves of Israeli democracy to wage a struggle for greater equality and integration. They are bilingual and bicultural, Israeli Palestinian in identity, and are in solidarity with the submerged Palestinian nation, but loyal to Israel. They support the PLO and a two-state solution to get their people settled and their own national aspirations fulfilled, but their fate and future are firmly linked to Israel.[72]

Once the uprising against Israeli rule broke out in the occupied territories in 1987, the ambivalence of Israel's Arabs became even more pronounced. To be sure, the Intifada unleashed strong feelings strengthening a sense of Palestinian identity and support for political Islamic movements.[73] A sense of sharing a common fate with Palestinians in the West Bank and Gaza became palpable.[74] At the same time, except for a slight increase in the number of individual hostile acts,[75] they did not join in the uprising directly. Even at the tensest moment in the midst of a clash with police during the general strike in December 1987 (named Peace Day), they were careful to draw a firm boundary between support for the Intifada—consisting for the most part of raising money for its

Arab victims—and their own participation in it, a caution that served to emphasize their separateness.[76]

In the difficult days of the Intifada, one prominent Arab summed up the tortured position of his community, a people relegated to marginality among both Palestinians and Israelis: "They will not manage to draw the Intifadeh into the Green Line [the armistice line after the 1948 war, which appeared on the maps in green]. There is a difference between players and fans. We are the fans. Our goal is to live in Israel with equal rights, while the aim of the residents in the West Bank is to form a separate state."[77] Only with renewed Israeli-Palestinian violence in 2000, as this book goes to press, have there been indications that Israeli Palestinians may indeed, after all, be drawn into the center of the conflict.

The Arabs of Israel made considerable gains in the country's strong economy and democratic political atmosphere. From a remnant of mostly fellaheen, shorn of leaders and institutions in 1948, they managed to rebuild a complex, stratified society, with a stable working class, a growing middle class of professionals and entrepreneurs, and its own talented cadre of intellectuals. As nearly one-fifth of Israeli society, the Arabs became more and more aware of themselves as a community and more articulate about their needs.

At the same time, they continued to suffer through personal and national humiliations. In 1990, the beatings of Arabs on the street after one terrorist attack or another sent shudders through their community. So, too, did the anti-Arab legislation proposed in the Knesset, although the laws were rarely passed. An example was an amendment to the Prevention of Terror ordinance of 1948, which would have allowed confiscation, without due process, of money from organizations receiving funds—knowingly or otherwise—from terrorist sources. Without defining the term *terrorist*, the amendment would have put many Arab social service agencies, which received financing from abroad, into serious jeopardy; one Jewish Knesset member argued that the amendment was "nothing but a tool for political persecution."[78]

Continued discrimination, both at the personal level and in official policy, contributed in the period after 1967 to what one Arab scholar has termed "an intensive process of re-Palestinization"[79]—a process led by the new Arab elite. Nevertheless, the central motifs and symbols that became the building blocks of the new Palestinism—longing for the homeland, the conception of the Lost Garden, even the glorification of a piece of land or an olive tree—could not evoke the same powerful feelings for the Arabs in Israel, living in their original villages, as for those in *ghurba*, including residents of the far-off refugee camps.

Even the poetry, now as much a part of Israeli as Palestinian life, could not be as evocative. When, for example, Fadwa Tuqan wrote

> How can I see my land, my rights usurped,
> And remain here, a wanderer, with my shame?
> Shall I live here and die in a foreign land?
> No! I will return to my beloved land.
> I will return, and there
>   will I close the book of my life.[80]

she could bring empathy but not visceral identification. Anton Shammas, the best known of Israel's Arab writers, wrote his best-selling novel *Arabesques* in eloquent Hebrew. In this autobiographical account recalling his childhood in the village of Fassuta, he indicates how closely the Arabs in Israel are wedded to the Jewish culture around them—how their Palestinism is laced with what we might call their Israelism:

> My Jew will be an educated Arab. But not an intellectual. He does not gallop on the back of a thoroughbred mare, as was the custom at the turn of the century, nor is he a prisoner of the IDF [the Israel Defense Forces], as was the custom at the turn of the state [of Israel]. . . . He speaks and writes excellent Hebrew, but within the bounds of the permissible. For there must be some areas that are out of bounds for him, so nobody will accuse me of producing the stereotype in reverse, the virtuous Arab. He might be permitted the *Kaddish* [the Jewish prayer of mourning], as it were, but not the *Kol Nidre* [the Yom Kippur prayer]. And so on and so forth. A real minefield.[81]

The pain of this ambivalence emerges as yet another echo of the myth of Scylla and Charybdis. Twenty years before Shammas, another Palestinian in Israel noted, "I sometimes think that we are neither real Arabs nor real Israelis, because in the Arab countries they call us traitors, and in Israel, spies."[82] More recently, this refrain has been articulated by a teacher: "When I educate my pupils toward loyalty to the State I am considered a traitor . . . and when I emphasize the national character of my pupils and try to nurture in them a sense of national pride, I am told I am a traitor."[83] Such a mutual ill fit has relegated the Arabs of Israel to the sidelines in the nearly half century after al-Nakba. The central task of national reconstruction has fallen to those remaining outside Israel—both in Arab Palestine and in the new Palestinian communities beyond the borders of the old British Mandate.

NOTES

CHAPTER 1. MYTHS AND MODELS

1. Joel S. Migdal, *Strong Societies and Weak States: State-Society Relations and State Capabilities in the Third World* (Princeton, N.J.: Princeton University Press, 1988); Joel S. Migdal, Atul Kohli, and Vivienne Shue, *State Power and Social Forces: Domination and Transformation in the Third World* (Cambridge: Cambridge University Press, 1994); and *State-in-Society: Studying How States and Societies Transform and Constitute One Another* (New York: Cambridge University Press, forthcoming).

2. James C. Scott, *Weapons of the Weak: Everyday Forms of Peasant Resistance* (New Haven: Yale University Press, 1985).

3. James C. Scott, *Domination and the Arts of Resistance: Hidden Transcripts* (New Haven: Yale University Press, 1990); Forrest Colburn, *Everyday Forms of Peasant Resistance* (New York: M.E. Sharpe, 1989).

4. On the challenges Israeli democracy faces, especially in light of the institutional inertia of the state, see Ehud Sprinzak and Larry Diamond, eds., *Israeli Democracy under Stress* (Boulder: Lynne Rienner, 1993).

5. For a related argument on the effect of the idea of the state as distinct from the rest of society, see Timothy Mitchell, "The Limits of the State: Beyond Statist Approaches and Their Critics," *American Political Science Review* 85(March 1991): 95.

6. One important exception is Charles Tilly, *Coercion, Capital, and European States, AD 990–1990* (Cambridge, Mass.: B. Blackwell, 1990).

7. Baruch Kimmerling, *Zionism and Territory: The Socio-Territorial Dimensions of Zionist Politics* (Berkeley: Institute of International Studies, University of California, 1983); Adriana Kemp, "'Talking Boundaries': The Making of Political Territory in Israel's First Years" (Ph.D. dissertation, Tel-Aviv University, 1997); Ian Lustick, *Unsettled States, Disputed Lands: Britain and Ireland, France and Algeria, Israel and the West Bank-Gaza* (Ithaca: Cornell University Press, 1993).

8. Asher Arian, *The Choosing People: Voting Behavior in Israel* (Cleveland: Press of Case Western Reserve University, 1973); Michal Shamir, "Political Intolerance Among Masses and Elites in Israel: A Reevalutation," *The Journal of Politics* 53, no. 4 (Nov. 1991): 1018–1044; Yohanan Peres, "Modernization and Nationalism in the Identity of the Israeli Arab," *Middle East Journal* 24 (Autumn 1970): 479–492; Asher Arian and Michal Shamir, "Collective Identity and Electoral Competition in Israel," *American Political Science Review* 92, 2 (June 1999): 265–278.

9. See, for example, Talcott Parsons, "The Political Aspect of Social Structure and Process," in David Easton, ed., *Varieties of Political Theory* (Englewood Cliffs, N.J.: Prentice-Hall, 1966); Talcott Parsons, *Societies: Evolutionary and Comparative Perspectives* (Englewood Cliffs, N.J.: Prentice-Hall, 1966); and Edward Shils, *Center and Periphery: Essays in Macrosociology* (Chicago: Chicago University Press, 1975); also his book with Parsons, *Toward a General Theory of Action* (Cambridge: Harvard University Press, 1951).

10. Talcott Parsons, *Societies: Evolutionary and Comparative Perspectives*, 10.

11. The words in the quotation are from Yoav Peled and Gershon Shafir, "The Roots of Peacemaking: The Dynamics of Citizenship in Israel, 1948–93," *International Journal of Middle East Studies* 28, no. 3 (August 1996): 394. Their critique is of what they call the dominant paradigm in the sociology of Israeli society. It focuses particularly on Eisentadt's colleagues, Dan Horowitz and Moshe Lissak, *Trouble in Utopia: The Overburdened Polity of Israel* (Albany: State University of New York Press, 1989).

12. S. N. Eisenstadt, *Israeli Society* (New York: Basic Books, 1967), 409.

13. Dan Horowitz and Moshe Lissak, *Origins of the Israeli Polity: Palestine under the Mandate* (Chicago: The University of Chicago Press, 1978), 10.

14. Max Gluckman, *Politics, Law, and Ritual in Tribal Society* (Oxford: Basil Blackwell, 1965), 23.

15. Max Gluckman, "Foreword," in Shlomo A. Deshen, *Immigrant Voters in Israel: Parties and Congregations in a Local Election Campaign* (Manchester: Manchester University Press, 1970), xix. Gluckman makes a similar point in his Foreword to the book of another of his students, Moshe Shokeid, *The Dual Heritage: Immigrants from the Atlas Mountains in an Israeli Village* (Manchester: Manchester University Press, 1971).

16. Gluckman in *Immigrant Voters in Israel*, xxvi.

17. Yonathan Shapiro, *The Formative Years of the Israeli Labour Party* (Beverly Hills: Sage, 1976).

18. Peter Evans, Theda Skocpol, and Dietrich Reuschemeyer, eds., *Bringing the State Back In* (New York: Cambridge University Press, 1985).

19. Shapiro, *The Formative Years of the Israeli Labour Party*.

20. Lev Luis Grinberg, "The Crisis of Statehood: A Weak State and Strong Political Institutions in Israel," *Journal of Theoretical Politics* 5(Jan. 1993): 95. Grinberg, as his title indicates, did not accept the view of Israel as a strong state fully. He points to the strength of political organizations, what he calls the Israeli Labor Institutional Complex, as forces that kept the state weak.

21. Shapiro, *The Formative Years of the Israeli Labour Party*.

22. On the historiographical battles, see Efraim Karsh, *In Search of Identity: Jewish Aspects in Israeli Culture* (London: Frank Cass, 1999); Benny Morris, "The New Historiography: Israel Confronts Its Past," *Tikkun* 4 (Nov/Dec 1988): 19–102; and his book *Righteous Victims: A History of the Zionist-Arab Conflict, 1881–1999* (New York: Knopf, 1999); Shabtai Teveth, *Ben-Gurion: The Burning Ground, 1886–1948* (Boston: Houghton Mifflin, 1987); Laurence J. Silberstein, *The PostZionism Debates: Knowledge and Power in Israeli Culture* (New York: Routledge, 1999). For a fascinating account of the convergence

of national myth and academic research in the state's early years, see Michael Keren, *Ben Gurion and the Intellectuals: Power, Knowledge, Charisma* (Dekallo: Northern University Press, 1983).

23. Michael Shalev, *Labour and the Political Economy in Israel* (New York Oxford University Press, 1992), 13. Shalev amplified his criticism in "Time for Theory: Critical Notes on Lissak and Sternhell," *Israel Studies* 1(Fall 1966): 170–188.

24. One recent attempt to revive the center-oriented approach for the study of Israel dropped the assumption of integration and replaced it with an ongoing "political struggle for the center." This change deals with some of the difficulties of the approach but still fails to deal with the point below, the special role of the state in processes of domination and change. Pierre M. Atlas, "The Struggle for the Center in Political Culture: A Cognitive-Institutionalist Examination of the Origins of the Israeli Mainstream and Fringe, 1905–1949" (Rutgers, The State University of New Jersey Ph.D. dissertation, 2000).

25. Joel Beinin, *Was the Red Flag Flying There? Marxist Politics and the Arab-Israeli Conflict in Egypt and Israel, 1948–1965* (Berkeley: University of California Press, 1990); Avi Shlaim, *The Iron Wall: Israel and the Arab World* (New York: W.W. Norton, 2000).

26. Aharon Klieman, *Israel and the World After 40 Years* (Washingon : Pergamon-Brassey's International Defense Publishers, 1990); Michael Barnett, *Confronting the Costs of War: Military Power, State and Society in Egypt and Israel* (Princeton: Princeton University Press, 1992); and *Dialogues in Arab Politics: Negotiations in Regional Order* (New York: Columbia University Press, 1998).

27. Teveth, *Ben-Gurion.*

28. For example, see the gloves-off debate in the pages of the journal *Israel Studies.* Moshe Lissak, "'Critical' Sociology and 'Establishment' Sociology in the Israeli Academic Community," *Israel Studies* 1(Spring 1996): 247–294; Michael Shalev, "Time for Theory": 170–188; and Gershon Shafir, "Israeli Society: A Counterview," Israel Studies 1(Fall 1996), 189–213.

29. This diversity is elaborated in Uri Ram, *The Changing Agenda of Israeli Sociology: Theory, Ideology, and Identity* (Albany: State University of New York Press, 1995).

30. Shalev, *Labour and the Political Economy in Israel,* 53.

31. Lissak, "'Critical' Sociology and 'Establishment' Sociology in the Israeli Academic Community."

32. Uri Ben-Eliezer, *The Making of Israel Militarism* (Bloomington: Indiana University Press, 1998) [Hebrew Edition: *The Emergence of Israel Militarism, 1936–1956* (Tel Aviv, Israel: Dvir Publishing House, 1995)].

33. See Baruch Kimmerling, "State Building, State Autonomy, and the Identity of Society: The Case of the Israeli State," *Journal of Historical Society* 6 (1993): 397–429; "Sovereignty, Ownership, and 'Presence' in the Jewish-Arab Territorial Conflict: The Case of Bir'm and Ikrit," *Comparative Political Studies* 19 (1977): 155–176; "On the Knowledge of the Place," *Alpayim* 6 (1992) (Hebrew); "Conclusions," in Kimmerling, ed., *The Israeli State and Society: Boundaries and Frontiers* (Albany: State University of New York Press, 1989).

34. Gershon Shafir, *Land, Labor, and the Origins of the Israeli-Palestinian Conflict* (Cambridge: Cambridge University Press, 1989); and Gad Barzilai, *Wars, Internal Conflicts, and Political Order: A Jewish Democracy in the Middle East* (Albany: State University of New York Press, 1996).

35. Efraim Ben-Zadok, ed., *Local Communities and the Israeli Polity: Conflict of Values and Interests* (Albany: State University of New York Press, 1993).

36. Yael Yishai, *Land of Paradoxes: Interest Politics in Israel* (Albany: State University of New York Press, 1991); and Gadi Wolfsfeld, *The Politics of Provocation: Participation and Protest in Israel* (Albany: State University of New York Press, 1988); also see Sam N. Lehman-Wilzig, *Wildfire: Grassroots Revolts in Israel in the Post-Socialist Era* (Albany: State University of New York Press, 1992).

37. See, for example, Abraham Doron and Ralph M. Kramer, *The Welfare State in Israel: The Evolution of Social Security Policy and Practice* (Tel Aviv: Am Oved, 1992) (Hebrew).

38. On the theoretical significance of "becoming," see the interview with Norbert Elias in Johan Goudsblom and Stephen Mennell, eds., *The Norbert Elias Reader* (Oxford: Blackwell, 1998), 143.

39. See, for example, Mitchell, "The Limits of the State."

40. Baruch Kimmerling, ed., *Boundaries of the Israeli System* (Albany: State University of New York Press, 1988); Michael Barnett, ed., *Israel in Comparative Perspective: Challenging the Conventional Wisdom* (Albany: State University of New York Press, 1996).

41. Tobe Shanok, "The Yishuv's Early Capabilities: Organization, Leadership, and Policies" in Laura Zitrain Eisenberg and Neil Caplan, eds., *Review Essays in Israel Studies, Books on Israel, Vol. V* (Albany: State University of New York Press, 2000), 40, makes the good point that not putting Israel into a comparative framework makes its history seem miraculous.

42. Shabtai Beit-Zvi, *Post-Ugandian Zionism in the Crucible of the Holocaust* (Tel-Aviv: Bronfman Publishers 1977) (Hebrew).

43. Kenneth Lawson, "War at the Grassroots: The Great War and the Nationalization of Civic Life," Ph.D. dissertation (University of Washington, 2000), 61.

44. Lawson, "War at the Grassroots," 62.

45. Grinberg, "The Crisis of Statehood."

46. Ben Smith, personal communication, October 13, 1999.

47. See Sam N. Lehman-Wilzig, *Stiff-Necked People, Bottle-Necked System.*

48. Baruch Kimmerling and Joel S. Migdal, *Palestinians: The Making of a People* (New York: The Free Press, 1993).

CHAPTER 2. THE CRYSTALLIZATION OF THE STATE AND THE STRUGGLES OVER RULE MAKING

1. Kenneth H. F. Dyson, *The State in Western Europe: A Study of an Idea and Institution* (Oxford: Martin Robinson, 1980).

2. Bertrand Badie and Pierre Birnbaum, *The Sociology of the State* (Chicago: University of Chicago Press, 1983).

3. Baruch Kimmerling, *Zionism and Territory.*

4. Dan Horowitz, "Dual Authority Polities," *Comparative Politics* 14 (1982): 329–349.

5. Badie and Birnbaum, 35.

6. Barrington Moore Jr., *Social Origins of Dictatorship and Democracy: Lord and Peasant in the Making of the Modern World* (Boston: Beacon Press, 1966).

7. J. P. Nettl, "The State as a Conceptual Variable," *World Politics* 20 (1968): 559–592.

8. Joseph R. Strayer, *On the Medieval Origins of the Modern State* (Princeton: Princeton University Press, 1970); Charles Tilly, *The Formation of National States in Western Europe* (Princeton: Princeton University Press, 1975); Gianfranco Poggi, *The Development of the Modern State: A Sociological Introduction* (Stanford, Cal.: Stanford University Press, 1978); Raymond Grew, *Crises of Political Development in Europe and the United States* (Princeton: Princeton University Press, 1978).

9. Immanuel Wallerstein, *The Modern World System: Capitalist Agriculture and the Origins of the European World-Economy in the Sixteenth Century* (New York: Academic Press, 1974).

10. Charles S. Liebman and Don-Yehiya Eliezer, *Civil Religion in Israel: Traditional Judaism and Political Culture in the Jewish State* (Berkeley: University of California Press, 1983), 23.

11. Bernard Wasserstein, *The British in Palestine: The Mandatory Government and the Arab-Jewish Conflict 1917–1929* (London: Royal Historical Society, 1978), 87.

12. Joel S. Migdal, *Palestinian Society and Politics* (Princeton: Princeton University Press, 1980).

13. Yonathan Shapiro. *The Formative Years of the Israeli Labour Party*, 79.

14. Ibid., 79.

15. David Ben-Gurion, *From Class to Nation* (Tel-Aviv: Am Oved, 1974) (Hebrew).

16. S. Zalman Abramov, *Perpetual Dilemma: Jewish Religion in the Jewish State* (Rutherford, N.J.: Fairleigh Dickinson University Press, 1976), 115.

17. Dan Horowitz, "The Yishuv and Israeli Society: Continuity and Change," *State, Government and International Relations* 21 (1983): 46.

18. Shapiro *The Formative Years of the Israeli Labour Party*, 56.

19. Richard Kraus and Reeve D. Vanneman. "Bureaucrats versus the State in Capitalist and Socialist Regimes," *Comparative Studies in Society and History* 27 (1985): 111–122.

20. Shapiro, *The Formative Years of the Israeli Labour Party*.

21. Ibid., 182–184.

22. Ira Sharkansky, *What Makes Israel Tick?: How Domestic Policy-Makers Cope with Constraints* (Chicago: Nelson-Hall, 1985).

CHAPTER 3. LAYING THE BASIS FOR A STRONG STATE

1. Dietmar Rothermund, "The Legacy of the British-Indian Empire in Independent India," in Wolfgang J. Mommsen and Jürgen Osterhammel, eds.,

Imperialism and After: Continuities and Discontinuities (London: Allen and Unwin, 1986), 141.

2. See, for example, Akhil Gupta, "Technology, Power, and the State in a Complex Agricultural Society: The Green Revolution in a North Indian Village." (Ph.D. diss., Stanford University, 1987).

3. David Vital, *The Origins of Zionism* (Oxford: Clarendon Press, 1975), 89.

4. Quoted in ibid., 90.

5. Theodor Herzl, *The Jewish State* (New York: Herzl Press, 1970), 110.

6. On the general methodological issue, see Arend Lijphart, "Comparative Politics and the Comparative Method," *American Political Science Review* 65 (September 1971): 682–693; on the specific case, see Dan Horowitz, "The Yishuv and Israel Society—Continuity and Change," 31–67 (text in Hebrew; title translated).

7. Ibid., 46 (my translation).

8. Migdal, *Palestinian Society and Politics.*

9. For the events leading up to the Balfour Declaration and the immediate reaction to it, see Leonard Stein, *The Balfour Declaration* (London: Vallentine, Mitchell, 1961). On British motivations in issuing the declaration, see Esco Foundation for Palestine, *Palestine*, vol. 1 (New Haven: Yale University Press, 1947), 114–118. Also, see Ronald Sanders, *The High Walls of Jerusalem: A History of the Balfour Declaration and the Birth of the British Mandate for Palestine* (New York: Holt, Rinehart and Winston, 1983).

10. Max Beloff, "Britain's Liberal Empire 1897–1921," vol. 1 in *Imperial Sunset* (London: Methuen, 1969).

11. Zionist leader Chaim Weizmann presented the idea of an agency to the Council of Ten at Paris during the peace conference in 1919. He spoke of a Jewish council or agency—representative of Jewish Palestine and world Jewry. His ideas echoed other Zionist proposals asking for a maximum degree of self-government for the Jews. See *Palestine*, vol. 1, pp. 156–164.

12. Aaron S. Klieman, *Foundations of British Policy in the Arab World* (Baltimore: Johns Hopkins University Press, 1970), 25. One British document, written during the Mandatory period, described the strategic value as follows: "Palestine is the bridge connecting Africa and Asia, part of the only practicable corridor between the Nile and the Euphrates. It is in a similar position to the Suez Canal on the one side as is Egypt on the other, for it affords the possibility of defence against land attack on the Canal from the North." Royal Institute of International Affairs, *Political and Strategic Interests of the United Kingdom* (London: Oxford University Press, 1939), 142.

13. Quoted in Elizabeth Monroe, *Britain's Moment in the Middle East 1914–1956* (London: Chatto and Windus, 1963), 79. Balfour himself, nonetheless, never relinquished his belief in the Jewish national homeland.

14. See Norman Bentwich, *England in Palestine* (London: Kegan Paul, 1932), 82. Bentwich, a Zionist sympathizer, was British attorney general of Palestine in the 1920s.

15. See Michael J. Cohen, *Palestine: Retreat from the Mandate* (New York: Holmes and Meier, 1978).

16. Bernard Wasserstein, *The British in Palestine*, 16.

17. Ibid., 87.

18. Joel S. Migdal, "Urbanization and Political Change: The Impact of Foreign Rule," *Comparative Studies in Society and History* 19 (July 1977): 328–349.

19. What I call in shorthand the Ben-Gurion strategy was the product, in fact, of a number of outstanding labor Zionist leaders in the Yishuv, including Yitzhak Ben-Zvi, Berl Katznelson, and Chaim Arlosoroff.

20. Wasserstein, *The British in Palestine*, 24.

21. Chaim Weizmann, *Trial and Error* (London: Hamish Hamilton, 1949), 407.

22. Yonathan Shapiro, *The Formative Years of the Israeli Labour Party*, 74.

23. Peter Y. Medding, *Mapai in Israel* (Cambridge: Cambridge University Press, 1972), 9.

24. See Dan Horowitz and Moshe Lissak, *Origins of the Israeli Polity*, 42ff.

25. Shapiro, *The Formative Years of the Israeli Labour Party*, 18.

26. Howard M. Sachar, *A History of Israel: From the Rise of Zionism to Our Time* (New York: Alfred A. Knopf, 1976), 159.

27. Quoted in Wasserstein, *The British in Palestine*, 134.

28. Shapiro, *The Formative Years of the Israeli Labour Party*, 72.

29. Ibid., 78–79.

30. Quoted in ibid., 79.

31. Ibid., 37.

32. See Ben-Gurion, *From Class to Nation*.

33. Shapiro, *The Formative Years of the Israeli Labour Party*, 233. The newfound position of the labor leaders was threatened in 1927 when an efficiency-minded executive under British Zionist Harry Zacher took a much more aggressive supervisory stance. By 1929, the laborers had established their preeminence.

34. Kimmerling, *Zionism and Territory*.

35. J. C. Hurewitz, *The Struggle for Palestine* (New York: Schocken Books, 1976), 41.

36. Medding, *Mapai in Israel*, 10.

37. Weizmann, *Trial and Error*, 42.

38. Ibid., 418–419.

39. Aaron S. Klieman, "The Divisiveness of Palestine: Foreign Office versus Colonial Office on the Issue of Partition, 1937," *The Historical Journal* 22, no. 2 (1979): 425.

40. Quoted in Cohen, *Palestine*, 15.

41. Quoted in ibid.

42. Quoted in ibid., 15–16.

43. Klieman, "The Divisiveness of Palestine," 438.

44. See, for example, Kenneth W. Stein, *The Land Question in Palestine, 1917–1939* (Chapel Hill: University of North Carolina Press, 1984).

45. Horowitz and Lissak, *Origins of the Israeli Polity*, 45.

46. Ibid., 42–43.

47. Shapiro, *The Formative Years of the Israeli Labour Party*, 31.

48. Migdal, *Palestinian Society and Politics*, ch. 2.

49. See Ian Lustick, *Arabs in the Jewish State: Israel's Control of a National Minority* (Austin: University of Texas Press, 1980).

50. Asher Arian, *Politics in Israel: The Second Generation* (Chatham, N.J.: Chatham House, 1985), 226–232.

51. See Sharkansky, *What Makes Israel Tick?*

52. For Arabs, firm control has been maintained but without reaching the level of high legitimacy and without personal identification as Israelis outweighing other identities. See Migdal, *Palestinian Society and Politics*; and Lustick, *Arabs in the Jewish State*. On identity of Jewish Israelis, see Uri Farago, "Stability and Change in the Jewish Identity of School-Age Youths in Israel (1965–1974)." (Paper distributed by Levi Eshkol Research Institute for Economics, Society and Policy in Israel, Hebrew University, 1977).

CHAPTER 4. VISION AND PRACTICE

1. R. A. Nisbet, *History of the Idea of Progress* (New York: Basic Books, 1980).

2. Gianfranco Poggi, *The Development of the Modern State*, 102.

3. J. P. Nettl, "The State as a Conceptual Variable": 559–592.

4. A. C. Lamborn, "Power and the Politics of Extraction," *International Studies Quarterly* 27 (1983), 126.

5. R. Mousnier, "The Fonde," in R. Foster and J. P. Greene, eds., *Precondition of Revolution in Early Modern Europe* (Baltimore: Johns Hopkins University Press, 1970), 132–133.

6. C. Richelieu, "Political Testament," in T. K. Rabb, ed., *The Thirty Years' War: Problems of Motive, Extent, and Effect* (Boston: D.C. Heath, 1964), 79.

7. V. Azarya and N. Chazan. "Diengagement from the State in Africa: Reflections on the Experience on Ghana and Guinea," *Comparative Studies in Society and History* 29 (1987): 106–161.

8. C. W. Reynolds, *The Mexican Economy* (New Haven: Yale University Press, 1970).

9. Raymond Vernon, *The Dilemma of Mexico's Development: The Roles of the Private and Public Sectors* (Cambridge: Harvard University Presss, 1965), 59.

10. N. Hamilton, *The Limits of State Autonomy: Post-Revolutionary Mexico* (Princeton: Princeton University Press, 1982), 100.

11. See Vernon, *The Dilemma of Mexico's Development*, 72 and Hamilton, *The Limits of State Autonomy*, 141.

12. R. D. Hansen, *The Politics of Mexican Development* (Baltimore: Johns Hopkins University Press, 1971), 32.

13. Hamilton, *The Limits of State Autonomy*, 178.

14. Migdal, *Strong Societies and Weak States: State-Society Relations and State Capabilities in the Third World*.

15. P. Friedrich, "The Legitimacy of a Cacique," in S. Schmidt, L. Guasti,

C. Lande, and J. C. Scott, eds., *Friends, Followers and Factions: A Reader in Political Clientelism* (Berkeley: University of California Press, 1977).

16. M. S. Grindle, *Bureaucrats, Politicians, and Peasants in Mexico: A Case Study in Public Policy* (Berkeley: University of California Press, 1977), 129.

17. Hamilton, *The Limits of State Autonomy.*

18. G. A. Nasser, *Egypt's Liberation: The Philosophy of Revolution* (Washington, D.C.: Public Affairs Press, 1955).

19. J. Waterbury, *The Egypt of Nasser and Sadat: The Political Economy of Two Regimes* (Princeton: Princeton University Press, 1983), 266–267.

20. M. Abdel-Fadil, *Development, Income Distribution, and Social Change in Rural Egypt 1952–1970: A Study in the Political Economy of Agrarian Transition* (Cambridge: Cambridge University Press, 1975).

21. R. H. Adams Jr., "Growth Without Development in Rural Egypt: A Local-Level Study of Insitutional and Social Change," *Mimeo* (1981): 124–125.

22. See R. W. Baker, *Egypt's Uncertain Revolution under Nasser and Sadat* (Cambridge: Harvard University Press, 1978), 205 and L. Binder, *In a Moment of Enthusiasm: Political Power and the Second Stratum in Egypt* (Chicago: University of Chicago Press, 1978), 7.

23. A. Marwick, *War and Social Change in the Twentieth Century: A Comparative Study of Britain, France, Germany, Russia, and the United States* (London: Macmillan, 1974), 25.

24. P. J. Vatikiotis, *The History of Egypt.* Second ed. (Baltimore: Johns Hopkins University Press, 1980), 406.

25. David Ben-Gurion, and I. Ben-Zvi. *Eretz Israel in the Past and in the Present* (Jerusalem: Yad Izhak Ben Zvi, 1975), 25 [Hebrew].

26. Baruch Kimmerling, *Zionism and Territory.*

27. Peter Y. Medding, *Mapai in Israel,* 9.

28. Howard M. Sachar, *A History of Israel,* 159.

29. Shapiro, *The Formative Years of the Israeli Labour Party,* 78–79.

CHAPTER 5. CIVIL SOCIETY IN ISRAEL

1. This point, indeed, has been a truism in political science. See, for example, Gabriel A. Almond and Sidney Verba, *The Civic Culture* (Princeton: Princeton University Press, 1963).

2. Bendix et al. note that "the independence of private associations is a synonym for civil society" and that for civil society to exist a "consensus" is required between state and society. "Reflections on Modern Western States and Civil Societies," *Research in Political Sociology* 3 (1987): 14–15.

3. Hegel put forth the notion of civil society as one that emerges from the interdependence of individuals, their conflicts and their needs for cooperation. Those needs give rise to the state, and it is the law, the principle of rightness, that links civil society to the state. G. W. F. Hegel, *Philosophy of Right* (Oxford: The Clarendon Press, 1942), 122–123 and 134–135. Marx reacted to Hegel's conception, arguing that the state is merely the mechanism to defend privileged propertied interests in civil society. He understood civil society in a material

sense, the expression of particular property rights. Gramsci noted that besides the educative agencies of the state helping maintain hegemony, there are, "in reality, a multitude of other so-called private initiatives and activities [that] tend to the same end—initiatives and activities that form the apparatus of the political and cultural hegemony of the ruling classes." This, for Gramsci, is civil society. Antonio Gramsci, *Selections from the Prison Notebooks* (New York: International Publishers, 1971), 258. Stepan wrote, "Following Gramsci, we stress that an important requirement for hegemony is a rough congruence between the dominant values of civil society and those of political society." Alfred Stepan, *The State and Society: Peru in Comparative Perspective* (Princeton: Princeton University Press, 1978), 97. Whereas Hegel believed that society created the demand for the state, others, including Stepan, have argued that the state can create civil society. Otto Hintze alluded to this mutuality of the state and civil society and the role of the state in creating its own civil society, using the term *nationalities* instead of civil society: "The European peoples have only gradually developed their nationalities; they are not a simple product of nature but are themselves a product of the creation of states." Otto Hintze, "The Formation of States and Constitutional Development: A Study in History and Politics," in *The Historical Essays of Otto Hintze*, ed. Felix Gilbert (New York: Oxford University Press, 1975), 161.

4. See, for example, Andrew Arato, "Empire vs. Civil Society: Poland 1981–82," *Telos* 14, no. 50 (1981–1982): 19–48. For a critique, see Zbigniew Rau, "Some Thoughts on Civil Society in Eastern Europe and the Lockean Contractarian Approach," *Political Studies*, 3.

5. Gadi Wolfsfeld, *The Politics of Provocation: Participation and Protest in Israel*.

6. See, for example, Asher Arian, *Consensus in Israel* (New York: General Learning Press, 1971); E. Etzioni-Halevy, *Political Culture in Israel* (New York: Praeger, 1977); and Itzhak Galnoor, *Steering the Polity: Political Communication in Israel* (Beverly Hills: Sage, 1982).

7. Brenda Danet, *Pulling Strings: Biculturalism in Israeli Bureaucracy* (Albany: State University of New York Press, 1989), 14.

8. Wolfsfeld, *The Politics of Provocation*, 15.

9. Marcia Drezon-Tepler, *Interest Groups and Political Change in Israel* (Albany: State University of New York Press, 1990), 1.

10. Yael Yishai, *Land of Paradoxes: Interest Politics in Israel*, 81.

11. Baruch Kimmerling, "Between the Primordial and the Civil Definitions of the Collective Identity: Eretz Israel or the State of Israel?" in Erik Cohen, Moshe Lissak, and Uri Almagor, eds., *Comparative Social Dynamics: Essays in Honor of S. N. Eisenstadt* (Boulder: Westview Press, 1985), 262–283.

12. Yael Yishai, personal correspondence, March 8, 1992.

13. See Walter Gelhorn, *Ombudsmen and Others* (Cambridge: Harvard University Press, 1966), as well as his *When Americans Complain* (Cambridge: Harvard University Press, 1966), and the volumes of the International Ombudsman Institute, *Ombudsman and Other Complaint-Handling Systems Survey* (Edmonton, Alberta, Law Center, University of Alberta).

14. Danet, *Pulling Strings*, 1.

15. This is the subject of Danet's excellent book *Pulling Strings*.

16. See Kimmerling, "Between the Primordial and the Civil Definitions of the Collective Identity."

17. Wolfsfeld, *The Politics of Provocation*, 17.

18. Ibid., 19.

19. Drezon-Tepler, *Interest Groups*, 47ff.

20. Yishai, *Land of Paradoxes*, 69.

21. Ibid., 335.

22. Ibid., 335–336. Bendix et al. do note that "civil society comprises only a segment of the population." Those not in civil society tend to be marginal sorts—those abandoned by their parents, homeless people who do not participate in the market, illegal immigrants, etc. "Reflections on Modern Western States and Civil Societies," 23.

23. Uri Ben-Eliezer, "Testing for Democracy in Israel," in Ian S. Lustick and Barry Rubin, eds., *Critical Essays on Israeli Society, Politics, and Culture, Books on Israel*, vol. 2, (Albany: State University of New York Press, 1991), 77.

24. Charles Liebman and Eliezer Don-Yehiya, *Civil Religion in Israel*.

25. Wolfsfeld, *The Politics of Provocation*, 14.

26. Uri Ben-Eliezer, "The Meaning of Political Participation in a Non-Liberal Democracy: The Example of Israel" (mimeo), 28, 19.

CHAPTER 6. SOCIETY FORMATION AND THE CASE OF ISRAEL

1. (Princeton: Princeton University Press, 1988).

2. Louis Hartz, *The Founding of New Societies* (New York: Harcourt Brace, 1964) and *The Liberal Tradition in America* (New York: Harcourt Brace, 1955).

3. Liah Greenfeld and Michel Martin, eds., *Center: Ideas and Institutions* (Chicago: The University of Chicago Press, 1988), viii.

4. Benedict Anderson, *Imagined Communities: Reflections on the Origin and Spread of Nationalism* (New York: Verso, 1991), 36.

5. On this blurring of the distinction between state and society through use of the term nation, we can note Michael Mann's statement made in a different context. "The theories," he noted, "are reductionist, reducing the state to pre-existent aspects of civil society. . . . They deny that the state possesses emergent properties of its own." Michael Mann, *The Sources of Social Power*, Vol. I., *A History of Power from the Beginning to* A.D. *1760* (New York: Cambridge University Press, 1986), 50.

6. As Anthony D. Smith noted, "The rise to prominence of some Third World states which clearly cannot be termed 'nations', countries like Nigeria, India and Indonesia, has undermined the near-universality of the modern belief in the 'naturalness' of nations." *The Ethnic Origins of Nations* (London: Basil Blackwell, 1986), 7–8.

7. Anderson, *Imagined Communities*, 4. Also, see John Breuilly, *Nationalism and the State* (Manchester: Manchester University Press, 1982), ch. 1.

8. Eugen Weber, *Peasants into Frenchmen: The Modernization of Rural France 1870–1914* (Stanford: Stanford University Press, 1976).

9. One observer noted, "Even in the West, the much-sought marriage of state and ethnie has not turned out to be all that happy and enduring." Anthony D. Smith, "State-Making and Nation-Building" in John A. Hall, ed., *States in History* (London: Basil Blackwell, 1986), 230.

10. Clifford Geertz, ed., *Old Societies and New States: The Quest for Modernity in Asia and Africa* (New York: The Free Press, 1963), vi.

11. Ibid., p.v.

12. Edward Shils, "On the Comparative Study of the New States" in Geertz, ed., *Old Societies and New States*, 2–3.

13. Joel S. Migdal, "The State in Society: An Approach to Struggles for Domination," in Migdal, Kohli, and Shue, eds., *State Power and Social Forces*.

14. On previous society-centered theories, see Theda Skocpol, "Bringing the State Back In: Strategies of Analysis in Current Research," in Evans, Rueschemeyer, and Skocpol, eds., *Bringing the State Back In*, 4.

15. Geertz, "The Integrative Revolution: Primordial Sentiments and Civil Politics in the New States" in Geertz, ed., *Old Societies and New States*, 108.

16. Ibid., 109.

17. Kimmerling, "Between the Primordial and the Civil Definitions of the Collective Identity, 262–283.

18. Also, see Liah Greenfeld, *Nationalism: Five Roads to Modernity* (Cambridge: Harvard University Press, 1992), 8–14.

19. Ernest Gellner, *Thought and Change* (Chicago: The University of Chicago Press, 1964), 156.

20. David Held, *Political Theory and the Modern State: Essays on State, Power, and Democracy* (Stanford: Stanford University Press, 1989), 6.

21. Horowitz and Lissak, *Origins of the Israeli Polity*, 33.

22. Ibid., 42–44.

23. Kimmerling and Migdal, *Palestinians*, 79.

24. Musa Kazim al-Husayni, cited in Yehoshua Porath, *The Emergence of the Palestinian-Arab National Movement, 1918–1929* (London: Frank Cass, 1974), 107.

25. Note Parsons's definition: "A society is a type of social system, in any universe of social systems which attains the highest level of self-sufficiency as a system in relation to its environment." He leaves out the territorial or boundedness dimensions altogether. Parsons, *Societies*, 9. Mann, *The Sources of Social Power*, 13, comes closer to the territorial issue: "A society is a network of social interaction at the boundaries of which is a certain level of interaction cleavage between it and its environment."

26. Horowitz and Lissak, *Origins of the Israeli Polity*, 33.

27. Yitzhak Galnoor, *The Partition of Palestine: Decision Crossroads in the Zionist Movement* (Albany: State University of New York Press, 1995).

28. Shmuel Sandler, "The Origins of the National and Statist Traditions in Zionist Foreign Policy," *Jewish Political Studies Review* 2 (Fall 1990): 129–130.

29. Yoav Peled, "Ethnic Democracy and the Legal Construction of Citizenship: Arab Citizens of the Jewish State," *American Political Science Review* 86 (June 1992): 434.

30. Ibid., 435.

31. For a related but more restricted view, see David L. Blaney and Mustapha Kamal Pasha, "Civil Society and Democracy in the Third World: Ambiguities and Historical Possibilities," *Studies in Comparative International Development* 28 (Spring 1993): 3–24.

32. Geertz, "The Integrative Revolution," 108–109.

CHAPTER 7. CHANGING BOUNDARIES AND SOCIAL CRISIS

1. Eric Hammel, Six *Days in June: How Israel Won the 1967 Arab-Israeli War* (New York: Charles Scribner's Sons, 1992), 33.

2. Itzhak Galnoor, "Israeli Society and Politics,'" in Stephen J. Roth, ed., *The Impact of the Six-Day War: A Twenty-Year Assessment* (New York: Macmillan, 1988), 179.

3. Richard Z. Chesnoff, Edward Klein, and Robert Littell, *If Israel Lost the War* (New York: Coward-McCann, 1969), frontmatter.

4. William Stevenson, *Strike Zion!* (New York: Bantam Books, 1967), 1.

5. Quoted in Stevenson, *Strike Zion!* in frontmatter.

6. Among the new works looking at the effects of the 1967 war on Israeli society are Gad Barzilai, *Wars, Internal Conflicts, and Political Order*; Yagil Levy, *Trial and Error: Israel's Route from War to De-escalation* (Albany: State University of New York Press, 1997); and Reuven Pedatzur, *The Triumph of Embarrassment: Israel and the Territories after the Six-Day War* (Tel-Aviv: Bitan, 1996) [Hebrew].

7. Liebman and Don-Yehiya write, "Statism affirms the centrality of state interests and the centralization of power at the expense of nongovernmental groups and institutions. In terms of symbols and style, statism reflects the effort to transform the state and its institutions into the central foci of loyalty and identification. Statism gives rise to values and symbols that point to the state, legitimate it, and mobilize the population to serve its goals." Charles S. Liebman and Eliezer Don-Yehiya, Civil *Religion in Israel: Traditional Judaism and Political Culture in the Jewish State*, 84.

8. See the discussion in Michael Keren, *The Pen and the Sword: Israeli Intellectuals and the Making of the Nation-State* (Boulder: Westview Press, 1989), 1–5.

9. Indeed, academics have written of the development of Israel's own civil religion, in which the state stands at the center. See Liebman and Don-Yehiyeh, *Civil Religion in Israel*, 84, where they write, "In its more extreme formulation statism cultivates an attitude of sanctity toward the state, affirming it as an ultimate value." They go on to note that "the establishment of an independent Jewish state only a few years after the Holocaust evoked an outburst of enthusiasm from Jews both in the Diaspora and the Land of Israel. . . . The joy and enthusiasm evoked by the creation of Israel had the character of Messianic sentiments. In this context many believed the state to be the fulfillment of the traditional Jewish vision of redemption" (pp. 85–86).

10. "During the prestate period it was possible to cultivate the civil religion of one subgroup without hampering the basic unity of the Jewish population.

The political leadership of the various camps interrelated through a complex network, compromising on some disputed issues and principles and ignoring many others. Avoiding issues was possible in the absence of statehood and political sovereignty. Available resources, money, and jobs were distributed by the political leadership according to a key; according to a negotiated formula, each group received an allocation based roughly on its voting strength." Ibid., 81.

11. S. N. Eisenstadt, *The Transformation of Israeli Society: An Essay in Interpretation* (London: Weidenfeld and Nicolson, 1985), 186.

12. Erik Cohen, "Ethnicity and Legitimation in Contemporary Israel," *The Jerusalem Quarterly* (Summer, 1983), 113.

13. Alan Dowty, *The Jewish State: A Century Later* (Berkeley: University of California Press, 1998), 61–73.

14. Ian S. Lustick, *Arabs in the Jewish State.*

15. See for example Yochaman Peres, "Modernization and Nationalism in the Identity of the Israeli Arab," *Middle East Journal* 24 (Autumn 1970): 479–492.

16. Yoav Peled, "Ethnic Democracy and the Legal Construction of Citizenship: Arab Citizens of the Jewish State," 435.

17. Itzhak Galnoor, *The Partition of Palestine.*

18. Shlomo Avineri, "Political Ideologies: From Consensus to Confrontation, in Roth, ed., *The Impact of the Six-Day War,* 198. A powerful argument about Israel's pre-1967 war boundaries is made by Adriana Kemp, "Talking Boundaries: The Making of a Political Territory in Israel's Early Years."

19. "Newcomers are expected to change cultural traditions and ways of life that are considered unsuitable or irrelevant to life in Israel. This social definition puts pressure on people who come from Asian or African countries to adopt Western codes of behavior." Hanna Herzog, "Political Ethnicity as a Socially Constructed Reality: The Case of Jews in Israel" in Milton J. Esman and Itamar Rabinovich, eds., *Ethnicity, Pluralism, and the State in the Middle East* (Ithaca: Cornell University Press, 1988), 140.

20. Yocheved Liron, *Deprivation and Socio-Economic Gap in Israel* (Jerusalem: Israel Economist, 1973), 12. The figures are for 1968–69.

21. A large number of studies were surveyed by Raphael Roter and Nira Shamai. See "Social Policy and the Israeli Economy, 1948–1980," in Moshe Sanbar, ed., *Economic and Social Policy in Israel: The First Generation* (New York: University Press of America, 1990), 162.

22. Erik Cohen, "The Black Panthers and Israeli Society," in Ernest Krausz, ed., *Studies of Israeli Society, Vol. 1, Migration, Ethnicity, and Community* (New Brunswick, N.J.: Transaction Books, 1983), 149.

23. Yosef Gorny, *The State of Israel in Jewish Public Thought: The Quest for Collective Identity* (London: Macmillan, 1994), 39.

24. Vered Kraus and Robert W. Hodge, *Promises in the Promised Land: Mobility and Inequality in Israel* (New York: Greenwood Press, 1990), 59.

25. See Donna Robinson Divine, "Political Legitimacy in Israel: How Important Is the State?" *International Journal of Middle East Studies* 10 (1979): 205–224.

26. Galnoor, "Israeli Society and Politics," 178.

27. Ibid., 181.

28. Gadi Wolfsfeld, *The Politics of Provocation*, 15.

29. See Joel S. Migdal, "Civil Society in Israel," in Ellis Goldberg, Reşat Kasaba, and Migdal, eds., *Rules and Rights in the Middle East: Democracy, Law, and Society* (Seattle: University of Washington Press, 1993), 125. On the manipulation of consensus in Israeli society by political elites, see Barzilai, *Wars, Internal Conflicts, and Political Order.*

30. Cohen, "The Black Panthers and Israeli Society," 147.

31. David Weisburd, *Jewish Settler Violence: Deviance as Social Reaction* (University Park: The Pennsylvania State University Press, 1989), 111.

32. Yakir Plessner, *The Political Economy of Israel: From Ideology to Stagnation* (Albany: State University of New York Press, 1994), 139, states that "in 1965 almost 63 percent of all workdays lost in strikes were in the public sector. Even more impressive, over 71 percent of all strikers were in the public sector, although its share in employment was only less than 23 percent."

33. Ibid., 139.

34. Michael Shalev, *Labour and the Political Economy in Israel*, 257.

35. Yair Aharoni, *The Israeli Economy: Dreams and Realities* (New York: Routledge, 1991), 195.

36. Plessner, *The Political Economy of Israel*, 177.

37. Aharoni, *The Israeli Economy*, 85–86; and Paul Rivlin, *The Israeli Economy* (Boulder: Westview Press, 1992), 3.

38. Plessner, *The Political Economy of Israel*, 178.

39. Avineri, "Political Ideologies," 199.

40. On the concept of ethnonationalism, see Walker Connor, *Ethnonationalism: The Quest for Understanding* (Princeton: Princeton University Press, 1994). While universalism implies rationalism in Weberian terms, ethnonationalism (a loyalty to one's own kind), Connor maintains, rests on passions and nonrational factors. On the growing debate between the civic and ethnonational models after the 1967 war, see Dowty, *The Jewish State*, ch. 10.

41. See two recent volumes, for example: Charles Liebman and Elihu Katz, *The Jewishness of Israelis: Responses to the Guttman Report* (Albany: State University of New York Press, 1997); and Dowty, *The Jewish State.*

42. Ibid., 13.

43. See Baruch Kimmerling, "Between the Primordial and the Civil Definitions of the Collective Identity: Eretz Israel or the State of Israel?" in Erik Cohen, Moshe Lissak, and Uri Almagor, eds., *Comparative Social Dynamics: Essays in Honor of S. N. Eisenstadt* (Boulder: Westview Press, 1985), 262–283.

44. Ilan Peleg, "The Arab-Israeli Conflict and the Victory of Otherness," in Walter P. Zenner, ed., *Critical Essays on Israeli Social Issues and Scholarship: Books on Israel*, Vol. III (Albany: State University of New York Press, 1994), 228. Also, see Cohen, "Ethnicity and Legitimation in Contemporary Israel," p. 114.

45. Shlomo Deshen, "Political Ethnicity and Cultural Ethnicity in Israel During the 1960s," in Krausz, ed., *Studies of Israeli Society*, Vol. 1, 142.

46. Raphael Roter and Nira Shamai, "Social Policy and the Israeli Economy, 1948–1980," in Moshe Sanbar, ed., *Economic and Social Policy in Israel: The First Generation* (New York: University Press of America, 1990), 163.

47. Oded Remba, "Income Inequality in Israel: Ethnic Aspects"' in Michael Curtis and Mordecai S. Chertoff, eds., *Israel: Social Structure and Change* (New Brunswick: Transaction Books, 1973), 203.

48. Shlomo Swirski, *Israel: The Oriental Majority*, (New Jersey: Zed Books, 1989).

49. Virginia Dominguez, *People as Subject, People as Object: Selfhood and Peoplehood in Contemporary Israel* (Madison: University of Wisconsin Press, 1989). Commenting on Dominguez, James Armstrong writes, "Ethnic divisions within Israeli society are only problematic insofar as there is some idealized, subject-constructed sense of peoplehood which is compatible with those divisions." "The Search for Israeliness: Toward an Anthropology of the Contemporary Mainstream," in Stone and Zenner, eds., *Critical Essays on Israeli Social Issues and Scholarship*, 123.

50. Sammy Smooha, *Israel: Pluralism and Conflict* (London: Routledge and Kegan Paul, 1978), 193.

51. See Avraharn Shama and Mark Iris, *Immigration Without Integration* (Cambridge, Mass.: Schenkman, 1977).

52. Y. Nini, quoted in Cohen, "The Black Panthers and Israeli Society," 154.

53. Cohen, "The Black Panthers and Israeli Society," 154.

54. See Herzog, "Political Ethnicity as a Socially Constructed Reality: The Case of Jews in Israel," 140–151. On the question of inclusion versus segregation, see the important work by Myron J. Aronoff, *Israeli Visions and Divisions: Cultural Change and Political Conflict* (New Brunswick, N.J.: Transaction, 1989).

55. "By institutions I mean established organizations and the rules and practices that govern how these organizations function internally and relate to one another and to society." Kathryn Sikkink, *Ideas and Institutions: Developmentalism in Brazil and Argentina* (Ithaca: Cornell University Press, 1991), 23.

56. Lustick, *Unsettled States, Disputed Lands*.

57. Peter Evans, Dietrich Reuschemeyer, and Theda Skocpol, *Bringing the State Back In*.

58. James N. Rosenau, "The State in an Era of Cascading Politics: Wavering Concept, Widening Competence, Withering Colossus, or Weathering Change?" *Comparative Political Studies* 21 (April 1988): 14.

59. Other examples of those looking at the state as a dependent variable are Robert H. Jackson, *Quasi-States: Sovereignty, International Relations, and the Third World* (New York: Cambridge University Press, 1990); Robert H. Jackson and Carl G. Rosberg, "Why Africa's Weak States Persist: The Empirical and the Juridical in Statehood," *World Politics* 35 (October 1982): 1–24; and Joel S. Migdal, Atul Kohli, and Vivienne Shue, eds., *State Power and Social Forces*. In the context of Israel, one book rejecting the notion of the state as a black box is Levy, *Trial and Error*.

60. On that enterprise, see Migdal, "Studying the State," in Mark I. Lichbach and Alan S. Zuckerman, eds., *Comparative Politics: Rationality, Culture, and Structure* (New York: Cambridge University Press, 1997).

61. Galnoor, "Israeli Society and Politics," 193–194.

62. Arnold Lewis, "Ethnic Politics and the Foreign Policy Debate in Israel," in Myron J. Aronoff, *Cross-Currents In Israeli Culture and Politics, Political Anthropology*, Vol. IV (New Brunswick: Transaction Books, 1984), 28.

63. Cohen, in "Ethnicity and Legitimation in Contemporary Israel," wrote, "It is claimed that Oriental Jews are entitled to gain such access—by sheer virtue of being Jews, and not because of some particular process of absorption and resocialization" (120). I am indebted to Ovadia Shapira for reminding me that Erik Cohen made this important point over fifteen years ago. Also, see Lewis, "Ethnic Politics and the Foreign Policy Debate in Israel," 33.

64. Brenda Danet, *Pulling Strings: Biculturalism in Israeli Bureaucracy*, 95.

65. Cohen, "The Black Panthers and Israeli Society," 149.

66. Cohen, "Ethnicity and Legitimation in Contemporary Israel," 116.

67. On the growing negativism toward Arabs, see Ehud Sprinzak, *The Ascendance of Israel's Radical Right* (New York: Oxford University Press, 1991). For a different explanation of the enmity that Middle Eastern Jews demonstrated toward Arabs, see Yoav Peled, "Mizrahi Jews and Palestinian Arabs: Exclusionist Attitudes in Development Towns," in Oren Yiftachel and Avinoarn Meir, eds., *Ethnic Frontiers and Peripheries: Landscapes of Development and Inequality in Israel* (Boulder: Westview Press, 1998), 87–111.

68. Danet, *Pulling Strings*, 243.

69. See Aziz Haidar, *On the Margins: The Arab Population in the Israeli Economy* (New York: St. Martin's Press, 1995), 97ff.

70. This point should not be overstated. The labor market, as Peled shows, continued to be split along ethnic lines after 1967, in certain ways. See Peled, "Mizrahi Jews and Palestinian Arabs."

71. Seyour Spilerman and Jack Habib, "Development Towns in Israel: The Role of Community in Creating Ethnic Disparities in Labor Force Characteristics"' in Krausz, ed., *Studies of Israeli Society*, 200.

72. Ibid., 203–207.

73. Ibid., 211–217.

74. Shama and Iris, in *Immigration without Integration*, 116, note the occupational concentration of Jews with Middle Eastern roots. The quote is from Orem Yiftachel, "The Internal Frontier: Territorial Control and Ethnic Relations in Israel," in Yiftachel and Meir, eds., *Ethnic Frontiers and Peripheries*, 39–67.

75. Shama and Iris, *Immigration without Integration*, 137–138.

76. Swirski, *Israel*, 28.

77. Spilerman and Habib, "Development Towns in Israel," 222.

78. See Levy, *Trial and Error,* ch. 4, on the change in social structure after the 1967 war. Levy ties this change in strategy by Israel to a de-escalation of its conflict with the Arabs. In my view, he underestimates the impact of the war itself on both these processes.

79. Amir Ben-Porat, *Divided We Stand: Class Structure in Israel from 1948 to the 1980s* (New York: Greenwood Press, 1989), 62.

80. Haidar, *On the Margins*, ch. 5–6, presents excellent data on the new mobility. Chapter 6 is titled "From Village to Dormitory Community."

81. For the relation between the two forms of protest, see Eva Etzioni-Halevey, "Patterns of Conflict Generation and Conflict Absorption: The Cases of Israeli Labor and Ethnic Conflicts," in Krausz, ed., *Studies of Israeli Society*, 231–254.

CHAPTER 8. THE ODD MAN OUT

1. George Kossaifi, "Demographic Characteristics of the Arab Palestinian People," in Khalil Nakleh and Elia Zureik, eds., *The Sociology of the Palestinians* (New York: St. Martin's Press, 1980), 25. On refugee numbers see United Nations, *Report of the Economic Survey Mission of the Middle East* (New York: United Nations, 1949), 22. Laurie A. Brand, *Palestinians in the Arab World: Institution Building and the Search for a State* (New York: Columbia University Press, 1988), 150, estimates 900,000 Palestinians in Jordan in 1949, including 70,000 who already were settled on the East Bank. Gad Gilbar, "Trends in the Demographic Development of the Palestinians," *Cathedra* 189 (1987): 42–56 [Hebrew], puts the number on the West Bank at 670,000. An estimate based on the 1950 Jordanian census was 742,000 on the West Bank and 184,700 Palestinians on the East Bank, demonstrating an already apparent tendency of Palestinians to migrate from the West Bank to the East.

2. Charles Liebman and Eliezer Don-Yehiya, *Civil Religion in Israel.*

3. The lower estimate is given by Charles S. Kamen, "After the Disaster: The Arabs in the State of Israel, 1948–1950," *Collections on Research and Critique*, No. 10 (December 1984), 18–20. The higher estimate is based on UNRWA data and is adopted by Ian Lustick, *Arabs in the Jewish State: Israel's Control of a National Minority*. The same ratio is given by Sammy Smooha, *The Orientation and the Politicization of the Arab Minority in Israel* (Haifa: The Jewish-Arab Center, Institute of Middle Eastern Studies, Haifa University, 1984), 79.

4. Moshe Dayan has suggested that as many 1,000 refugees a month infiltrated back into Israel, some for brief periods but some to stay permanently. See "Israel's Border Problems," *Foreign Affairs* 23 (January, 1955): 261.

5. Documentation is cited in Kamen, "After the Catastrophe I," *Middle Eastern Studies* 23 (October, 1987): 453–495.

6. Baruch Kimmerling, "Sovereignty, Ownership and 'Presence' in the Jewish-Arab Territorial Conflict—The Case of Bir'm and Ikrit," *Comparative Political Studies* 10 (July 1977): 155–176.

7. Kamen, "After the Catastrophe I," 476, estimates that 14 percent of the male population of military age (15–60) was in prison.

8. Don Peretz, *Israel and the Palestine Arabs* (Washington, D.C.: The Middle East Institute, 1958), 142. See also Sabri Jiryis, *The Arabs in Israel* (New York: Monthly Review Press, 1976).

9. Baruch Kimmerling, *Zionism and Territory: The Socioterritorial Dimensions of Zionist Politics.*

10. The state gave a high priority to these forms, which were part of a nation-building process. It heavily subsidized the new immigrants' rural settle-

ments and protected them from the competition of cheap agricultural labor economy of the Arabs. Baruch Kimmerling, *Zionism and Economy* (Cambridge, Mass.: Schenkman, 1983). For the structure of Arab labor and its development in the first decade of the existence of Israel, see Yoram Ben-Porath, *The Arab Labor Force in Israel* (Jerusalem: Falk Institute for Economic Research, 1966) [Hebrew].

11. See Raja Khalidi, "The Economy of the Palestinian Arabs in Israel," in George T. Abed, ed., *The Palestinian Economy: Studies in Development Under Prolonged Occupation* (New York: Routledge, 1989), 42–49. For an analysis of small villagers' entrepreneurship see Aziz Haidar, *Types and Patterns of Economic Entrepreneurship in Arab Villages in Israel—1950–1980* (Jerusalem: Unpublished Ph.D. thesis, The Hebrew University of Jerusalem, 1985) [Hebrew].

12. Elia T. Zureik, *The Palestinians in Israel: A Study in Internal Colonialism* (Boston: Routledge and Kegan Paul, 1979), 131–141. Zureik analyzes the situation of the Arabs in the framework of the Jewish nation-state from the beginning in terms of "settler" or "internal colonialism" (viz. "colonies of exploitation" supported by an external power). Also see Herbert Adam, *Modernizing Racial Domination* (Berkeley, University of California Press, 1972) 31, and Najwa Makhoul, "Changes in the Employment Structure of Arabs in Israel," *Journal of Palestine Studies* 3 (1982): 77–102.

13. Itzhak Arnon and Michael Raviv, *From Fellah to Farmer: A Study on Change in Arab Villages* (Rehovot, Israel: Settlement Study Center, Agricultural Research Organization, The Volcani Center, Bet-Dagan, 1980 [Publication on Problems of Regional Development, no. 31]).

14. Sami F. Geraisy, *Arab Village Youth in Jewish Urban Centers* (Ann Arbor: University Microfilms, 1971), 82.

15. By 1963, more Arabs worked in construction-related jobs than in agriculture. See State of Israel, *Labor Power Survey, 1963* (Jerusalem: Central Bureau of Statistics, 1964), 52–53.

16. See Edna Bonacich, "The Past, Present, and Future of Split Labor Market Theory," *Research in Race and Ethnic Relations* 1 (1979): 17–64. See also Shlomo Swirski and Deborah Bernstein, "The Rapid Economic Development of Israel and the Emergence of the Ethnic Division of Labor," *British Journal of Sociology* 33 (1982): 64–85.

17. Michael Shalev, "Jewish Organized Labor and the Palestinians: A Study of State/Society Relations in Israel," in Baruch Kimmerling, ed., *The Israeli State and Society*, 93–134.

18. Sami Khalil Mar'i, *Arab Education in Israel* (Syracuse: Syracuse University Press, 1978), xii.

19. Yehoshua Talmon (the first Israeli adviser to the prime minister on Arab affairs), cited in Lustick, *Arabs in the Jewish State*, 48.

20. Abner Cohen, *Arab Border Villages: A Study of Continuity and Change in Social Organization* (Manchester: Manchester University Press, 1965), 118; and Subhi Abu Ghosh, "The Politics of an Arab Village in Israel" (Princeton: Princeton University, unpublished Ph.D. Dissertation, 1965), 33.

21. Jiryis, *The Arabs in Israel*, 9–71. (This book was first published in Israel

in 1966, the Israeli authorities later trying to prevent its publication in France keeping the author in administrative custody.)

22. Fouzi El-Asmar, *To Be an Arab in Israel* (London: Frances Pinter, 1975), 23.

23. Ibid., 52.

24. Lustick, *Arabs in the Jewish State,* passim.

25. Sammy Smooha, *Arabs and Jews in Israel: Conflicting and Shared Attitudes in a Divided Society* (Boulder: Westview, 1989), 130–139.

26. Baruch Kimmerling found a built-in tension in the Israeli collective identity between its religious/primordial ingredients and the civil/modern ones. See "Between the Primordial and the Civil Definitions of the Collective Identity: Eretz Israel or the State of Israel," 262–283.

27. Nadim Rouhana, "The Civic and National Subidentities of the Arabs in Israel: A Psycho Political Approach," in John E. Hofman et al., eds., *Arab-Jewish Relations in Israel: A Quest in Human Understanding* (Bristol, Indiana: Wyndham Hall Press, 1988), 123–153.

28. It appeared 13 times beginning in October 1959, using different names, since the authorities refused to grant permission for a regular journal. Changing the title was the only way to circumvent the legal obstacles. However, the suffix of each title was, "al-Ard" (the land). Circulated in runs of about 2,000 copies, it was finally banned in March, 1960, following the publisher's use of the same title twice.

29. Lustick, *Arabs in the Jewish State,* 128.

30. See Yaacov Landau, *The Arabs in Israel* (London: Oxford University Press, 1969), chapter 4, and Jiryis, *The Arabs in Israel,* chapter 4. Jiryis himself was a young lawyer, a graduate of the Hebrew University, and one of the founders and leaders of this group. His book was the first on the Arab situation in Israel after 1948. Later, he left the country and became one of the most prominent intellectuals of the Palestinian resistance movement. He is considered an expert on the internal policy of Israel.

31. This policy was rooted in tradition: "In the agrarian, peasant society of eighteenth-, nineteenth-, and early twentieth-century Palestine, strong village patrilineages gained recognition from the government and/or representatives of power (military governors, tax officials, administrators) in the form of derived local authority and titles (muhktar, shaikh) for its dominant personages/leaders and/or enjoyed minor economic advantages." Henry Rosenfeld, "Men and Women in Arab Peasant to Proletariat Transformation," in Stanley Diamond, ed., *Theory and Practice: Essays Presented to Gene Weltfish* (New York: Mouton, 1989), 196.

32. On this faith being maintained by a minority of an Arab minority, see Gabriel Ben-Dor, "Intellectuals in Israeli Druze Society," in Elie Kedourie and Sylvia G. Haim, eds., *Palestine and Israel in the 19th and 20th Centuries* (London: Frank Cass, 1982), 232.

33. Although many of the problems have eased, overcrowding of classrooms, lack of qualified teachers, a shortage of vocational education, and other problems have continued to plague the Arab educational sector. See Mar'i, *Arab Education in Israel,* chapter 1.

34. All the textbooks of the mandatory period were outlawed, not only because they included expressions of hostility towards the Jewish community and Zionism, but also because most of them included some expression of Arab Palestinian political identity.

35. Mar'i, *Arab Education in Israel*, 19–20.

36. Ibid., 50.

37. Yochanan Peres, Avishai Ehrlich, and Nira Yuval-Davis, "National Education for Arab Youth in Israel: A Comparative Analysis of Curricula," *Jewish Journal of Sociology* 12 (1970): 156.

38. See Zuriek, *The Palestinians in Israel*, 157–158.

39. For a content analysis of teaching materials in different classes, see Muhammad Miyari, *Contents of Teaching in Arab Schools* (Jerusalem: Ministry of Education, Educational Planning Project, 1975) [Hebrew]; and Peres, Ehrlich, and Yuval-Davis, "National Education for Arab Youth in Israel." Also see Mar'i, *Arab Education in Israel*, 70–89.

40. Ibid., 229. The categories on religious self-identification were added to the 1967 survey.

41. Khalil Nakhleh, "Palestinian Intellectuals and Revolutionary Transformation," in Nakhleh and Elia Zureik, eds., *The Sociology of the Palestinians* (New York: St. Martin's Press, 1980), 188–189.

42. Anton Shammas describes the poetry of Arabs in Israel as "bad," because thematically it never left the village to try to meet the real and much more complex "new Arab experience" in Israel. See *The Arab Literature in Israel* (Tel Aviv: Shiloach Center for Research of Middle East, Tel Aviv University, 1976), 42

43. Aziz Haidar, "The Different Levels of Palestinian Ethnicity," in M. S. Esman and I. Rabinovich, eds., *Ethnicity, Pluralism and the State in Middle East* (Ithaca: Cornell University Press, 1988), 108.

44. Zureik, *The Palestinians in Israel*, 183

45. See Landau, *The Arabs in Israel*, 195–198.

46. Called Maki until 1965, the Communist party ended up entirely Jewish, as it denied the legitimacy of both Zionism and Arab nationalism and Zionism— and thereafter Rakah, which drew both its rank-and-file and its voters largely from the Arab community. See Elie Rekhess, "Jews and Arabs in the Israeli Communist Party" in Esman and Rabinovich, eds., *Ethnicity, Pluralism, and the State in the Middle East*, 121–139. On Jews and Arabs in Mapam, see Yael Yishai, "Integration of Arabs in an Israeli Party: The Case of Mapam, 1948–54," in Elie Kedourie and Sylvia G. Haim, eds., *Zionism and Arabism in Palestine and Israel* (London: Frank Cass, 1982), 240–255.

47. A cadre of these lawyers later became central figures in the military courts, defending those arrested in the occupied territories. See George Emile Bisharat, *Palestinian Lawyers and Israeli Rule: Law and Disorder in the West Bank* (Austin: University of Texas Press, 1989), 92–95.

48. Mark Tessler, "Arabs in Israel," in Ann Mosely Lesch and Tessler, *Israel, Egypt, and the Palestinians: From Camp David to Intifada* (Bloomington: Indiana University Press, 1989), 101.

49. al-Haj, *Social Change and Family Processes*.

50. Rosenfeld, "Men and Women in Arab Peasant to Proletariat Transformation," 200, 205.

51. One survey showed that by the 1980s as many as 85 percent of Arab households consisted of nuclear families. See al-Haj, *Social Change and Family Processes*, 93. In the 1970s, suveys showed the figure to be about 55 percent. See Smooha, *Arabs and Jews in Israel* I: 37.

52. Henry Rosenfeld, "The Class Situation of the Arab National Minority in Israel," *Comparative Studies in Society and History* 20 (January, 1978): 395.

53. Ibid. On the move to wage labor starting in the earliest years of the state, see Arnihoud Israely, "The Employment Revolution Among Non-Jewish Minorities of Israel," *Hamizrah Hehadash* 26 (1976): 232–239 [Hebrew].

54. Ahmad S. Khalidi, *The Arab Economy in Israel: The Dynamics of a Region's Development* (New York: Croom Helm, 1988), 172.

55. Ibid., 191.

56. Arnon and Raviv, *From Fellah to Farmer*, 23–25.

57. Aziz Haidar, *The Arab Population in the Israeli Economy* (Tel Aviv: International Center for Peace in the Middle East, 1990) and Ruth Klinov, "Arabs and Jews in the Israeli Labor Force" (Jerusalem: Department of Economics, Hebrew University, Working Paper No. 214, 1989).

58. A. S. Khalidi, *The Arab Economy in Israel*, 182, has put it, that economy has been "subservient to the interests and capacities of national capital. . . ."

59. Kimmerling, *Zionism and Economy*, 189–204.

60. Haidar, *The Arab Population in the Israeli Economy*, 131.

61. Aziz Haidar, *The Emergence of the Arab Bourgeoisie in Israel* (Jerusalem: Arab Thought Forum, 1986), chapter 1 [Arabic].

62. al-Haj, *Social Change and Family Processes*, 111.

63. Ibid., chapter 5.

64. Lustick, *Arabs in the Jewish State*, 258.

65. See Zureik, *The Palestinians in Israel*, 175. In 1979, the Arab students at the five Israeli universities called a day of protest to express their indignation at the discrimination they said they faced.

66. Even local organizations such as the League for Jaffa Arabs and the Nazareth Heritage Society furthered this process. See Tessler, "Arabs in Israel," 115.

67. Control over local municipalities was the only autonomous focus of power for Israeli Arabs and, especially, for the Communist party. However, the party failed to manage the municipalities effectively. They were not only discriminated against by the Israeli authorities, but they neglected local problems, such as unpopular tax collection, to deal with "high politics." See Majid Al-Hajj and Henry Rosenfeld, *Arab Local Government in Israel* (Boulder: Westview, 1990), 66–68.

68. Smooha, *Arabs and Jews in Israel*, xvi. See also K. Nakleh, "Cultural Determinants of Palestinian Collective Identity: The Case of the Arabs in Israel," *New Outlook* 18 (1975): 54–57.

69. The survey was of 427 male Arab adults, commissioned by the newspaper, *Davar*, and executed by DAHAF, a professional polling institute. *Davar*,

September 22, 1868. Haidar, "The Different Levels of Palestinian Ethnicity," 109–110, found that Arabs in Israel felt superior in some realms and inferior in others (for instance, socioculturally). See also Sharif Kanaana, *Change and Continuity: Studies on the Effect of Occupation on Arab Palestinian Society* (Jerusalem: Arab Studies Society, 1983) [Arabic].

70. Smooha, *Arabs and Jews in Israel*, 209.

71. Smooha, *The Orientation and Politicization of the Arab Minority in Israel*, 34, 39; and *Arabs and Jews in Israel*, 54, 137.

72. Ibid., xvii.

73. See Elie Rekhes, "Israeli Arabs and the Arabs of the West Bank and Gaza: Political Affinity and National Solidarity," *Asian and African Studies* 23 (1989): 119–154; Aziz Haidar, "The Different Levels of Palestinian Identity." Also see Aharon Layish, ed., Special Issue on "The Arabs in Israel: Between Religious Revival and National Awakening," *HaMizrach HeHasdash* 32 (1989): 125–128 [Hebrew]. From this issue, see specifically the articles of Thomas Mayer, "The Muslim Youth in Israel," 10–20; Elie Rekhes, "Israeli Arabs and the Arabs of the West Bank and Gaza Strip: Political Ties and National Identification," 165–191; George Kanazi, "Ideologies in Palestinian Literatures in Israel," 129–138. In the 1992 Israeli elections, up to 50 percent of Arab votes went for Jewish parties, attempting to re-enter the Jewish-dominated Israeli political arena. They were a major factor in the victory of the left bloc, contributing about five seats to it (in addition to five seats for the Arab parties, which constituted an integral, but unofficial, part of the Israeli left parliamentary bloc).

74. Sample surveys indicated that the proportion of Israeli Arabs who identified themselves in Palestinian terms was:

1976	1980	1985	1988
57.5	54.5	68.0	67.0

The endorsement of general strikes as a means of Arab struggle was:

1976	1980	1985	1988
63.0	55.0	61.0	74.0

Support of the Committee of the Heads of Arab Local Councils was:

1976	1980	1985	1988
48.0	55.0	63.0	71.0

The data are from Sammy Smooha, "The Divergent Fate of the Palestinians on Both Sides of the Green Line: The Intifada as a Test," paper presented at the International Sociological Association, XII World Congress of Sociology, Madrid, July 12, 1990.

75. According to Israeli officials, sabotage committed by Arabs in Israel increased from 69 incidences in 1987 to 238 in 1988, but then decreased to 187 the following year. Of these 187 incidents, there were 91 acts of arson, 28 Molotov cocktails, 17 explosives, 8 stabbings, 8 violent assaults, 6 shootings, and 3 hand grenade attacks. More frequent were "subversive nationalistic incidents"—in 1989 they included 119 stone throwings, 104 writings of anti-Israeli

or pro-PLO slogans, 92 hoistings of Palestinian flags, 15 road blockings, 14 acts of destruction of state emblems, 4 layings of false explosives, etc. Idem, 19–20.

76. Asa Ghanim and Sara Osetzki-Lasar, *Green Line, Red Lines and the Israeli Arabs Facing the Intifada* (Givat Haviva: Institute of Arab Studies, 1990) [Hebrew]; also Smooha, "The Divergent Fate of the Palestinians," 5.

77. Suleiman Shakur, cited in Ibid, 12.

78. David Libai cited in Thea Buxbaum and Marla Brettschneider, "Amendment No. 3: Protector of Israeli National Security or Threat to Israeli Arabs?" *Israel Horizons* 37 (1989) and 38 (1990): 9.

79. Mar'i, *Arab Education in Israel*, x.

80. Cited in A. L. Tibawi, "Visions of the Return: The Palestinian Arab Refugees in Arab Poetry and Art," *Middle East Journal* 17 (1963): 517.

81. Anton Shammas, *Arabesques* (New York: Harper and Row, 1988), 91. In 1992 the prestigious Israel Prize for Literature went to Emile Habibi, the first time it was awarded to an Arab (in protest, the leader of the Tehiya party, Yuval Ne'eman, returned his own prize in physics).

82. Cited in Yochanan Peres and Nira Yuval-Davis, "Some Observations on National Identity of the Israeli Arab," *Human Relations* 22 (1969): 219.

83. Cited in Zureik, *The Palestinians in Israel*, 178.

BIBLIOGRAPHY

Abdel-Fadil, M. *Development, Income Distribution, and Social Change in Rural Egypt 1952–1970: A Study in the Political Economy of Agrarian Transition.* Cambridge: Cambridge University Press, 1975.

Abramov, S. Zalman. *Perpetual Dilemma: Jewish Religion in the Jewish State.* Rutherford, N.J.: Fairleigh Dickinson University Press, 1976.

Abu Ghosh, Subhi. "The Politics of an Arab Village in Israel." Unpublished Ph.D. dissertation. Princeton University, 1965.

Adam, Herbert. *Modernizing Racial Domination.* Berkeley: University of California Press, 1972.

Adams, R. H. Jr. "Growth Without Development in Rural Egypt: A Local-Level Study of Institutional and Social Change." *Mimeo* (1981): 124–125.

Aharoni, Yair. *The Israeli Economy: Dreams and Realities.* New York: Routledge, 1991.

Almond, Gabriel A., and Sidney Verba. *The Civic Culture.* Princeton: Princeton University Press, 1963.

Anderson, Benedict. *Imagined Communities: Reflections on the Origin and Spread of Nationalism.* New York: Verso, 1991.

Arato, Andrew. "Empire vs. Civil Society: Poland 1981–82." *Telos* 14, no. 50 (1981–1982): 19–48.

Arian, Asher. *The Choosing People: Voting Behavior in Israel.* Cleveland: Press of Case Western Reserve University, 1973.

———. *Consensus in Israel.* New York: General Learning Press, 1971.

———. *Politics in Israel: The Second Generation.* Chatham, N.J.: Chatham House, 1985.

———. *The Second Republic Politics in Israel.* New Jersey: Chatham House, 1998.

Arian, Asher, and Michal Shamir. "Collective Identity and Electoral Competition in Israel." *American Political Science Review* 93, 2 (June 1999): 265–278.

———. *The Elections in Israel, 1992.* Albany: State University of New York Press, 1995.

Armstrong, James. "The Search for Israeliness: Toward an Anthropology of the Contemporary Mainstream"' in Stone and Zenner, eds., *Critical Essays on Israeli Social Issues and Scholarship.* Books on Israel, Vol. III. Albany: State University of New York Press, 1994.

Arnon, Itzhak, and Michael Raviv. *From Fellah to Farmer: A Study on Change in Arab Villages.* Rehovot, Israel: The Volcani Center, Bet-Dagan, 1980.

Aronoff, Myron Joel. *Frontiertown: The Politics of Community Building in Israel.* Manchester: Manchester University Press, 1974.

————. *Israeli Visions and Divisions: Cultural Change and Political Conflict.* New Brunswick, N.J: Transaction, 1989.

————. *Power and Ritual in the Israeli Labor Party: A Study in Political Anthropology.* Armonk: M. E. Sharpe, 1993.

el-Asmar, Fouzi. To *Be an Arab in Israel.* London: Frances Pinter, 1975.

Atlas, Pierre M. "The Struggle for the Center in Political Culture: A Cognitive-Institutionalist Examination of the Origins of the Israeli Mainstream and Fringe, 1905–1949." Ph.D. dissertation. Rutgers, The State University of New Jersey, 2000.

Avineri, Shlomo. *The Making of Modem Zionism: The Intellectual Origins of the Jewish State.* New York: Basic Books Publishers, 1981.

————. "Political Ideologies: From Consensus to Confrontation." In *The Impact of the Six-Day War: A Twenty-Year Assessment,* ed. Stephen J. Roth. New York: Macmillan, 1988.

Azarya, Victor, and Naomi Chazan. "Disengagement from the State in Africa: Reflections on the Experience of Ghana and Guinea," *Comparative Studies in Society and History* 29 (1987): 106–161.

Badie, Bertrand, and Pierre Birnbaum. *The Sociology of the State.* Chicago: University of Chicago Press, 1983.

Baker, Raymond William. *Egypt's Uncertain Revolution under Nasser and Sadat.* Cambridge: Harvard University Press, 1978.

Barnett, Michael N. *Confronting the Costs of War: Military Power, State, and Society in Egypt and Israel.* Princeton: Princeton University Press, 1992.

————. *Dialogues in Arab Politics: Negotiations in Regional Order.* New York: Columbia University Press, 1998.

————. ed. *Israel in Comparative Perspective: Challenging the Conventional Wisdom.* Albany: State University of New York Press, 1996.

Barzilai, Gad. *Wars, Internal Conflicts, and Political Order: A Jewish Democracy in the Middle East.* Albany: State University of New York Press, 1996.

Beinin, Joel. *Was the Red Flag Flying There? Marxist Politics and the Arab-Israeli Conflict in Egypt and Israel, 1948–1965.* Berkeley: University of California Press, 1990.

Beit-Zvi, Shabtai B. *Post-Ugandian Zionism in the Crucible of the Holocaust.* Tel-Aviv: Bronfman Publishers, 1977 [Hebrew].

Beloff, Max. *Imperial Sunset.* London: Methuen, 1969.

Ben-Dor, Gabriel. "Intellectuals in Israeli Druze Society." In *Palestine and Israel in the 19th and 20th Centuries,* eds. Elie Kedourie and Sylvia G. Haim. London: Frank Cass, 1982.

Ben-Eliezer, Uri. *The Making of Israeli Militarism.* Bloomington: Indiana University Press, 1998. [Hebrew Edition. *The Emergence of Israel Militarism, 1936–1956.* Tel-Aviv, Israel: Dvir Publishing House, 1995.]

————. "The Meaning of Political Participation in a Non-Liberal Democracy: The Example of Israel." *Comparative Politics* 25, 4 (1993): 397–413.

————. "Testing for Democracy in Israel." In *Critical Essays on Israeli Society, Politics, and Culture,* Books on Israel, vol. 2, eds. Ian S. Lustick and Barry Rubin. Albany: State University of New York Press, 1991.

Ben-Gurion, David. *From Class to Nation.* Tel-Aviv: Am Oved, 1974 [Hebrew].

Ben-Gurion, David, and I. Ben Zvi. *Eretz Israel in the Past and in the Present.* Jerusalem: Yad Izhak Ben Zvi, 1979 [Hebrew].

Ben-Porat, Amir. *Divided We Stand: Class Structure in Israel from 1948 to the 1980s.* New York: Greenwood Press, 1989.

Ben-Porath, Yoram. *The Arab Labor Force in Israel.* Jerusalem: Falk Institute for Economic Research, 1966 [Hebrew].

Ben-Zadok, Efraim. *Local Communities and the Israeli Polity: Conflict of Values and Interests.* Albany: State University of New York Press, 1993.

Bentwich, Norman. *England in Palestine.* London: Kegan Paul, 1932.

Binder, Leonard. *In a Moment of Enthusiasm: Political Power and the Second Stratum in Egypt.* Chicago: University of Chicago Press, 1978.

Bisharat, George Emile. *Palestinian Lawyers and Israeli Rule: Law and Disorder in the West Bank.* Austin: University of Texas Press, 1989.

Blaney, David L., and Mustapha Kamal Pasha. "Civil Society and Democracy in the Third World: Ambiguities and Historical Possibilities." *Studies in Comparative International Development* 28 (Spring 1993): 3–24.

Bonacich, Edna. "The Past, Present, and Future of Split Labor Market Theory." *Research in Race and Ethnic Relations* 1 (1979): 17–64.

Brand, Laurie A. *Palestinians in the Arab World: Institution Building and the Search for State.* New York: Columbia University Press, 1988.

Breuilly, John. *Nationalism and the State.* Manchester: Manchester University Press, 1982.

Buxbaum, Thea, and Marla Brettschneider. "Amendment No. 3: Protector of Israeli National Security or Threat to Israeli Arabs?" *Israel Horizons* 37 (1989) and 38 (1990): 9.

Chesnoff, Richard Z., Edward Klein, and Robert Littell. *If Israel Lost the War.* New York: Coward-McCann, 1969.

Cohen, Abner. *Arab-Border Villages: A Study of Continuity and Change in Social Organization.* Manchester: Manchester University Press, 1965.

Cohen, Erik. "The Black Panthers and Israeli Society." In *Studies of Israeli Society*, Vol. I, *Migration, Ethnicity and Community,* ed. Ernest Krausz. New Bruswick, N.J.: Transaction Books, 1980.

———. "Ethnicity and Legitimation in Contemporary Israel." *The Jerusalem Quarterly* 28 (Summer, 1983): 111–144.

Cohen, Michael J. *Palestine: Retreat from the Mandate.* New York: Holmes and Meier, 1978.

Colburn, Forrest. *Everyday Forms of Peasant Resistance.* New York: M. E. Sharpe, 1989.

Connor, Walker. *Ethnonationalism: The Quest for Understanding.* Princeton: Princeton University Press, 1994.

Danet, Brenda. *Pulling Strings: Biculturalism in Israeli Bureaucracy.* Albany: State University of New York Press, 1989.

Dayan, Moshe. "Israel's Border Problems," *Foreign Affairs* 33 (1955): 250–267.

Deshen, Shlomo. *Immigrant Voters in Israel: Parties and Congregations in a Local Election Campaign.* Manchester: Manchester University Press, 1970.

——. "Political Ethnicity and Cultural Ethnicity in Israel During the 1960s." In *Studies of Israeli Society*, Vol. I, *Migration, Ethnicity and Community*, ed. Ernest Krausz. New Bruswick, N.J.: Transaction Books, 1980.

Deshen, Shlomo, and Moshe Shokeid. *Distant Relations: Ethnicity and Politics Among Arabs and North African Jews in Israel*. New York: Praeger, 1982.

Dietmar, Rothermund. "The Legacy of the British-Indian Empire in Independent India." In *Imperialism and After: Continuities and Discontinuities*, eds. Wolfgang J. Mommsen and Eirgen Osterhammel. London: Allen and Unwin, 1986.

Divine, Donna Robinson. "Political Legitimacy in Israel: How Important is the State?" *International Journal of Middle East Studies*, 10 (1979): 205–224.

Dominguez, Virginia. *People as Subject, People as Object: Selfhood and Peoplehood in Contemporary Israel*. Madison: University of Wisconsin Press, 1989.

Doron, Abraham, and Ralph M. Kramer. *The Welfare State in Israel: The Evolution of Social Security Policy and Practice*. Tel Aviv: Am Oved, 1992 [Hebrew].

Dowty, Alan. *The Jewish State: A Century Later*. Berkeley: University of California Press, 1998.

Drezon-Tepler, Marcia. *Interest Groups and Political Change in Israel*. Albany: State University of New York Press, 1990.

Dyson, Kenneth H. F. *The State in Western Europe: A Study of an Idea and Institution*. Oxford: Martin Robertson, 1980.

Eisenstadt, S. N. *Israeli Society*. New York: Basic Books, 1967.

——. *The Transformation of Israeli Society: An Essay in Interpretation*. London: Weidenfeld and Nicolson, 1985.

Esco Foundation for Palestine. *Palestine*, vol. 1. New Haven: Yale University Press, 1947.

Etzioni-Halevy, Eva. *Political Culture in Israel*. New York: Praeger, 1977.

——. "Patterns of Conflict Generation and Conflict 'Absorbtion': The Cases of Israeli Labor and Ethnic Conflicts." In *Studies of Israeli Society*, Vol. 1, *Migration, Ethnicity and Community*, ed. Ernest Krausz. New Bruswick, N.J.: Transaction Books, 1980.

Evans, Peter B., Dietrich Rueschemeyer, and Theda Skocpol. *Bringing the State Back In*. New York: Cambridge University Press, 1985.

Farago, Uri. "Stability and Change in the Jewish Identity of School-Age Youths in Israel (1965–1974)." Paper distributed by Levi Eshkol Research Institute for Economics, Society and Policy in Israel. Hebrew University, 1977.

Friedrich, P. "The Legitimacy of a Cacique." In *Friends, Followers, and Factions: A Reader in Political Clientelism*, eds. S. Schmidt., L. Guasti., C. Lande, and J. C. Scott. Berkeley: University of California Press, 1977.

Frisch, Hillel. *Countdown to Statehood: Palestinian State Formation in the West Bank and Gaza*. Albany: State University of New York Press, 1998.

Galnoor, Itzhak. "Israeli Society and Politics." In *The Impact of the Six-Day War: A Twenty-Year Assessment*, ed. Stephen J. Roth. New York: Macmillan, 1988.

——. *The Partition of Palestine: Decision Crossroads in the Zionist Movement*. Albany: State University of New York Press, 1995.

———. *Steering the Polity: Political Communication in Israel*. Beverly Hills: Sage, 1982.

Geertz, Clifford, ed.. *Old Societies and New States: The Quest for Modernity in Asia and Africa*. New York: The Free Press, 1963.

Gelhorn, Walter. *Ombudsmen and Others*. Cambridge: Harvard University Press, 1966.

———. *When Americans Complain*. Cambridge: Harvard University Press, 1966.

Gellner, Ernest. *Thought and Change*. Chicago: The University of Chicago Press, 1964.

Geraisy, Sami F. *Arab Village Youth in Jewish Urban Centers*. Unpublished Ph.D. dissertation, Brandeis University, 1970.

Ghanim, Asa, and Sara Osetzki-Lasar. *Green Line, Red Lines and the Israeli Arabs Face the Intifada*. Givat Haviva: Institute of Arab Studies, 1990 [Hebrew].

Gilbar, Gad. "Trends in the Demographic Developments of the Palestinian Arabs, 1870–1948." *Cathedra* 45 (1987): 42–56 [Hebrew].

Gluckman, Max. *Order and Rebellion in Tribal Africa: Collected Essays with an Autobiographical Introduction*. London: Cohen and West, 1963.

———. *Politics, Law, and Ritual in Tribal Society*. Oxford: Basil Blackwell, 1965.

Goldberg, Ellis, Reşat Kasaba, and Joel S. Migdal. *Rules and Rights in the Middle East: Democracy, Law, and Society*. Seattle: University of Washington Press, 1993.

Gorny, Yosef. *The State of Israel in Jewish Public Thought: The Quest for Collective Identity*. London: Macmillan, 1994.

Gouldsblom, Johan, and Stephen Mennell., eds. *The Norbert Elias Reader: A Biographical Selection*. Oxford: Blackwell, 1998.

Gramsci, Antonio. *Selections from the Prison Notebooks*. New York: International Publishers, 1971.

Greenfeld, Liah. *Nationalism: Five Roads to Modernity*. Cambridge: Harvard University Press, 1992.

Greenfeld, Liah, and Michel Martin. *Center: Ideas and Institutions*. Chicago: The University of Chicago Press, 1988.

Grew, Raymond. *Crises of Political Development in Europe and the United States*. Princeton: Princeton University Press, 1978.

Grinberg, Lev Luis. "The Crisis of Statehood: A Weak State and Strong Political Institutions in Israel." *Journal of Theoretical Politics* 5, no. 1 (Jan. 1993): 89–107.

Grindle, Merilee Seffil. *Bureaucrats, Politicians, and Peasants in Mexico: A Case Study in Public Policy*. Berkeley: University of California Press, 1977.

Gupta, Akhil. "Technology, Power, and the State in a Complex Agricultural Society: The Green Revolution in a North Indian Village." Unpublished Ph.D. dissertation, Stanford University, 1987.

Haidar, Aziz. *The Arab Population in the Israeli Economy*. Tel Aviv: International Center for Peace in the Middle East, 1990.

———. "The Different Levels of Palestinian Ethnicity." In *Ethnicity, Pluralism and the State in the Middle East*, eds. M. S. Esman and 1. Rabinovich. Ithaca: Cornell University Press, 1988.

———. *The Emergence of the Arab Bourgeoisie in Israel.* Jerusalem: Arab Thought Forum, 1986 [Arabic].

———. *On the Margins: The Arab Population in the Israeli Economy.* New York: St. Martin's Press, 1995.

———. *Types and Patterns of Economic Entrepreneurship in Arab Villages in Israel—1950–1980.* Unpublished Ph.D. dissertation, Jerusalem: Hebrew University, 1985 [Hebrew].

al-Haj, Majid. *Social Change and Family Processes : Arab Communities in Shefar-A'm.* Boulder: Westview Press, 1987.

al-Haj, Majid, and Henry Rosenfeld. *Arab Local Government in Israel.* Boulder: Westview, 1990.

Hamilton, Nora. *The Limits of State Autonomy: Post-Revolutionary Mexico.* Princeton: Princeton University Press, 1982.

Hammel, Eric. *Six Days in June: How Israel Won the 1967 Arab-Israeli War.* New York: Charles Scribner's Sons, 1992.

Hansen, Roger D. *The Politics of Mexican Development.* Baltimore: Johns Hopkins University Press, 1971.

Hartz, Louis. *The Founding of New Societies.* New York: Harcourt Brace, 1964.

———. *The Liberal Tradition in America.* New York: Harcourt Brace, 1955.

Hegel, Georg Wilhelm Friedrich. *Philosophy of Right.* Oxford: The Clarendon Press, 1942.

Held, David. *Political Theory and the Modern State: Essays on State, Power, and Democracy.* Stanford: Stanford University Press, 1989.

Herzl, Theodor. *The Jewish State.* New York: Herzl Press, 1970.

Herzog, Hanna. "Political Ethnicity as a Socially Constructed Reality: The Case of Jews in Israel." In *Ethnicity, Pluralism, and the State in the Middle East,* eds. Milton J. Esman and Itamar Rabinovich. Ithaca: Cornell University Press, 1988.

Hintze, Otto. "The Formation of States and Constitutional Development: A Study in History and Politics." In *The Historical Essays of Otto Hintze,* ed. Felix Gilbert. New York: Oxford University Press, 1975.

Horowitz, Dan. "Dual Authority Polities." *Comparative Politics* 14 (1982): 329–349.

———. "The Yishuv and Israeli Society: Continuity and Change." *State, Government and International Relations* 21 (1983): 31–68 [Hebrew].

Horowitz, Dan, and Moshe Lissak. *Origins of the Israeli Polity: Palestinian under the Mandate.* Chicago: University of Chicago Press, 1978.

———. *Trouble in Utopia: The Overburdened Polity of Israel.* Albany: State University of New York Press, 1989.

Horowitz, Donald L. *Ethnic Groups in Conflict.* Berkeley: University of California Press, 1985.

Hurewitz, J. C. *The Struggle for Palestine.* New York: Schocken Books, 1976.

Israely, Amihoud. "The Employment Revolution among Non-Jewish Minorities of Israel," *Hamizrah Hehadash* 26 (1976): 232–239 [Hebrew].

Jackson, Robert H., *Quasi-States: Sovereignty, International Relations, and the Third World.* New York: Cambridge University Press, 1990.

Jackson, Robert H., and Carl G. Rosberg, "Why Africa's Weak States Persist: The Empirical and the Juridical in Statehood." *World Politics* 35 (October 1982): 1–24.

Jiryis, Sabri. *The Arabs in Israel.* New York: Monthly Review Press, 1976.

Kamen, Charles S. "After the Disaster: The Arabs in the State of Israel, 1948–1950." *Collections on Research and Critique* 10 (December 1984): 18–20.

———. "After the Catastrophe I: The Arabs in Israel, 1948–51." *Middle Eastern Studies* 23 (1987): 453–495.

Kanaana, Sharif. *Change and Continuity: Studies on the Effect of the Occupation on Arab Palestinian Society.* Jerusalem: Arab Studies Society, 1983 [Arabic].

Kanazi, George. "Ideologies in Palestinian Literature in Israel," *HaMizrah HeHadash* 32 (1989): 129–138 [Hebrew].

Karsh, Efraim. *In Search of Identity: Jewish Aspects in Israeli Culture.* London: Frank Cass, 1999.

Kemp, Adriana. "Talking Boundaries: The Making of Political Territory in Israel's Early Years." Unpublished Ph.D. dissertation, Tel-Aviv University, 1998.

Keren, Michael. *Ben Gurion and the Intellectuals: Power, Knowledge, Charisma.* Dekallo: Northern University Press, 1983.

———. *The Pen and the Sword; Israeli Intellectuals and the Making of the Nation-State.* Boulder: Westview Press, 1989.

Khalidi, Ahmad S. *The Arab Economy in Israel: The Dynamics of a Region's Development.* New York: Croom Helm, 1988.

Khalidi, Raja. "The Economy of the Palestinian Arabs in Israel." In *The Palestinian Economy: Studies in Development under Prolonged Occupation,* ed. George T. Abed. New York: Routledge and Kegan Paul, 1989.

Kimmerling, Baruch. "Between the Primordial and the Civil Definitions of the Collective Identity: Eretz Israel or the State of Israel?" In *Comparative Social Dynamics: Essays in Honor of S. N. Eisenstadt,* eds. Erik Cohen, Moshe Lissak, and Uri Almagor. Boulder: Westview Press, 1985.

———. *The Israeli State and Society: Boundaries and Frontiers.* Albany: State University of New York Press, 1989.

———. "On the Knowledge of the Place." *Alpayim* 6 (1992): 57–68 [Hebrew].

———. "Sovereignty, Ownership, and 'Presence' in the Jewish-Arab Territorial Conflict—The Case of Bir'm and Ikrit." *Comparative Political Studies* 10 (1977): 155–176.

———. "State Building, State Autonomy, and the Identity of Society: The Case of the Israeli State." *Journal of Historical Society* 6, no. 4 (1993): 397–429.

———. *Zionism and Economy.* Cambridge, Mass.: Schenkman, 1983.

———. *Zionism and Territory: The Socio-Territorial Dimensions of Zionist Politics.* Berkeley: University of California Berkeley Press, 1983.

Kimmerling, Baruch, and Joel S. Migdal. *Palestinians: The Making of a People.* New York: The Free Press, 1993.

Klieman, Aaron S. "The Divisiveness of Palestine: Foreign Office versus Colonial Office on the Issue of Partition, 1937." *The Historical Journal* 22, no. 2 (June 1979): 423–441.

———. *Foundations of British Policy in the Arab World.* Baltimore: Johns Hopkins University Press, 1970.

———. *Israel and the World After 40 Years.* Washingon: Pergamon-Brassey's International Defense Publishers, 1990.

Klinov, Ruth. "Arabs and Jews in the Israeli Labor Force." Jerusalem: Department of Economics, Hebrew University, 1989 [Working Paper no. 214].

———. *Israel and the World After 40 Years.* Washington: Pergamon-Brassey's International Defense Publishers, 1990.

Kossaifi, George. "Demographic Characteristics of the Arab Palestinian People." In *The Sociology of the Palestinians,* eds. Khalil Nakleh and Elia Zureik. New York: St. Martin's Press, 1980.

Kraus, Richard, and Reeve D. Vanneman. "Bureaucrats versus the State in Capitalist and Socialist Regimes." *Comparative Studies in Society and History* 27 (1985): 111–122.

Kraus, Vered, and Robert W. Hodge. *Promises in the Promised Land: Mobility and Inequality in Israel.* New York: Greenwood Press, 1990.

Lamborn, A. C. "Power and the Politics of Extraction," *International Studies Quarterly* 27 (1983): 123–146.

Landau, Yaacov. *The Arabs in Israel.* London: Oxford University Press, 1969.

Lawson, Kenneth. "War at the Grassroots: The Great War and the Nationalization of Civic Life." Unpublished Ph.D. dissertation, University of Washington, 2000.

Layish, Aharon. "The Arabs in Israel: Between Religious Revival and National Awakening." *HaMizrah HeHadash* 32 (1989) [Hebrew].

Lehman-Wilzig, Sam N. *Stiff-Necked People, Bottle-Necked System: The Evolution and Roots of Israeli Public Protest, 1949–1986.* Bloomington: Indiana University Press, 1990.

———. *Wildfire: Grassroots Revolts in Israel in the Post-Socialist Era.* Albany: State University of New York Press, 1992.

Levy, Yagil. *Trial and Error: Israel's Route from War to De-escalation.* Albany: State University of New York Press, 1997.

Lewis, Arnold. "Ethnic Politics and the Foreign Policy Debate in Israel." In *Cross-Currents In Israeli Culture and Politics, Political Anthropology,* vol. IV, ed. Myron J. Aronoff. New Brunswick, N.J.: Transaction Books, 1984, 25–38.

Liebman, Charles S., and Eliezer Don-Yehiya. *Civil Religion in Israel: Traditional Judaism and Political Culture in the Jewish State.* Berkeley: University of California Press, 1983.

Liebman, Charles S., and Elihu Katz, eds. *The Jewishness of Israelis: Responses to the Guttman Report.* Albany: State University of New York Press, 1997.

Lijphart, Arend. "Comparative Politics and the Comparative Method." *American Political Science Review* 65 (September 1971): 682–693.

Liron, Yocheved. *Deprivation and Socio-Economic Gap in Israel.* Jerusalem: Israel Economist, 1973.

Lissak, Moshe. "'Critical' Sociology and 'Establishment' Sociology in the Israeli Academic Community: Ideological Struggles or Academic Discourse?" *Israel Studies* 1, no. 1 (Spring 1996): 247–294.

Lustick, Ian. *Arabs in the Jewish State: Israel's Control of a National Minority.* Austin: University of Texas Press, 1980.

——. *Unsettled States, Disputed Lands: Britain and Ireland, France and Algeria, Israel and the West Bank-Gaza.* Ithaca: Cornell University Press, 1993.

Makhoul, Najwa. "Changes in the Employment Structure of Arabs in Israel." *Journal of Palestine Studies* 3 (1982): 77–102.

Mann, Michael. *The Sources of Social Power.* New York: Cambridge University Press, 1986.

Mar'i, Sami Khalil. *Arab Education in Israel.* Syracuse: Syracuse University Press, 1978.

Marwick, Arthur. *War and Social Change in the Twentieth Century: A Comparative Study of Britain. France, Germany, Russia, and the United States.* London: Macmillan, 1974.

Mayer, Thomas. "The Muslim Youth in Israel." *HaMizrah HeHadash* 32 (1989): 10–20 [Hebrew].

Medding, Peter Y. *Mapai in Israel.* Cambridge: Cambridge University Press, 1972.

Migdal, Joel S. "Civil Society in Israel" in Ellis Goldberg, Reşat Kasaba, and Migdal, eds., *Rules and Rights in the Middle East: Democracy, Law, and Society.* Seattle: University of Washington Press, 1993.

——. *Palestinian Society and Politics.* Princeton: Princeton University Press, 1980.

——. *State-in-Society: Studying How States and Societies Transform and Constitute One Another.* New York: Cambridge University Press, forthcoming.

——. *Strong Societies and Weak States: State-Society Relations and State Capabilities in the Third World.* Princeton, N.J.: Princeton University Press, 1988.

——. "Studying the State." In *Comparative Politics: Rationality, Culture, and Structure,* eds. Mark I. Lichbach and Alan S. Zuckerman. New York: Cambridge University Press, 1997.

——. "Urbanization and Political Change: The Impact of Foreign Rule." *Comparative Studies in Society and History* 19 (July 1977): 328–349.

Migdal, Joel S., Atul Kohli and Vivienne Shue, eds. *State Power and Social Forces: Domination and Transformation in the Third World.* Cambridge: Cambridge University Press, 1994.

Mitchell, Timothy. "The Limits of the State: Beyond Statist Approaches and Their Critics." *American Political Science Review* 85 (March 1991): 77–90.

Miyari, Muhammad. *Contents of Teaching in Arab Schools.* Jerusalem: Ministry of Education, Educational Planning Project, 1975 [Hebrew].

Monroe, Elizabeth. *Britain's Moment in the Middle East 1914–1956.* London: Chatto and Windus, 1963.

Moore, Barrington Jr. *Social Origins of Dictatorship and Democracy: Lord and Peasant in the Making of the Modem World.* Boston: Beacon Press, 1966.

Morris, Benny. "The Eel and History: A Reply to Shabtai Teveth." *Tikkun* 5 (Mar/Apr 1990): 19–86.

——. "The New Historiography: Israel Confronts Its Past." *Tikkun* 4 (Nov/Dec 1988): 19–102.

————. *Righteous Victims: A History of the Zionist-Arab Conflict, 1881–1999.* New York: Knopf, 1999.

Mousnier, R. "The Fronde." In *Precondition of Revolution in Early Modern Europe,* eds. R. Foster and J. P. Greene. Baltimore: Johns Hopkins University Press, 1970.

Nakleh, K. "Cultural Determinants of Palestinian Collective Identity: The Case of the Arabs in Israel." *New Outlook* 18 (1975): 54–57.

Nakleh, Khalil, and Elia Zureik, eds. *The Sociology of the Palestinians.* New York: St. Martin's Press, 1980.

Nasser, Gamal Abdul. *Egypt's Liberation: The Philosophy of Revolution.* Washington, D.C.: Public Affairs Press, 1933.

Nettl, J. P. "The State as a Conceptual Variable." *World Politics* 20 (1968): 559–592.

Nisbet, Robert A. *History of the Idea of Progress.* New York: Basic Books, 1980.

Pappe, Ilan. *The Making of the Arab-Israeli Conflict 1947–1951.* London: I. B. Tauris, 1994.

Parsons, Talcott. "The Political Aspect of Social Stucture and Process." In *Varieties of Political Theory,* ed. David Easton. Englewood Cliffs, N.J.: Prentice-Hall, 1966.

————. *Societies: Evolutionary and Comparative Perspectives.* Englewood Cliffs, N.J.: Prentice-Hall, 1966.

Parsons, Talcott, and Edward Shils. *Toward a General Theory of Action.* Cambridge: Harvard University Press, 1951.

Pedatzur, Reuven. *The Triumph of Embarassment: Israel and the Territories After the Six-Day War.* Tel-Aviv: Bitan, 1996 [Hebrew].

Peled, Yoav. "Ethnic Democracy and the Legal Construction of Citizenship: Arab Citizens of the Jewish State." *American Political Science Review* 86 (June 1992): 434–452.

————. "Mizrahi Jews and Palestinian Arabs: Exclusionist Attitudes in Development Towns." In *Ethnic Frontiers and Peripheries: Landscapes of Development and Inequality in Israel,* eds. Oren Yiftachel and Avinoam Meir. Boulder: Westview Press, 1998.

Peled, Yoav, and Gershon Shafir. "The Roots of Peacemaking: The Dynamics of Citizenship in Israel, 1948–93." *International Journal of Middle East Studies* 28, no. 3 (August 1996): 391–412.

Peleg, Ilan. "The Arab-Israeli Conflict and the Victory of Otherness." In *Critical Essays on Israeli Social Issues and Scholarship: Books on Israel, Vol. III,* ed. Walter P. Zenner. Albany: State University of New York Press, 1994.

Peres, Yohanan. "Modernization and Nationalism in the Identity of the Israeli Arab." *Middle East Journal* 24 (Autumn 1970): 479–492.

Peres, Yohanan, and Ephraim Yuchtman-Yaar. *Trends in Israeli Democracy: The Public's View.* Boulder: Lynne Rienner Publishers, 1992.

Peres, Yohanan, and Nira Yuval-Davis. "Some Observations on National Identity of the Israeli Arab." *Human Relations* 22, no. 3 (June 1969): 219–233.

Peres, Yohanan, Avishai Ehrlich, and Nira Yuval-Davis. "National Education for Arab Youth in Israel: A Comparative Analysis of Curricula." *Jewish Journal of Sociology* 12, no. 2 (Dec 1970): 147–163.

Peretz, Don. *Israel and the Palestine Arabs.* Washington, D.C.: The Middle East Institute, 1958.

Plessner, Yakir. *The Political Economy of Israel: From Ideology to Stagnation.* Albany: State University of New York Press, 1994.

Poggi, Gianfranco. *The Development of the Modem State: A Sociological Introduction.* Stanford: Stanford University Press, 1978.

Porath, Yehoshua. *The Emergence of the Palestinian-Arab National Movement, 1918–1929.* London: Frank Cass, 1974.

Ram, Uri. *The Changing Agenda of Israeli Sociology: Theory, Ideology, and Identity.* Albany: State of University of New York Press, 1995.

Rau, Zbigniew. "Some Thoughts on Civil Society in Eastern Europe and the Lockean Contractarian Approach," *Political Studies* 30 (1987): 573–592.

Rekhes, Elie. "Israeli Arabs and the Arabs of the West Bank and Gaza: Political Affinity and National Solidarity." *Asian and African Studies* 23 (1989): 119–154.

———. "Israeli Arabs of the West Bank and Gaza Strip: Political Ties and National Identification," *HaMizrah HeHadash* 32 (1989): 165–191 [Hebrew].

———. "Jews and Arabs in the Israeli Communist Party." In *Ethnicity, Pluralism, and the State,* eds. Milton J. Esman and Itamar Rabinovich. Ithaca: Cornell University Press.

Remba, Oded. "Income Inequality in Israel: Ethnic Aspects." In *Israel: Social Structure and Change,* eds. Michael Curtis and Mordecai S. Chertoff. New Brunswick, N.J.: Transaction Books, 1973.

Reynolds, Clark Winton. *The Mexican Economy.* New Haven: Yale University Press, 1970.

Richelieu, C. (1964). "Political Testament." In *The Thirty Years' War: Problems of Motive, Extent, and Effect,* ed. T. K. Rabb. Boston: D. C. Heath, 1964.

Robinson, Glenn. *Building a Palestinian State: The Incomplete Revolution.* Bloomington: Indiana University Press, 1997.

Rosenau, James N. "The State in an Era of Cascading Politics: Wavering Concept, Widening Competence, Withering Colossus, or Weathering Change?" *Comparative Political Studies* 21, no. 1 (April 1988): 13–44.

Rosenfeld, Henry. "The Class Situation of the Arab National Minority in Israel." *Comparative Studies in Society and History* 20, no. 3 (July 1978): 374–407.

———. "Men and Women in Arab Peasant to Proletariat Transformation." In *Theory and Practice: Essays Presented to Gene Weltfish,* ed. Stanley Diamond. New York: Mouton, 1989.

Roter, Raphael, and Nira Shamai, "Social Policy and the Israeli Economy, 1948–1980." In *Economic and Social Policy in Israel: The First Generation,* ed. Moshe Sanbar. New York: University Press of America, 1990.

Rothermund, Dietmar. "The Legacy of the British-Indian Empire in Independent India." In *Imperialism After Continuities and Discontinuities,* eds. Wolfgang M. Mommsen and Jürgen Osterhammel. London: Allen and Unwin, 1986.

Rouhana, Nadim. "The Civic and National Subidentities of the Arabs in Israel: A Psycho-Political Approach." In *Arab-Jewish Relations in Israel: A Quest in*

Human Understanding, ed. John E. Hofman. Bristol, Ind.: Wyndham Hall Press, 1988.

Royal Institute of International Affairs. *Political and Strategic Interests of the United Kingdom.* London: Oxford University Press, 1939.

Sachar, Howard M. *A History of Israel: From the Rise of Zionism to Our Time.* New York: Alfred A. Knopf, 1979.

Sanders, Ronald. *The High Walls of Jerusalem: A History of the Balfour Declaration and the Birth of the British Mandate for Palestine.* New York: Holt, Rinehart and Winston, 1983.

Sandler, Shmuel. "The Origins of the National and Statist Traditions in Zionist Foreign Policy." *Jewish Political Studies Review* 2 (Fall 1990): 129–130.

Scott, James C. *Domination and the Arts of Resistance: Hidden Transcripts.* New Haven: Yale University Press, 1990.

———. *Weapons of the Weak: Everyday Forms of Peasant Resistance.* New Haven: Yale University Press, 1985.

Shafir, Gershon. "Israeli Society: A Counterview." *Israel Studies* 1 (Fall 1995): 189–213.

———. *Land, Labor, and the Origins of the Israeli-Palestinian Conflict.* Cambridge: Cambridge University Press, 1989.

Shalev, Michael. "Jewish Organized Labor and the Palestinians: A Study of State/Society Relations in Israel." In *The Israeli State and Society: Boundaries and Frontiers,* ed. Baruch Kimmerling. Albany: State University of New York Press, 1989.

———. *Labour and the Political Economy in Israel.* New York: Oxford University Press, 1992.

———. "Time for Theory: Critical Notes on Lissak and Sternhell." *Israel Studies* 1 (Fall 1996): 170–188.

Shama, Avraham, and Mark Iris. *Immigration Without Integration: Third World Jews in Israel.* Cambridge, Mass.: Schenkman, 1977.

Shamir, Michal. "Political Intolerance Among Masses and Elites in Israel: A Reevalutation of the Elitist Theory of Democracy." *The Journal of Politics* 53, no. 4 (Nov 1991): 1018–1044.

Shammas, Anton. *The Arab Literature in Israel.* Tel Aviv: Shiloach Institute, Tel Aviv University, 1976.

———. *Arabesques.* New York: Harper and Row, 1988.

Shanok, Tobe. "The Yishuv's Early Capabilities: Organization, Leadership, and Policies." In *Review Essays in Israel Studies, Books on Israel,* Vol. V, eds. Laura Zitrain Eisenberg and Neil Caplan. Albany: State University of New York Press, 2000.

Shapiro, Yonathan. *The Formative Years of the Israeli Labour Party.* Beverly Hills: Sage, 1976.

Sharkansky, Ira. *What Makes Israel Tick?: How Domestic Policy-Makers Cope with Constraints.* Chicago: Nelson-Hall, 1985.

Shils, Edward. *Center and Periphery: Essays in Macrosociology.* Chicago: Chicago University Press, 1975.

———. "On the Comparative Study of the New States. " In *Old Societies and New States,* ed. Clifford Geertz. New York: The Free Press, 1963.

Shlaim, Avi. *The Iron Wall: Israel and the Arab World.* New York: W. W. Norton, 2000.

Shokeid, Moshe. *The Dual Heritage: Immigrants from the Atlas Mountains in an Israeli Village.* Manchester: Manchester University Press, 1971.

Sikkink, Kathryn. *Ideas and Institutions: Developmentalism in Brazil and Argentina.* Ithaca: Cornell University Press, 1991.

Silberstein, Laurence J. *The Post-Zionism Debates: Knowledge and Power in Israeli Culture.* New York: Routledge, 1999.

Smith, Anthony D. *The Ethnic Origins of Nations.* London: Basil Blackwell, 1986.

———. "State-Making and Nation-Building." In *States in History,* ed. John A. Hall. London: Basil Blackwell, 1986.

Smooha, Sammy. *Arabs and Jews in Israel I: Conflicting and Shared Attitudes in a Divided Society.* Boulder: Westview, 1989.

———. *The Divergent Fate of the Palestinians on Both Sides of the Green Line: The Intifada as a Test.* Paper presented at the International Sociological Association, XII World Congress of Sociology, Madrid, July 12, 1990.

———. *Israel: Pluralism and Conflict.* London: Routledge and Kegan Paul, 1978.

———. *The Orientation and the Politicization of the Arab Minority in Israel.* The Jewish-Arab Center, Institute of Middle Eastern Studies, Haifa University, 1984.

Spilerman, Seymour, and Jack Habib. "Development Towns in Israel: The Role of Community in Creating Ethnic Disparities in Labor Force Characteristics." In *Studies of Israeli Society,* Vol. I, *Migration, Ethnicity and Community,* ed. Ernest Krausz. New Bruswick, N.J.: Transaction Books, 1980.

Sprinzak, Ehud. *The Ascendance of Israel's Radical Right.* New York: Oxford University Press, 1991.

Sprinzak, Ehud and Larry Diamond. eds. *Israeli Democracy under Stress.* Boulder: Lynne Rienner, 1993.

State of Israel. *Labor Power Survey, 1963* (Jerusalem: Central Bureau of Statistics, 1964).

Stein, Kenneth W. *The Land Question in Palestine, 1917–1939.* Chapel Hill: University of North Carolina Press, 1984.

Stein, Leonard. *The Balfour Declaration.* London: Vallentine, Mitchell, 1961.

Stepan, Alfred. *The State and Society: Peru in Comparative Perspective.* Princeton: Princeton University Press, 1978.

Sternhell, Zeev. *The Founding Myths of Israeli: Nationalism, Socialism and the Making of the Jewish State.* Princeton, N.J.: Princeton University Press, 1998.

Stevenson, William. *Strike Zion!* New York: Bantam Books, 1967.

Stone, Russell A., and Walter P. Zenner. *Critical Essays on Israeli Social Issues and Scholarship.* Albany: State University of New York Press, 1994.

Strayer, Joseph R. *On the Medieval Origins of the Modern State.* Princeton: Princeton University Press, 1970.

Swirski, Shlomo. *Israel: The Oriental Majority.* New Jersey: Zed Books, 1989.

Swirski, Shlomo, and Deborah Bernstein. "The Rapid Economic Development of Israel and the Emergence of the Ethnic Division of Labor." *British Journal of Sociology* 33 (1982): 64–85.

Tessler, Mark. "Arabs in Israel." In *Israel, Egypt, and the Palestinians: From Camp David to Intifada,* eds. Ann Mosely Lesch and Mark Tessler. Bloomington: Indiana University Press, 1998.

Teveth, Shabtai. *Ben-Gurion: The Burning Ground, 1886–1948.* Boston: Houghton Mifflin, 1987.

Tibawi, A. L. "Visions of the Return: The Palestinian Arab Refugees in Arab Poetry and Art." *Middle East Journal* 17 (1963): 507–540.

Tilly, Charles. *Coercion, Capital, and European States, AD 990–1990.* Cambridge, Mass.: B. Blackwell, 1990.

———. *The Formation of National States in Western Europe.* Princeton: Princeton University Press, 1975.

United Nations. *Report of the Economic Survey Mission of the Middle East.* New York: United Nations, 1949.

Vatikiotis, Panayiotis J. *The History of Egypt.* Second ed. Baltimore: Johns Hopkins University Press, 1980.

Vernon, Raymond. *The Dilemma of Mexico's Development: The Roles of the Private and Public Sectors.* Cambridge: Harvard University Press, 1963.

Vital, David. *The Origins of Zionism.* Oxford: Clarendon Press, 1975.

Wallerstein, Immanuel. *The Modern World-System: Capitalist Agriculture and the Origins of the European World-Economy in the Sixteenth Century.* New York: Academic Press, 1974.

Wasserstein, Bernard. *The British in Palestine: The Mandatory Government and the Arab-Jewish Conflict 1917–1929.* London: Royal Historical Society, 1978.

Waterbury, John. *The Egypt of Nasser and Sadat: The Political Economy of Two Regimes.* Princeton: Princeton University Press, 1983.

Weber, Eugene. *Peasants into Frenchmen: The Modernization of Rural France 1870–1914.* Stanford: Stanford University Press, 1976.

Weisburd, David. *Jewish Settler Violence: Deviance as Social Reaction.* University Park: The Pennsylvania State University Press, 1989.

Weizmann, Chaim. *Trial and Error.* London: Hamish Hamilton, 1949.

Wolfsfeld, Gadi. *The Politics of Provocation: Participation and Protest in Israel.* Albany: State University of New York Press, 1988.

Yiftachel, Oren. "The Internal Frontier: Territorial Control and Ethnic Relations in Israel." In *Ethnic Frontiers and Peripheries: Landscape of Inequality and Development in Israel,* eds. Oren Yiftachel and Avinoam Meir. Boulder: Westview Press, 1998.

Yishai, Yael. "Integration of Arabs in an Israeli Party: The Case of Mapam, 1948–54." In *Zionism and Arabism in Palestine and Israel,* eds. Elie Kedourie and Slyvia G. Haim. Totowa, N.J.: F. Cass, 1982.

———. *Land of Paradoxes: Interest Politics in Israel.* Albany: State University of New York Press, 1991.

Zureik, Elia T. *The Palestinians in Israel: A Study in Internal Colonialism.* Boston: Routledge and Kegan Paul, 1979.

INDEX